VIA Folios 154

Preston Street
Corso Italia

PRESTON STREET
AN INFORMAL HISTORY OF ITALIANS IN OTTAWA
CORSO ITALIA

Franco Ricci

BORDIGHERA PRESS

All rights reserved. Parts of this book may be reprinted only by written permission from the authors, and may not be reproduced for publication in book, magazine, or electronic media of any kind, except in quotations for purposes of literary reviews by critics.

© 2022, Franco Ricci
Cover painting by Lucia Alloggia.

Library of Congress Cataloging-in-Publication Data

Names: Ricci, Franco, 1953- author.
Title: Preston Street, Corso Italia : an informal history of Italians in Ottawa / Franco Ricci.
Other titles: Informal history of Italians in Ottawa
Description: New York, NY : Bordighera Press, [2022] | Series: VIA Folios ; 154 | Includes bibliographical references. | Summary: "Chronicling the history of Preston Street and the Italian Canadian community in Ottawa, Professor Franco Ricci thoroughly researches and recounts the social history, the people, and the many institutions of Ottawa's Italian community"-- Provided by publisher.
Identifiers: LCCN 2021055825 | ISBN 9781599541631 (paperback)
Subjects: LCSH: Italians--Ontario--Ottawa--History. | Italians--Ontario--Ottawa--Social life and customs. | Italians--Ontario--Ottawa--Ethnic identity. | Preston Street (Ottawa, Ont.)--History. | Little Italies--Ontario--Ottawa--History. | Ottawa (Ont.)--History--20th century.
Classification: LCC F1059.7.I8 R51 2022 | DDC 305.85/10971384--dc23/eng/20220112
LC record available at https://lccn.loc.gov/2021055825

Printed with Ingram Lightning Source.

Published by
BORDIGHERA PRESS
John D. Calandra Italian American Institute
25 W. 43rd Street, 17th Floor
New York, NY 10036

VIA Folios 154
ISBN 978-1-59954-163-1

TABLE OF CONTENTS

An Ottawa Italian Story	11
"It takes a village to raise a child . . ."	15
Preface	19
Introduction	21
Beginnings	25
First Italians	39
Community	53
Early Migration to Ottawa	69
Ethnicity and Institutions	105
Social Groups: Conserving a Past, Reshaping Ethnic Identities	163
Construction: Building a Nation and an Identity	193
The Villa Marconi Centre: Elder Care, an Enduring Legacy	213
Preston Street Today: Updating Identity	243
Afterword: The Future and Sustainability	283
Bibliography	289
Acknowledgements	297
About the Author	299

Per tutti quelli che cercano:
Una terra promessa
Un mondo diverso
Dove crescere i loro pensieri

For all those that seek:
A promised land
A different world
A place to grow their spirit

> EROS RAMAZZOTTI, *Una terra promessa*

Laudamus veteres, sed nostri utemur annis.
Lodiamo i tempi antichi, ma sappiamoci muovere nei nostri.
Praise ancient times, but move well in our own.

OVIDIO [PUBLIO OVIDIO NASONE]

AN OTTAWA ITALIAN STORY

Born in Ottawa's *Little Italy* in 1941, the youngest of eight children, growing up on the corner of Rochester and Pamilla Streets, and being intimately connected to the Italian community socially and professionally in my adult years, I was pleased when Professor Franco Ricci called me to let me know of the book he was preparing on the history of Ottawa's Italian-Canadian community, its people, and its institutions. It is my pleasure to provide a Forward to this welcome work.

Professor Ricci has thoroughly researched and chronicled the social history, the people, and the many institutions of Ottawa's Italian-Canadian community, a task that was long overdue, and accomplished in the nick of time as community development and the passage of time have relegated much of our community's history to the memory of octogenarians. Thanks go to Professor Ricci for capturing so much of our lore just in time before all their memories fade.

I was born in *Little Italy* close to the half-century point of its existence. This allowed me and my contemporaries to experience the rich and incredible reality of the first generation of landed immigrants from Italy, who arrived in the early 1900s, and to witness the often difficult transition challenges for them and their families during the second half of the century. The list of early immigrants includes three Italian brothers from Calabria: Eugenio, my father, who arrived in Canada in 1924, and his younger brothers Antonio and Alfredo. The three individually owned and operated separate businesses in *Little Italy* for a combined 120 years. Because of their community profile, I was well integrated into the vibrant life of this unique and thriving community.

I can truly appreciate Professor Ricci's chronicling this original Italian community and the unfortunate transitioning of my *Little Italy* from the place where hundreds of Italian families were also living this unique experience to one where eventual government expropriations in the 1960s diminished the presence of many of the original founding families and divided the community and the heartfelt connectedness between lifelong neighbours.

It was a body blow to everyone in the Italian community when the Federal Government first expropriated Lebreton Flats in the 1960s and razed all the homes and businesses of 7,500 people to make way for government buildings. The Flats, as it was known, encompassed 50 acres and, although it was home primarily to Franco-Ontarians, many Italian-Canadians lived in the Flats area that were contiguous to *Little Italy*. The expropriated area remains vacant to this day.

Then the Federal Government turned its sights to significant parts of *Little Italy* itself and expropriated many family homes and small family businesses adjacent to Saint Anthony's Church.

The third blow came when the Federal Government purchased and then razed the Booth Street Stadium, a fully autonomous sports park with bleachers. The stadium had served and animated *Little Italy* and the broader Ottawa community with semi-professional and community baseball, softball, football, soccer, as well as other social and professional events. It occupied the equivalent of four municipal blocks and was replaced by faceless government buildings that had no affinity with the realities, culture, and *feel* of *Little Italy*.

Professor Ricci superbly captures the shrinkage of *our Little Italy* after these expropriations and the dispersal of many families to other Ottawa neighbourhoods. This included the loss of my family's residence and our general store that included a dairy and butcher shop on the corner of Rochester and Pamilla Streets in 1957. My uncle Alfredo also lost his grocery store and residence.

He also ably chronicles the rise of the Villa Marconi Long Term Care Home and associated Community Centre and Canadian Italian Historical Centre, a product of the determined commitment and sound leadership of Ottawa's Italian community leaders. Villa Marconi provides palliative care for our aging seniors and a second, and long needed, gathering place for Ottawa's Italian-Canadian community in the Fisher Heights area. The new focal point attracted many Italian families into the already *Italianized* neighbourhood as well as a second Italian church, the Madonna della Risurrezione. This broadened the Ottawa Italian community into a comfortable duality of Villa Marconi-Fisher Heights and the reality of a diminished *Little Italy* in and around the area of Preston Street and St. Anthony of Padua Church.

The historical reality of *Little Italy* had been one of a giant extended family. I remember growing up amongst what seemed like dozens of acquired aunts and uncles, attending St. Anthony Elementary School, located across the street from the parish, along with all of my older siblings when it was known as The Dante Academy. We were taught by nuns and lay teachers, one of which included my sister Mary.

Much has not been documented from that period, such as the annual Spring "end of school year" picnic held at the Arboretum at Dows Lake where mothers and teachers celebrated along with the younger children. Or the Friday 2:30 p.m. walk of the entire student body across Gladstone Avenue to St Anthony's Church to participate in the weekly novena, after which the students would be released to go home.

Memories and mementos from that simpler time are many and personal; too few of them have been commemorated. For example, I still have a photograph of myself as an infant at my christening. My godfather had been replaced by his son who acted as proxy because his father had been arrested and taken away to an internment camp; or one of my earliest memories as a four year old remembering that 1945 day when the entire population of *Little Italy* poured out onto the streets marching and celebrating with every noise maker conceivable shouting repeatedly "the war is over." Who could ever forget that memory? And so I was proud to approve, when as the Mayor of Ottawa in 2005, a significant infrastructure package to help renew and upgrade that very street that had seen so much jubilation, love, and joy ... Preston Street.

Looking back, it is clear to me that both the 20th Century Italian immigration and the later arrival of immigrants between the 1950s and 1970s together created a dynamic and meaningful Italian-Canadian community that has contributed to the City of Ottawa's evolving identity and growth. What has evolved, however, over the last three decades are two significant and independent Italian neighbourhoods, each with an Italian-Canadian footprint and vitality. These two *Little Italys* have become an attraction to Italian-Canadians who thrive in the broader community of Ottawa, yet who regularly return to these neighborhoods to experience a return to their roots.

On the one hand, Fisher Heights has become home to a stable and exciting neighbourhood, populated by countless Italian-Canadian families who comprise The Madonna Della Risurrezione parish, the Villa Marconi Community Centre and Day Care, the Canadian Italian Historical Centre, and the Villa Marconi Long Term Care Centre for the elderly.

On the other, the reshaping and redefining of the Preston Street landscape, together with St. Anthony School and iconic St. Anthony of Padua church today represent a "go to place" for Ottawans. Indeed, Preston Street/Corso Italia and *Little Italy*, continue to highlight and promote an Italian flavour and ambiance in the city as well as a recognizable and significant iconic cultural presence that is certain not only to survive but grow. Although the recent erection of the area-defining archway sits in the shadow of a 40-storey high condominium tower, it cannot erase the memories of the spot where the Cardillo brothers served the community for decades with an Esso service centre and auto repair shop.

There is so much to read about these memories and passings, but also of future growth of my *Little Italy* in Professor Ricci's wonderful book. So let me end by saying again, thank you for your work, your dedication to our community, and your help in preserving our collective history.

GRAZIE!!!

Robert Chiarelli
Lawyer, former Regional Chair of Ottawa-Carleton,
former Mayor of Ottawa, and former Ontario Cabinet Minister.

"IT TAKES A VILLAGE TO RAISE A CHILD . . ."

When Professor Franco Ricci first approached me in early January 2020 to write the Forward to his book chronicling the history of Preston Street and the Italian-Canadian community in Ottawa, I was very honoured. I was proud to help my friend weave the story of this very interesting community, my community, and capture its history, rich traditions, social intricacies, personal stories, and evolving challenges as it moves forward in the ever changing multicultural Capital city of Ottawa.

I was aware, through our many informal talks, that the professor had a keen interest in Italian and Italian-American culture, given his Italian and Italian-American background, and his course curriculum at the University of Ottawa attested to those personal and academic pursuits.

This book has been a long time in the making for Professor Ricci. Having shared many stories, articles and pictures with Franco from my own personal collection and that of the Italian Canadian Historical Centre imbued me with a strong sense of pride in realizing that his book would be the first to fully chronicle the Ottawa Italian community, of which I am so proud. There have indeed been other shorter studies and memorial volumes. One in particular, published in 2015, was titled *A Journey of Faith: A History of St. Anthony of Padua Church 1913-2013*. That wonderful volume, chock-full of photographs and local family stories, chronicled the growth of this community pillar and its parish. But a history of the entire community, a description of its experiences, its many establishments, indeed of its humanity, was long in coming.

As President of the National Congress of Italian-Canadians (National Capital District) with a strong familial allegiance and emotional connection to Preston Street and its Village, it was most important to me that the story be told of the area's wondrous and now almost mythical past, but that it also addressed questions of its evolving future. What happens, indeed, in years to come, to the distinctive flavour and character of my ethnic enclave, one that the early generations of Italian immigrants struggled so hard to build and now see their descendants struggle to preserve? Can this ethnic building block of Canadian Multiculturalism provide enrichment for successive generations to come?

This book, in its many chapters, recounts the history, stories, lives, and character of a very special community and its people. It is a community that has thrived and survived, has grown and evolved despite the economic instability of the depression in the early 1930s, the nightmare of two world wars, the internment of some of its most respected leaders in the 1940s (listed as enemy aliens by their own government), the new wave of immigration in the 1950s and 1960s that resurfaced dormant issues of assimilation, language, education and culture. It has persevered despite the highly controversial expropriation of property and displacement of long-time residents to the suburban neighborhoods of Nepean, Alta Vista and Carleton Heights in the early 1960s. This unfortunate and forced migration from the center of ethnic comfort nevertheless symbolized the coming of age of the Ottawa Italian community - a very close-knit section of the city where everyone knew their neighbours, sometimes came from the same area of Italy, and held shared values of trust, respect, and reliance.

It depicts Ottawa's first Italian citizens who settled in the Lowertown (present day market) area of Ottawa, especially along Murray and St. Patrick streets, in the second half of the 19TH century. We rediscover family names like Graziadei, Calderone and Mandia, early musicians, merchants and fruit peddlars; true pioneers who laid the foundation for future arrivals. Other immigrants became labourers for private contractors. Some, learning the process, became very large contractors and honored their origins as astute businessmen and benevolent community citizens. A small church appeared in 1908 on Murray Street to provide spiritual guidance to this small but spreading sector of immigrants. Five years later in 1913, the cornerstone of St. Anthony of Padua church is laid in what was then known as Rochesterville. The church became the bedrock, heart and soul of the growing community while the many individuals, sports teams, banquet halls, grocery stores, restaurants, and small businesses helped shape the multicultural enclave that is Preston Street/*Corso Italia* today.

And so, the Italian colony of Ottawa begins to take shape amongst the many other ethno-cultural communities in the Preston Street area and . . . the rest is history as told in these subsequent pages.

Professor Ricci ably describes this historical process and the more recent formation of the many social clubs, regional and cultural organizations and their presence in today's Italian community. Are they still relevant? What inherent challenges do they face with successive generations? Do they have an enduring base, and can they remain sustainable? Can they evolve and remain evergreen? Does wanting to cook like *nonna*, travel to the hometown regions of Abruzzo, Calabria, and Friuli, or supporting A.C. Milan or Juventus during soccer matches provide enough for community spirit to survive, or do third and fourth generation youth mark their rich cultural heritage in other ways? Is community media, both print and broadcast, important in helping to disseminate awareness in a world dominated by fluid social media? These are questions that permeate the community and provide fodder for ongoing discussion. The murals and monuments projects, painted and sculpted over the past twenty years, act as an old family snapshot, worn with time. Are they enough to disseminate awareness and pride in the community when descendants of the pioneer families return for the occasional gelato and espresso? Does the presence of these artworks and beautification projects provide a historical relevance that leads to a further appreciation? These are questions pondered and analyzed in this book.

As such it also provides a very thorough analysis of the revered place that is Villa Marconi, the most recent icon and revered emblem of community unity. Its 25-year presence has provided a new sociocultural focal point for a possible future. It is a loving legacy bequeathed to our seniors and their families, to those intrepid many who came as young men and women to make a better life for themselves and successive generations.

But beyond legacy and caring for our elderly, what indeed lies ahead for Preston Street and *The Village*?

Will the gentrification of these older neighbourhoods bring challenges that invariably threaten the fabric and makeup of that "neighbourhood feel." Will new residents respect the heritage and history of their environs? Will their offspring produce National Hockey League and Canadian Football League professional players as the area did in the 1940s? And how about an Olympic gold medallist? Will there be another Italian-Canadian Mayor of the Capital city of Canada? In today's radically sanitized world, will neighborhood nicknames such as *cement*, *cootsie* and *tomato* even be possible? In these pages, you are invited to look back into another time when these names readily identified an individual and everyone knew of whom they spoke.

Professor Ricci has done an exhaustive study on his subject and has written a very interesting book on Preston Street and its Italian community. Laying-out lengthy tentacles in any community is not an easy task. But this book is indeed a valued, welcome, and worthwhile read.

On a final note, I agreed to write this Foreword because I am a student of history and the content of this book is near and dear to my heart and to my family's history. I sat around many a table growing up, listening to my parents and their friends recounting stories of foreign places, harrowing experiences and intrepid individuals, many of whom I reencountered in this book. By osmosis, those stories remained within me. I hope the same happens to you as you learn of a very special time and place on Preston Street.

Enjoy!

Trina Costantini-Powell
President, National Congress of Italian-Canadians
(National Capital District) Ottawa, Ontario, Canada

PREFACE

The following study is both a labor of love and frustration. Love for a community that often demonstrates heartfelt resolve, unrelenting drive, and the sagacious hope that its has provided the best of itself to its adopted home and coming generations; frustration for that same community that too often resides in the shadows of its own studied indifference, unwitting indolence, and undeserved pettiness towards itself and its potential.

Government towns everywhere are notoriously self-centered and wilfully immobile. More often than not, seminal infrastructure initiatives, worthwhile community projects, and the best-laid plans of elected local leaders are too often drowned beneath layers of carefully crafted bureaucratic apologies that are the norm of men of pseudo power. As a capital city, Ottawa faces the challenge of balancing effective modern growth and cultural prosperity with the machinery of governance that stalls opportunity and sanctions patience.

The hyphenated ethnic communities that live in this government town are too often afflicted with the same pedigree of official lethargy. Living in the shadow of the Peace Tower, the Italian-Canadian community of Ottawa has been forced to cope with the many limitations that the local bureaucracy has erected while at the same time creating many of its own making. These practical impediments have forged the community's socio-politically variegated character. Though many individuals, families, companies, and larger corporations have thrived, too often the weight of self-inflicted squabbles have limited the considerable potential of the community. Too often, self-serving individuals have outweighed and divided the predominantly unselfish and benevolent group into uncompromising rival factions. All too often, inherent and merited ethnic pride has been reduced to unwanted submission and spoiling indifference, ultimately resulting in cultural stagnation and inevitable sociopolitical and economic decline.

What follows is an attempt to measure the century or so of Italian and Italian-Canadian influence in the Capital Region. All attempts were made to include every single individual, member, and/or group that has in any way influenced the neighborhood now known as *Little Italy* as well as the community beyond. My efforts were often greeted with outright love, support, and a cautious enthusiasm that was always counterbalanced with an equal amount of indifference and skepticism.

I thank everyone who took the time to support my efforts of chronicling the history of the community but am also most grateful to those whose silence simply spurred this chronicler to delve further into the corners of our community. By no means is this study complete. I have not focussed on individual families or single members and their accomplishments. When proper names are mentioned, they are intended as a part of the community narrative. There are indeed many important and colorful actors in this community play and I hope one day to add to this present study with a story that highlights their inimitable contributions to community solidarity. In this present work I have instead attempted to measure those institutions that any community slowly constructs to both invent and sustain itself as a viable sociocultural co-community to the larger Canadian context. Pundits will thus find ample opportunities to highlight omissions and errors on each-and-every page. Any-and-all exclusions, errors, omissions, interpretations, and misconceptions are mine alone. I simply hope that my personal reading of the years I have spent in Ottawa spur other, more competent and fleshed interpretations of this wonderful community.

SEMPER AD MELIORA

INTRODUCTION

Moments, Documents, and Monuments

The primary focus of this study is the Ottawa roadway named Preston Street. For those old enough to remember, Preston Street is the main thoroughfare of a neighborhood area once known as *The Village*. The street is thus an important vestige of a long-standing community; a visual memory replete with the historical experiences of displacement and immigration, finding jobs, and raising families. For the younger set, Preston Street is a contemporary asphalt pavement; a present space that is often not very relevant to their lives beyond the entertainment the local establishments seek to provide. When considering the image of the street that emerges from these past and present memory places it is necessary to consider the epistemological essence of the sources used to construct the neighborhood's current panorama. For the older members of the Italian-Canadian community, family histories, recalled events, and shared memories are the vital monuments that evoke former times and give the street a comfortable humane essence. For the younger crowd, contemporary food spots, upbeat events and outdoor activities that animate the street supply the fodder for emotions that will become those future recollections of their youth.

While documents such as photographs, newspaper articles, civil and church archives are the documents that provide the social historian with a notion of the practical lore and customs of a place, it is the visceral details of the humanity that spawned those heartfelt documents that subtend the Preston Street narrative. This collective narrative is like a colorful patchwork that assembles all of the past individual histories into a manageable group chronicle. When seen from this perspective, the practical and often haphazard events of this collective narrative vouchsafe the foundations of our definition of the local character of the Italian-Canadian community that was, and remains, an essential element of the area. Any of my notions that may seem contrived from these authentic sources are totally independent of predefined or predetermined interpretations. They remain a product of wilfully objective investigation over the course of many years.

This study, then, can be said to constitute a reality of its own. A major contribution to my evaluation of the Italian-Canadian community was a series of interviews with members of the community. These testimonies gained more and more relevance as the work progressed. Photographs, charts, facts, figures, life stories of individuals provided by families and members of the community became useful informants of the evolving historical reality of the Italian-Canadian community of Ottawa. Relevant relationships between the historical or family events related to me and the characters narrating the stories became part of my written representation of them. At a moment in contemporary culture that is constructed through social memes and determined more and more by pictures and impressions of the past, it became important to be led less by impressions and more by real accounts of that past.

In this study, I have therefore attempted to distinguish between documents and monuments. Used in the broad sense, documents are *testimonials* of the past. These include real texts (letters, photographs), genuine testimony (interviews, commentary). These are the *tracks* of human making that guarantee real and enduring memory. Monuments, on the other hand, are *traces* of the past. They are often more subliminal and may include partial impressions, hazily recalled images, sporadic events or fragmented ideas that gain meaning in the present (or at least demand the most recognition) but can be clouded by present political or emotional obligations. A document can become a monument when it contributes to the formation of a universally accepted social image that is transmitted to future generations as real collective memory.[1]

I treat each document, or testimonial, as a monumental trace of the recalled past of the community. Taken together, these elements bring to the surface the character of the collective unconscious of the

---

1 Two terms first employed by Erwin Panofsky in an essay originally published in 1940, titled "The History of Art as a Humanistic Discipline." Now in Erwin Panofsky, *Meaning in the Visual Arts* (Woodstock, NY: Overlook, 1974).

Ottawa Italian-Canadian community as it is externally symbolized by the streetscape and history of Preston Street now *Corso Italia*.[2]

As will quickly become apparent to the reader, this study of Preston Street is more a foreword or initial attempt to define tendencies, rather than a conclusive study of the area and its inhabitants. Much more work needs to be done by others to examine and interpret the individual tales, events, and institutions into a fuller socio-historical account.

Thus, while the tone of the study is that of an historical chronicle, I will orient myself towards a celebration of the community that created that life history and gloss personal differences between members of the community in favor of the positive common mental pictures nurtured by the Italian-Canadians of Ottawa. I will focus on those images of meaning (landmarks, institutions, professions) and systems of orientation (associations, celebrations) that present consistent perceptions of social unity, commonality, and community relationship. The image of Preston Street and its Italian-Canadian community may display vitality and hope just as it may reveal decadence and despair. That image develops without direct guidance; it merely evolves within the annals of time.

This study will therefore concentrate on the identity that the Italian-Canadian community has created *of and for* itself as reflected in the nature of the street that has come to symbolize its existence. It is hoped that these reflections will allow a more coherent *imageability*

---

2 In 1986, local resident Angelo Germano collected over 1000 signatures from Preston Street neighborhood families and businesses that supported his idea of renaming the street to *Corso Italia*.

The petition met resistance from then Mayor Jim Durrell, from Regional Chair Andy Hayden, and from Gord Hunter, Chair of the Regional Planning Committee. Their concerns were both financial, the expense of changing signage for the city as well as the personal expense of changing addresses for local businesses, and practical; they feared that other ethnic enclaves would claim the same privilege.

But Mac Harb, Alderman for the area, was overwhelmingly enthusiastic. "Italians have made an important contribution to this city and this is the least we could do." He believed the change would lure more business to the street and also inspire the community to revitalize the area.

A compromise was eventually achieved with commemorative (non-official) names given to Preston Street (*Corso Italia*) and Gladstone Avenue (*Via Marconi*).

(those entities that may be read or perceived or seen as belonging to a unique culture) of the Italian-Canadian community of Ottawa, allowing the community to better locate itself within the Canadian mosaic of which it is a vital part.

And so, the ultimate purpose of this written account is to produce a visual realm of monumental memory for the Italian-Canadian community of Ottawa before that memory forever dissipates into the realm of youthful forgetfulness and disregard. More importantly, it wishes to give a voice to those that have remained silent, if not often forgotten, in the hope that one day their story might not have been unremembered.

BEGINNINGS

Cars, trucks, and heavy transports bustle down the busy thoroughfare known as Preston Street. A vital link between the city proper and the once nearby countryside, a highway link between the Province of Quebec and local Ontario industry, the traffic is often deafening, swallowing up the street in rush hour madness. But once a year, the street assumes shades of its other more benevolent half; *Corso Italia* comes alive with people as motor traffic is supplanted by a promenading multitude that saunters amidst food booths glistening with roasted sausages, speakers blaring Italian pop music, running smiling children that scurry between their parents and visiting out of town relatives. During the annual event known as Italian Week, 500,000 pairs of feet pound the pavement usually reserved for spinning tires. And so, Preston Street/*Corso Italia* lives its schizophrenic nature: half transportation artery, half pedestrian mall, in an uneasy balance of Mediterranean pedestrian pleasure and North American economic utility.

At any instant, the street is more than the eye can see, more that any ear can hear. It is a setting waiting to be explored and explained. It is a place whose value lies in the events leading up to its present-day reality. There really is no result or defining end, only a succession of stages, some good some bad, that characterize the nature of the street. Every Italian that has ever lived in Ottawa has an uncertain, sometimes ambivalent, association with Preston Street; the very image of the Italian-Canadian community as perceived by others is steeped in its inhabitants' often troubled memories and too often spoiled good intentions.

The capital city of Ottawa is an environ of distinctive and distinct districts. For the most part, one usually knows where one is simply by the general characteristics of the surrounding area. The Sandy Hill district, with its turn of the century freehold Victorian latticed homes, holds nothing in common with the clapboard, shotgun box architecture of Mechanicsville, though both were developed in the late 1800s. Nestled between the Rideau Canal and turn-of-the-century business district, the tree-lined streets of The Glebe are often considered to be the most nostalgic, charming, and liveable of Ottawa neighborhoods. The irresistibly trendy vibes of Glebites, however, would lose any physical tumble with the grimier, shadier (as in character), and seedier (as in economic) side of the city, notably Vanier, although the latter district rests in the shade of the Parliament buildings. Neighborhoods in Ottawa are thus as multi-culturally and economically diverse as the politicos that call the city their home.

The Preston Street area also displays characteristics that make it a unique and distinctive neighborhood. The uninspired architecture is at first overpowering for its drabness. This, of course, is the first superficial view of an outsider. Little on the street can be cited as aesthetically distinctive with any critical concensus. When I asked people for a general visual description and impressions of the street, one of the most common remarks given was that it was missing something, that it has no alluring center; that it needs, in other words, a heart. The recent sprouting of block-long office towers has done little to soften the street's concrete physiognomy. The attempt to create a food district (comparable to the stretch of restaurants located in the Somerset Village area) is motley and tired.

Preston Street is thus often physically decried as formless; an endless and uneven spread of restaurants, caffe's, hairdressers, and, up until the recent infill of new buildings, parking lots. Yet, the metaphorical and symbolic personality and perceived identity of the street seems to be quite different. When pressed for information, these same people describe the area as a collection of family names and of recognizably shared memories. Undoubtedly, this is due to the emblematic nature of the street and the locales that constitute its Italian-Canadian history. People remembered personal and public events that filled-out the bleak grey landscape of the street, bringing it to life in the subtle hues of colored memory.

The bane of automobile traffic, however, was dominant in many conversations. Frequent derogatory references were made to the highway overpass that divides the street into two distinct areas. (It is interesting that older citizens who remember the overpass as a railroad bridge spoke in more romantic terms of this area once known as *The Village*). All in all, Preston Street is considered an essential linear node, an edge (a rather rough one), or path in the Ottawa cityscape. The street is a primary junction between northern and southern Ottawa suburbs; the customary route of physical transition between urban life and what was once rural countryside. It broached the limits, therefore, between traditional wealth and unassuming poverty. It remains, however, an unassuming temporal node that will permit us to initiate a spiritual journey between its congested vehicular present and a simpler, memorable past. For Preston Street was not always a narrow two-lane and cluttered thoroughfare . . .

Name

Preston Street derives its name from George H. Preston, a partner of William Young Rochester. Both had jointly purchased land in the present Preston Street area in 1859. The vainglorious habit of the time was to name parcels of land after oneself. The two divided the area into lots and sold the land for profit. The area that came to be known as *The Village* was part of this partitioning. It ideally extends from the intersection of Preston and Gladstone Avenue, travels south along Preston Street to current day Carling Avenue. But we rush ahead of our story, a story that must indeed begin in the area known as Lebreton (originally and often still written LeBreton) Flats.

Contrary to popular belief, very few Italians ever lived in the Flats area. Inhabited primarily by working class families, the early inhabitants of the Flats were Irish-Catholic mill-hands who had moved to the area during the economic boom of the late 1860s and early 1870s. By the 1950s, however, most of the 500 homes on the Flats were inhabited by working class French-Canadians.[1]

---

1   See Bruce S. Elliott, *The City Beyond* (Ottawa: Tri-graphic Printing, 1991): 82.

Library and Archives Canada PA-008354.

Lebreton Flats is just south of the river's edge on part of what was once called the Richmond Landing because of the Richmond settlers who had once settled there and also because it was the terminus of the Richmond Road that began in the Village of Richmond. This was a primitive and rutted country dirt road, one of the first such routes in the county, one of the earliest in Upper Canada.[2]

Located just below the Chaudiere Falls, the landing was owned by an enterprising American named Robert Randal, a Loyalist, who moved to Upper Canada in 1798 from Maryland, U.S.A.. He first settled in Niagara Falls where he became a local industrialist involved with mining ore and mercantile commerce. In 1807, having heard about land for sale along the Ottawa River, he took an exploratory trip and was impressed by the boiling cauldron that was the Chaudiere Falls. In 1809 he purchased the land, known as Lot 40, and planned to develop mills and smelters near the water's edge. The future seemed bright and profitable. But, after a series of legal and economic misfortunes (it seems the area was rift with ne'er-do-wells), he was arrested and eventually wound-up in debtor's prison in Montreal. The property was subsequently posted for public auction.

The site was eventually purchased by Captain John LeBreton of Nepean and District Registrar Livius P. Sherwood of Brockville, in December 1820. Sherwood financed the deal as LeBreton was

---

2 The first road in the district was the Aylmer road, in 1818 and was called Britannia Road by Philemon Wright.

short (eternally) of funds and needed financial assistance. The two entrepreneurs divided the parcel. The land was purchased for 499 pounds. LeBreton kept the more lucrative western half of the flats for himself; Sherwood retained the eastern half. As a natural bend on the then highly trafficked river, the parcel of land seemed a promising spot to begin a permanent settlement. The bend in the river was formed by the rocks and churning waters of the Chaudiere Falls. An impressive site indeed. Once called the "second Niagara," the Falls was baptized *Asticou* by the Algonquin Indians and translated as *Chaudière* in French ("Big Kettle" in English) because the rising spray of the teeming water resembled the steam from a boiling cauldron. Their presence on the river determined the future location of the cities of Ottawa and Hull. But the visionary investors had more pressing interests. The challenging waters impeded the progress of moving logs to sawmills and pulp mills down river. Subsequently, the waterways leading to the Falls directly in front of the river bend were eternally jamed with rafts of lumber. Indeed, at the Chaudieere Falls, the log drive normally came to a halt with millions of board feet of lumber backed-up for miles upriver. To circumvent the Falls it was necessary to take the timber out of the water and haul it, by wagon, overland and past the Falls to what became known as the Richmond Landing. Delays of weeks that stretched to months due to weather were not infrequent. Loggers needed to wait their turns to move their logs beyond the rapids. Smelling profit, an enterprising LeBreton took advantage of the growing bottleneck by providing accommodation and generous libation (amongst other pursuits) for the hundreds of idle loggers.

The ambitious enterprise was sideswiped, however, by an equally determined General George Ramsay, 9th Earl of Dalhousie, Governor General of British North America from 1820 to 1828, who plotted to oppose his hated rival. It seems that the antipathy of Dalhousie towards Captain LeBreton knew no bounds. The reasons were both economic and personal: both were stumbling over each other as each sought to increase their property and wealth in the New World. Both Dalhousie and LeBreton had had keen interest in the waterfront parcel of land when it was owned by Randall. LeBreton wished the land for profit, while Dalhousie regarded the site a British government investment for military storage and supplies. When the land was unexpectedly auctioned, LeBreton hurried by horseback to Brockville where he arranged the necessary capital to purchase the land. There were few bidders and he obtained the 900 acres for the sum of 490 pounds. Imagine Lord Dalhousie's consternation when LeBreton immediately offered the land for purchase to him for the sum of 3000 pounds!

Chaudière Falls, Ottawa River, Upper Canada (Ottawa, Ontario), c. 1815?

The two parted, accusing each other of breach of confidence and malfeasance and vowing to meet in court. The lengthy 8-year dispute was settled in 1828 when the Court of Kings Bench held at Perth awarded undisputable title to the tract of land in the township of Nepean formerly known as the Richmond Landing to Capt. LeBreton. In the meanwhile, the enterprising Captain continued to improve the property; he built a sawmill and had begun to operate a grist mill. The area was now populated with small log dwellings and a large establishment known as the Union Hotel, a rather impressive building, it seems, for the area and times. LeBreton had also partitioned the land, ambitiously renamed the landing the Town of Sherwood, and waited for the profits to amass.

Viewed from Dalhousie's perspective, LeBreton's plans for the Town of Sherwood would draw commerce away from his own burgeoning property and commercial interests. Perched on the high land further east and, importantly upriver and well above the Chaudiere Falls[3], he had purchased the land in 1823 while awaiting word of the court settlement. According to contemporary historians, the purchase was meant to spite his upstart rival LeBreton. Dalhousie reserved the land for government use and set about to construct a village of his own on this eastern parcel.

An 1824 map drawn by Lord Dalhousie. It shows 'Lot 40', with the names Lebreton and Sherwood below. To the east is 'Lot C', owned by Nicholas Sparks. Above Sparks' property is a lot marked as 'government purchase'. This is "the Fraser Parcel," the land purchased by Dalhousie that eventually became the village of Bytown. The 'Road to Richmond' is at the bottom left. The two buildings marked as 'Gov't Stores' near the Chaudiere are the storehouses built by Dalhousie. - Library and Archives Canada C-16156.

The development of this village, eventually known as Bytown, was given to Lieutenant Colonel John By, a friend and business associate of Lord Dalhousie. The future growth of Bytown essentially stifled any possible real growth of the Town of Sherwood (the present-day Lebreton Flats)

To further consolidate the political and commercial viability of his territorial position, in 1826 Dalhousie authorized the opening of a timber channel *around* the Chaudiere Falls, effectively depriving LeBreton of a profitable mill site and any remuneration from logging

---

3   Elliot, *The City Beyond*, 85-99.

roads. In the fall of the same year, he recommended the building of bridges linking the Chaudiere Falls with Wright's Town, todays Hull. These measures effectively squelched the growth of the Town of Sherwood, an area that would certainly have developed into an important commercial center had it not been for the opening of the canal several hundred meters up-river.

In the meantime, in the Spring of 1826 Colonel By received orders to oversee the construction of a navigable waterway that stretched southward 130 miles to the town of Kingston, a Loyalist citadel on the banks of Lake Ontario.[4] Beyond the exploration and surveying and inspection of the planned route of the canal through unbroken wilderness, marshes, lakes, rivers, and streams, the Royal Engineers needed to establish the placement of the Ottawa locks. After considerable study and exploration of the local terrain along the Ottawa River, it was determined that the best location for the entrance locks on the Ottawa River would be west of the Richmond Landing. Indeed, the terrain was flat and, as an added premium, a natural gully (that ran along today's Preston Street) reached south to what was known as Dow's Great Swamp. This would not only expedite construction (imperitive because of the war with the neighboring United States) but save considerable costs. Furthermore, navigation would finally become possible on both the Upper Ottawa River and the Rideau River since the projected canal would connect to a branch of the Rideau River near present day Dow's Lake, thereby creating a great interior waterway.

Instead, it was determined (officially) that a better drain for the canal would be at Sleigh Bay, (changed in 1826 to Entrance Bay)

---

4 Built primarily for strategic military purposes at a time when Great Britain and the United States vied for control of the region. It was intended to provide a secure supply route from the Ottawa River to Kingston, thereby avoiding the St. Lawrence River route that was prone to American attack. The Rideau Canal made Kingston the primary military outpost and economic centre of Upper Canada. It extends 202 km and was opened in 1832. Although the original intent of the Rideau Canal as a military supply route in time of war were never realized, (the canal never saw military activity) it remains a fully functioning waterway without interruption since its construction. Many of its lock gates and sluice valves are still operated by hand-powered winches.

between what are now Parliament Hill and Major Hill Park. When the Crown determined that the future Rideau Canal would enter the Ottawa River on land owned (surprise!) by Governor General Lord Dalhousie, the fate of the Town of Sherwood (and LeBreton) was cast. With the lucrative (expensive and untimely) construction of the Rideau Canal underway, all plans for viable development of the Flats site became a pipedream. Indeed, the foundation of Bytown (later Ottawa) dates from this moment, 26 September 1826.[5]

It was not until the 1840s, with the continuing growth of what had become known as Bytown and its expansion westward, that renewed interest returned to the neglected Flats. A new suspension bridge from the Flats to Hull brought traffic to the heretofore neglected Richmond Landing. A still determined LeBreton surveyed new lots, cleared the forested land for new streets, and extended Wellington and Albert Streets westward so that they crossed the southeast corner of his property. The Flats thus became a geographical extension of Upper Town and the Sparks Estate, setting the stage for settlement and growth. The proximity to a growing downtown commercial Bytown district also brought a renewed interest to the area. Respectable tradesmen looking for profit turned the waterfront site into a service center for the lumber industry. Despite the economic injection, milling operations remained modest as the booming lumber trade was better served by the largest mill in Upper Canada which was located at the Rideau Falls just east of Bytown (and upriver).

Nevertheless, homes and trading posts on the Flats continued to grow in the 1850s, extending the reaches of the burgeoning town westward. By that time, however, Capt. LeBreton was dead, leaving his five nieces the beneficiaries of continuing expansion towards the future Richmond Road and suburban development. But it is the area just south of the Flats that merits our attention.

Bytown became the incorporated town of Ottawa 1855. It became the capital of the Province of Canada in 1857 by decree of Queen Victoria.[6] The Parliament Buildings, the region's major employer for

---

5   Furthermore, had the canal proceeded from the Richmond Landing, Preston Street may never have existed as we know it today.

6   In reality, Queen Victoria's choice was guided by John A. Macdonald

years to come, were under construction by 1859. Expansion as a capital city was now inevitable. The Richmond Road was macadamized, allowing for the gentrification of the thoroughfare with large country homesteads. Bank Street was also extended beyond the city limits and into the farming and laboring communities immediately south of the city. This provided a new (and needed) southern access route into the capital area.

What can be considered the first true city suburb of Ottawa was Rochesterville, just south of Lebreton Flats. The area had been formerly subdivided into sellable real estate house lots for the owners William Young Rochester and his son-in-law George H. Preston in 1859. Real growth was not to occur, however, until the boom years of the 1870s. This development began in Lebreton Flats but soon leaped the then city limits and spilled into the lots of Rochesterville. This area attracted the mushrooming legion of civil servants and corporate managers eager to live in estates in proximity of their offices. A selling point for the subdivided land was its healthful climate, views of the Chaudiere Falls, and stands of native evergreens. The notion of country living within city limits was reinforced with streets named for Canadian forest trees: Elm, Spruce, Maple, Cedar, Balsam, and Pine Streets.[7]

The greatest request for the popularly priced lots, however, came from mill-hands and by the early 1870s the demand far outstripped the available land. By then, a good portion of the inhabitants were French-Canadians. They formed an enclave in the southern part of the subdivision that became known as *The French Village*. Further west along the Richmond Road, disparate industrial villages and small hamlets prospered. The most successful and closest to the town of Rochesterville was the French-Canadian village of small wood-frame houses known as Mechanicsville. The blossoming of these out-laying ring properties and commerce coupled with the completion of the long-awaited railroad connection to the Chaudiere Falls, allowed Rochesterville to prosper. In 1870, when the Canada Central Railway began service from Broad Street (from the western end of Lebreton

---

and his government.

7   Elliot, *The City Beyond*, 115.

Flats to Carleton Place), it ran along present-day Scott Street. By 1881 a flourishing Rochesterville was home to 273 families.

Most of the area we now consider the Preston Street neighborhood was developed between 1866 and 1890; it was annexed to the newly incorporated City of Ottawa in 1889. On 26 April 1900, a good parcel of land between Preston Street and Rochester Street was destroyed by fire. The conflagration began around 10:00 am when a small chimney fire on St. Redempteur Street across the river in the City of Hull became uncontrollable. When fireman arrived, the flames were already lapping at neighboring shingles and had engulfed several homes. As wind velocity increased, all of Hull was ablaze within an hour. By one o'clock that afternoon the fire had swept across the Chaudiere Bridge engulfing the lumberyards of H.F. Bronson and J.R. Booth. Fire brigades from Smith's Falls, Brockville, Peterborough and distant Toronto were dispatched to aid the local Ottawa brigades. By five o'clock p.m., Montreal fire crews arrived to find dense clouds of black smoke blanketing the area of Lebreton Flats and a raging fire covering an area of two-and-one half miles south to Carling Avenue. By the time the fire burned itself out at midnight, three thousand buildings had been destroyed, 15,000 persons were homeless, seven were dead. The limestone cliffs that separate upper town from its lower rural districts were all that saved the Parliament Buildings. The entire western end of Preston Street, however, had been destroyed.

Rebuilding the site took place over the following two decades. The best part of the existing buildings in the Preston Street neighborhood were built between 1905 and 1920. The structures were basic, clapboard homes for the most part though some two-story apartment style brick clad buildings with stoops dotted the main street. The area has traditionally been inhabited by lower middleclass wage earners typically working in the nearby train yards. These French, Irish, and English workers were a hearty lot and maintained a steady population growth up until the beginning of WWII. Since 1941, however, the area has experienced a steady decline in population and an increase in the age of its residents. Between 1941-1951 the population decreased at a rate of 0.8% per year. By 1956-1961, the rate of decline had increased to

1.2% per year. Changes in land use did much to promote the decline, but a change in the character of the population also contributed to a devolving demographic profile. The neighborhood, like the rest of the City of Ottawa, was aging. On a whole, however, the general profile of the population in the Preston Street area was younger than the city average. The percentage of inhabitants over the age of 55 was 1.2% lower in 1951 and 1.7% lower in 1961 than the general population of the region. In fact, from 1951 onwards the percentage of the neighborhood population under 35 years of age was 3% higher than the City of Ottawa average. By 1961 the average was 5% higher. Though the area was losing its elderly, it was gaining a rejuvenated population base.

In relative terms, persons of French, Irish, and English origin were decreasing at a rate of 16%, 28%, and 39% respectively over the 1950s. On the other hand, the Italian component in the area grew a whopping 256%. In 1951, inhabitants claiming Italian origin numbered 400; by 1961 that number had increased to 1400. The Italian component of the neighborhood had increased its relative size from 6% of the local population to 23% in the same period. It should be noted that although the Preston area contained the largest single concentration of Italians in the City of Ottawa, during the same time period the number of Italians outside the Preston Street area increased from 1% of the general population in 1951 to 3% in 1961. This represents an overall increase of 284%.

The arriving Italians settled amongst the already established French and English families. The French, however (and eventually the Italians) became the two distinctive groups in the area lying west of LeBreton Street and north of Balsam Street. Notable concentrations of Italian families also lived along Bell Street between Eccles Street and Gladstone Avenue as well as near Christie Street. A French predominance lived along the area south of Gladstone Avenue and west of Bell Street.

Whatever their number or location within the neighborhood, the Italian diasporic experience was more than a relocation of an aggregate migrant population from one underdeveloped nation to another developing one. As the arriving individuals coalesced into collective forms of group life, a distinct community emerged with its own definite character, growing institutions, and an unmistakeable social and cultural life.

FIRST ITALIANS

The earliest contact of Italians with what would become Canada dates from 1497 when Giovanni Caboto, a Venetian, explored and claimed for England the territory of Newfoundland. There followed a litany of capable Italian explorers on loan to either England or France. They included Giovanni Verrazzano, in the service of King Francis of France, known as the first European to explore the east coast of North America (the Verrazzano-Narrows bridge in New York is named in his honor); Giuseppe Bressani, a Jesuit missionary who explored the area of New France and the Huron, the present-day north shore of Lake Ontario; and Enrico di Tonti, an associate of René Robert Cavelier, Sieur de La Salle. Tonti was La Salle's "right-hand man," enjoyed great favor with the Frenchman and journeyed with him on his famous exploration of the Mississippi River.

What spurred these men, our first *bone fide* immigrants, to sail in the service of foreign lands?

While the Italian *Rinascimento* (1300-1600) produced one of the most exhilarating sociopolitical and cultural periods in human history, laying the foundations for contemporary Western Civilization with unrivaled achievements in art, philosophy, architecture, literature, and politics, these glory days were soon met with an economic and political downturn. As the European economy turned its gaze westward towards the Americas, the Mediterranean economy went into a deep decline. This, coupled with the Spanish domination of the Iberian peninsula, the rise of Protestantism in Europe and subsequent Counter-Reformation measures by the Church of Rome, the ultra-conservative fear of heresy and torture by the ministers of the Church, the Inquisition, produced a climate of repression and orthodoxy that stifled any sort of growth. The Italian peninsula still produced great thinkers, but they sought and made their fortunes elsewhere. This soon-to-be turned into a backwater of Europe thus provided the intellectual and political underpinnings, as well as the practical know-how, that transformed the newly discovered and expanding territories of the freshly discovered Americas.

Because of its historically advantageous position in the Mediterranean Sea, Italian maritime traders had ruled the area and were the traditional middlemen between the Asian and European markets. Being a land of seafarers, a now dispirited and increasingly depressed Italian peninsula provided a steady supply of adventurers eager to leave its recession-stricken ports. The most famous of these is Cristoforo Colombo, who sailed for Spain under the banner of King Ferdinand II and Queen Isabella. Along with Colombo we must recall Amerigo Vespucci, a Florentine explorer, financier, navigator, and cartographer. The name *America* (the feminine form of the Latinized version of his name, *Americus Vespucius*), or Land of Americus, was used by the German publisher Martin Waldseemüller to baptize the newly found continents he presented in his world maps in the atlas *Cosmographiae Introductio* (1507).[1]

Indeed, many other valorous Italian explorers and adventurers, too many to mention here, and many not mentioned in the annals of history for their exploits, paid the price of anonymity as they lent service to foreign powers in order to escape the depressed conditions back home.[2]

---

1   The full title of the work pays homage to Vespucci: *Introduction to Cosmography with Certain Necessary Principles of Geometry and Astronomy to which are added The Four Voyages of Amerigo Vespucci and A Representation of the Entire World.*

2   This is a partial list of Italian explorers and navigators from *Wikepedia*: Giuseppe Acerbi; Enrico Alberto d'Albertis; Carlo Amoretti (1741–1816); Paolo Andreani; Orazio Antinori; Giosafat Barbaro (1413–1494); Giacomo Beltrami (1779–1855); Scipione Borghese; Vittorio Bottego; Giacomo Bove; Sebastiano Caboto (1474–1557); Umberto Cagni; Giovanni Caboto (1450–1500); Alvise Cadamosto (1432–1483); Gaetano Casati (1838–1902); Giuseppe Castiglione (1688–1766); Cristoforo Colombo (1451–1506); Ambrogio Contarini (1429–1499); Niccolò de' Conti (1395–1469); Andrea Corsali; Giovanni da Pian del Carpine (1185–1252); Ardito Desio (1897–2001); Alfonso de Tonti; Enrico de Tonti; Andrea Doria; Eusebio Kino; Alessandro Malaspina; Lancelotto Malocello; Reinhold Messner; Umberto Nobile; Antonio Pigafetta; Emmanuel Piloti; Marco Polo; Domenico Potorti; Niccolò and Maffeo Polo; Matteo Ricci; Prince Luigi

In the following centuries, motivated by political, ideological, or other considerations, Italians can be found advising the courts of Europe, educating the children of English aristocrats, preforming in the major arenas of Austrian music, enlisting in the foreign military campaigns of rising world powers.[3]

While mass migration from Italy did not begin until after the unification of the peninsula in the 1870s, we can ascertain with relative certainty that some immigration from the northern regions of the peninsula took place in the second half of the 19th Century, between the years 1850 and 1900. It was endemic poverty, however, especially in the southern part of the peninsula, that provided the steady flow of immigrants that ultimately burst into the great diaspora that would inundate the Americas. For the most part, these were seasonal peasant laborers who found that opportunities were better and wages were higher in the Americas, North and South, than in the traditional worker havens of Austria, Switzerland, and France. Cheaper transatlantic steamer fares and a full-fledged propaganda campaign by American job recruiters (usually Italian nationals hired to spread the fable that the streets were paved with gold) also fanned the hopes of the poor with dreams of monetary opportunity.

Some, however, were craftsmen and professionals from the more

---

Amedeo, Duke of the Abruzzi; Pietro Paolo Savorgnan di Brazzà; Giovanni da Verrazzano; Amerigo Vespucci; Ugolino Vivaldi; Vadino Vivaldi.

3   These Italian adventurers, whether dedicated to cultural or military pursuits, gained fame *fuori patria*. One such figure, Giuseppe Garibaldi, best known to Italians as a major figure of the Italian *Risorgimento,* was also a guerilla fighter in the wars for indepedance in Brazil and Uruguay in the 1830s and 1840s. He was particularly revered in the Americas and, during the American Civil War, was offered a commission as a major general with independent command by the Lincoln administratln. Garibaldi never accepted the offer because Lincoln would not declare the war as one against slavery. But perhaps he also preferred to remain in Italy during its own attempt of emancipation from the Austrians. Interestingly, however, the spirit of the freedom fighter remained alive in the Union's fight against Southern secessation. The 'Garibaldi Guard' was the nickname given to the 39th New York Volunteer Infantry Regiment that fought in the American Civil War. The regiment included many Italian-Americans who had also served under Giuseppe Garibaldi in Italy.

prosperous northern regions of the peninsula. Like their unskilled southern laboring counterparts, they too traveled to the Americas in search of better economic opportunities. Political insecurity at home (Italy was in the throes of nation building) and the coming of war (WWI) played a significant role in the decisions of these more affluent Northern Italians to seek a more secure place to live. Many settled in Boston, others in California and were responsible for the growth of the California wine industry. For the most part, the laborers traveled to the ports of New Orleans, Boston, and New York where they became an essential cog in both the emerging cultural milieu and growing industrial complex. Some traveled inland, finding labor in the marble quarries of Vermont and New Hampshire; others settled in the burgeoning cities along the many rivers of North America, laboring in the steel mills of Pittsburgh, extracting clay in the factories of St. Louis; many became railroad laborers and followed the tracks to North Dakota, Montana, Idaho, Washington State or even British Columbia. Their masonry and woodworking skills were instrumental in building the grand churches for the masses, the elite mansions of the new world riche, the Palladian style banks we still see today as part of the North American cityscape. But many were also musicians, teachers, and lawyers who educated the children of the upper class and conveyed Italian sensibilities to Western frontier towns.

The very first Italians that landed in Canada as immigrants served in the British army during the War of 1812, many of them settling in lots granted by Britain to its soldiers in the eastern townships of Quebec and in Southern Ontario. Besides the aforementioned explorers of note and those adventurous soldiers of fortune that found their way into the Canadian wilderness, Canada first witnessed the arrival of professional artisans, teachers, craftsmen, and musicians from Northern Italy in the mid-1800s. It is estimated that by 1881 over 2000 Italians resided in Canada, primarily in the urban centers of the growing metropolises of Montreal and Toronto finding work in construction and manufacturing. In the capital city of Canada, Ottawa, however, the situation was quite different. Hampered primarily by its location in the rugged glacial hills and deep river valleys formed by the confluence of the Ottawa and Rideau Rivers, and saddled with a stagnant single-source lumber-based outback economy, the attractiveness of the region as an immigrant destination never caught fire.

It is difficult to account for the number of Italians living in Ottawa at the beginning of the 1800s. Reliance on church records for births, deaths, baptisms, citizenship pledges, worker lists, musicians, bands, artists, job ads in papers, ads for music or language teachers, and Gatineau lumber camp logbooks, are all interesting historical artefacts but provide little real, hard, and dependable evidence. Never accurate, this information is often biased, inaccurate, often altered. Furthermore, a perusal of city and church records reveal that valuable records have been lost; victim of natural catastrophes such as flood, fire, or simple human neglect.

In 1855, the newly named capital City of Ottawa was incorporated and extricated itself from Carleton County in order to amalgamate and form a proper tax base. The construction of the Rideau Canal connecting Bytown to the St. Lawrence, the Ottawa Railway and the Bytown and Prescott Railway had created a link for the now burgeoning town with the outside world.

The area was further determined by the railways whose meanderings separated neighborhoods and created others. The Bytown and Prescott Railway (narrow gauge) entered the town from Manotick Station and proceeded through today's Gloucester, across the Rideau River to Taggart Street in Lowertown, where there was a station. J. R. Booth's railway, on the other hand, entered the city from the western town or Renfrew and ran along a path that eventually became the Queensway today. From this Queensway footprint the railway tracks ran north to LeBreton Flats; another spur followed the east side of the Rideau Canal, ran past the original Canadian National Railway Station (today's renovated Conference Centre) in front of the future site of the Chateau Laurier Hotel (inaugurated by its namesake, Sir Wilfrid Laurier, on 12 June 12 1912). The tracks then crossed Wellington/ Rideau Street and travelled along the east side of the 8 entrance locks of the Rideau Canal.[4]

---

[4] The magnificent ascending flight of 8 locks rising from the Ottawa River is now framed by Canada's Parliament Buildings on one side and the towering Chateau Laurier Hotel (now Fairmont Château Laurier)

At this juncture in its growth, there were discernable neighborhoods in the Bytown/Ottawa district. The large estate bequeathed to the town by Colonel John By at his death in 1836 was acquired by a land development company owned by group of local speculators who began what would become a business district. The area began immediately south of Nicholas Sparks' property and extended as far south as Gladstone Avenue and Mann Avenue.

In the years 1850-1900, Uppertown (Vittoria Avenue, Wellington Street and Sparks Streets) was inhabited by the English, Scottish, and Irish Protestants; the Irish Catholics and French lived in Lowertown; Lebreton Flats was home to blue collar mill workers but a settlement of workers crouched around the mills run by Thomas McKay in New Edinburgh. These neighborhoods were united by social class and not ethnicity, a reality that was to foster the cosmopolitan, if not elitist, character, of the evolving City of Ottawa.

The newly incorporated City of Ottawa saw its first Italians settle close to the city core. Here they formed small, class specific, worker communities with other immigrants. The employment opportunities for these first intrepid individuals were scant. Ottawa did not boast a diversified economy similar to the already established cities of Toronto and Montreal, or the grand metropolises south of the Canadian border. Subsequently, most newly arrived immigrants worked in the service industry as cooks, waiters, and tailors. Very few became loggers. Fewer still were skilled craftsmen. Some settled in Lowertown, near the growing elite Sandy Hill district.[5]

---

on the other. This is the largest single set of locks on the entire Rideau system providing a lift of 24 m (79 ft.). The old Commissariat building (the business/supply office used during the building of the Rideau Canal), sits nestled on the promontory created by the locks. Built in 1827, it is the oldest surviving building in Ottawa. It now houses the Bytown Museum.

5   Sandy Hill was the name given to the promontory of sandy soil that sits between the Rideau River and the Rideau Canal. The area, east of the downtown district, was originally the estate of Louis-Theodore Besserer, a retired notary from Quebec City who was a veteran of the War of 1812 and then member of the Legislative Assembly of Lower Canada who purchased the property in 1845. He eventually subdivided this large property and sold off building lots, transforming the barren hilly topography into rectangular streets. In 1876,

The Sandy Hill district is located immediately east of the downtown core. Known for its uneven terrain and sandy soil due to its being wedged between the Rideau Canal and Rideau River, the area was Ottawa's wealthiest enclave up until the migration of its notable lumber baron families to the higher Rockliffe bluffs in the early 1900s. White-collar government workers then settled the area but a large infusion of relatively wealthy home buyers remained attracted to the area's many life-style advantages. These included proximity to government buildings, a viable downtown commercial district, and the Lowertown farmers' markets. The area boasted a varied architectural style with flourishes of European romantic formalism. The mansion size Victorian Gothic, Georgian and Romanesque style buildings attracted a diversity of skilled masons and wood workers from France, Scotland, Ireland, Germany, USA, Russia, and of course, Italy.

Several Italian names sprinkled Sandy Hill. Of note is the name Guttadoria. The newly arrived immigrant family operated a small convenience store on the corner of Nelson and Wilbrod Streets. The

---

a portion of the area was purchased by the Freehold Association of Ottawa, a partnership of three Ottawa businessmen that included the lumber baron James Maclaren, banker Charles Magee and industrialist, and also former Member of Parliament Robert Blackburn. These men transformed Sandy Hill into an area of luxury residences. Institutions also played an important role in the shaping of the Sandy Hill area. The College de Bytown (now known as the University of Ottawa) for example, was built with the idea of attracting white-collar workers to the area. The institutions also served to attract other businesses and institutions thereby establishing Sandy Hill as an important place, not just an average little community. The homes and buildings were often built (not owned) by skilled Italian tradesman. Many of these buildings are now owned by the Heritage Canada Foundation. One such Heritage Home, locatred at 5 Blackburn Avenue was owned by William Fraser and his family until 1911; then passed to Ewan McLachlin of McLachlin Bros. Limited. Another lumber magnate, David G. Gilmour took up residence from 1921-1924. Between 1940 and 1945, Captain William "Billy" Avery Bishop, World War I flying ace and first Canadian airman to receive the Victoria Cross, resided at the house with his family. It is said that Winston Churchill joined him here for drinks and cigars on more than one occasion. From 1947-1956, the house served as the offices of the Italian embassy. Katherine Fletcher, *Capital Walks: Walking Tours of Ottawa* (Toronto: McClelland &Stewart, 1993).

Imbros name has also remained associated with the area as their grocery market and restaurant remained a Lowertown landmark up to the late 1970s. Most blue-collar workers, however, lived, as we shall see, in what would become known as *The Village*.

What is historically noteworthy is that the initial presence of Italians in Ottawa went almost unnoticed. Hard working, not prone to trouble, inconspicuous in public affairs, they set the tone for future generations of Italian-Canadians conspicuous for their many silent accomplishments in all fields of professional endeavor.

Numbers

By 1880, the first immigrants from Southern Italy were arriving in Ottawa, settling first in Ottawa Ward. The 1881 census reported 8 Italian households in the city of Ottawa for a total of 36 persons of Italian origin. Names of heads of households include: Francis Biagi, Stefano Muscardino, and John Varalo. These men were all born in Italy between the years 1836 and 1854 and represent the earliest migrants from Italy to the Ottawa region. No other city ward included Italians in the 1881 census.[6]

Table Source: The 1881 census.

Name	Born	Sex	Origin
BAIGI, Francis	born 1844	Male	Italian
Birth: Italy (Painter)			
BEZANO, Alfred	born 1836	Male	Italian
Birth: Italy (Plasterer)			
COURSOLLE, Jacob	born 1840	Male	Italian
Birth: Italy (Cab Driver Horse and Buggy)			
GRECAU, Raphael	born 1850	Male	Italian
Birth: Italy (name is GRECO)			
LAUREN, Joseph	born 1854	Male	Italian
Birth: Italy (Marble Worker)			
LA MOTHE, Hemo G.	born 1851	Male	French
Birth: Italy (note: French)			
MUSCARDINO, Stefano	born 1854	Male	Italian
Birth: Italy (Coalporter)			
VARALO, Gianni	born 1839	Male	Italian
Birth: Italy (Musician)			

---

6 The 1881 census is available online at www.familysearch.org.

According to the same census, household records list these men as already married or married locally.

Alfred Bezano	Male	45 years	Born in: Italy
Marguerite Bezano	Female	33 years	Born in: Quebec
Joseph Bezano	Male	15 years	Born in: Quebec
Jean Bezano	Male	12 years	Born in: Ontario
Elmire Bezano	Female	14 years	Born in: Ontario
Adele Bezano	Female	10 years	Born in: Ontario
Marie Louise Bezano	Female	6 years	Born in: Ontario
Denise Bezano	Female	4 years	Born in: Ontario

The 1881 census, for instance, notes that Alfred Bezano (above) married a French-Canadian woman; their offspring were all born in Canada.

In 1901, persons claiming Italian origin had increased to 305. By 1913, the number of households listed as Italian had increased to 150.[7] By 1911, the Italian community has expanded and has moved to the Preston Street neighborhood. Sojourners now appear as boarders in Italian homes. The family of Dominic and Mary Calculina contains four single male borders of working age.[8]

44	35	Calculina Dominck	M	Head	M	Sep 1883	27
45	35	Calculina Mary	F	Wife	M	May 1896	25
46	35	Lipuma Salvatore	M	Lodger	S	May 1865	46
47	35	Mondi Guiseppe	M	Lodger	S	Mar 1872	39
48	35	Canado Francesco	M	Lodger	S	Apr 1868	43
49	35	In**acesa Gaetano	M	Lodger	S	Feb 1877	34

Tightened immigration policy and a general political hostility towards Fascism restricted the number of entries to Canada from Italy before WWII. Nevertheless, by 1930 over 29,000 Italian immigrants called Canada their home. Laborers and unskilled farmers and peasants from central and southern Italy, especially from the regions of Calabria,

---

7 By comparison, the 1911 Census recorded over 7000 of persons claiming Italian origin in Montreal and over 4600 in Toronto.

8 Source: 1911 Census of Victoria Ward, Ottawa, Canada. www.automatedgenealogy.com.

Abruzzo, Molise, and Sicily overwhelmed Canadian immigration statistics. Strong family and village ties provided a network for immigration that attracted an ever-growing number of laborers and their families to Canadian cities. Fueled by both an expanding economy and a widespread shortage of male labor following WWII, Canada became a prime destination for the Italian diaspora. Indeed, Italy ranked as the top country of origin for immigration to Canada after the United Kingdom.[9] Principal destinations for the increasing wave of immigrants became the metropolitan areas of Ontario (62%), Quebec (20%), and British Colombia (10%), with majority concentrations, again, in the burgeoning cities of Toronto, Montreal, and a growing Vancouver.

The number of Italians in Ottawa increased in the years during and after WWII. In 1941, 1622 persons claiming Italian heritage lived in Ottawa; that number reached 2,150 by 1951. Ottawa began receiving the bulk of its Italian immigrant population between 1950 and 1970 with the years 1957-1958 showing the greatest immigration. Close to 80% of these newly arriving Italians were sponsored by relatives already living in Ottawa. In 1961, 8,263 persons of Italian origin called Ottawa home. The decade of the 1960s was the most prolific for immigration as numbers soared to 14,680 by 1971.

Though earlier migration to Ottawa was typically from Northern Italian areas, the great majority of Italians who came to Ottawa in the 1950s and 1960s were from Central and Southern Italian rural villages. These emigrants were concentrated in two Italian regions: the central region of Abruzzo (Pretoro, Rapino, and surrounding zone) and the southern region of Calabria (Cleto, Cosenza, Reggio Calabria). Other regions, including Lazio, Campania, Veneto, Piemonte, Molise, and Sicily are represented but to a much lesser extent.

It is interesting that immigration to Ottawa was never of a recurrent nature. This in contrast to earlier migrations to the new world that saw migrant men arrive for short work periods, save money, return to Italy, then migrate alone again. Possibly due to distance and/or relative

---

9   *Immigrants in Ottawa; Socio-cultural Composition and Socio-economic Conditions,* Social Planning Council of Ottawa, December 2004. ISBN# 1895732-36-0.

comfort and stable employment opportunities, Italian immigrants to Ottawa tended to settle the area and eventually raise families.

In 1976 the Canadian government decided to include the Mother-Tongue option on the official census questionnaire. This was done to rectify possible misinterpretations of evolving ethnic profiles. Statistics could now be used to determine the inference of increasing Anglicization or enduring cultural identification within original ethnic minority groups. In other words, and according to Statistics Canada:

"'Mother tongue' refers to the first language learned at home in childhood and still understood by the person at the time the data was collected. If the person no longer understands the first language learned, the mother tongue is the second language learned. For a person who learned two languages at the same time in early childhood, the mother tongue is the language this person spoke most often at home before starting school. The person has two mother tongues only if the two languages were used equally often and are still understood by the person. For a child who has not yet learned to speak, the mother tongue is the language spoken most often to this child at home. The child has two mother tongues only if both languages are spoken equally often so that the child learns both languages at the same time."[10]

If we consider language as the primary identity marker for an ethnic community, in 1996, 11,760 (1.6%) Ottawa citizens reported speaking Italian as a mother tongue. By 2001 this number had declined to 11,215 or 1.4% of the Ottawa population. When counting Ethnic Origin (those who consider themselves as having an Italian identity or heritage but do not consider Italian as their mother tongue) however, the 2001 number rises to 37,435 or 3.56% of the Ottawa population. For comparison, in the same 2001 census, Chinese (23,785; 3%) replaced Arabic (22,735; 2.9%) as the most spoken Non-official mother tongue in Ottawa while Italian became a distant third.

The 2006 Census reaffirmed the position of Chinese as the third most spoken language in Canada after English and French. Italian remained in fourth place Canada-wide though numbers declined. Similar results were reported in Ontario where Chinese languages

---

10 Statistics Canada. http://www12.statcan.gc.ca/census-recensement/2016/ref/dict/pop095-eng.cfm.

represented 4.1% (500,000) of Ontario's population, up from 3.7%. Italian claimed a fourth place standing with numbers declining to 4.7% of Ontario's population.

In Ottawa, Arabic (30,890) replaced Italian as the third most common mother tongue after English and French. Chinese (26,890) and Spanish (13,280) moved ahead of Italian (11,510) reflecting a dwindling number of citizens claiming Italian ancestry, Italian mother-tongue, or Italian identity. According to the 2006 Census, therefore, citizens of Italian origin represent 3.56% of the Ottawa population of 774,072.

Acculturation

Urbanization, generalized schooling, occupational and geographic mobility, as well as increased contact between different social and ethnic groups, all contribute to a weakened identification with the original immigrant group and a greater tolerance towards loss of mother language (shifting language use) and intermarriage (shifting cultural identity). It was not until 1981, however, when the inclusion of both mother-tongue and current home language questions in the 1981 Canada Census, that statistics provided a better statistical measure to evaluate the ethno-cultural profile of the evolving Italian population into a maturing Italian-Canadian community.

The profile question on the 1981 Census asked the following: "To which ethnic or cultural group did you or your ancestors belong on *first coming* to this continent?" Then a list of choices was offered. Respondents were asked to select from 17 categories; Italian was number 9. Census numbers, from this census forward, would now better reflect ethnic origin. In the evolving multicultural Canadian context, *ethnics* would now be classified as either immigrants or descendants of immigrants from countries other than Britain or France. Demographic data from each *ethnic* group could now be compared to the entire population in terms of location, age, occupation, income, mother-tongue, etc..

It must be noted that in 1986 the Employment Equity Act came into force. Subsequently, the politically charged reference to *"first coming"* of the 1981 census was removed from future enumerations, thus changing the meaning of the question, which now dealt more with an idiosyncratic personal identity rather than with original group origin. This effectively increased the number of respondents who considered themselves as maintaining a duel identity for whatever reason. It also increased Canada's advancing reputation as a pluralistic and cosmopolitan nation.

In 1991, statistics on visible minorities were counted fot the first time as required by Canada's Equity Act. The Employment Equity Act states that "members of visible minorities" means persons, other than aboriginal peoples, who are non-Caucasian in race or non-white in color. Since the 1991 census, Statistics Canada has used this definition in Census questionnaires.

The 2001 Census showed 726,725 Canadians listing Italian as their mother tongue; 544,090 claimed Italian as part of their ethnic origin, for a total of 1.2 million Italian-Canadians nationwide. We note that Italian is listed as a Non-official Mother Tongue (mother tongue is the first language learned in the home) on the Census form.

If we jump to the Census figures of 2016, where Italy is listed as a Southern European nation, a total of 1,587,965 Canadians claim Italian origin. Only 375,635, however, list Italian as their mother tongue. In Ontario, a total of 72,960 persons claim the Italian language in the Non-official Mother Tongue category, 9,030 of which lived in Ottawa. Members of the Ottawa community who claim Italy as their place of birth numbered 5,410. If we consider the number of Ottawa households in which Italian is spoken in the home, the number falls to 2,500 (1,110 males, 1,390 females).

The profile of the Italian and Italian-Canadian community reflects the evolving ethnocultural characteristics of the general population. As first waves of immigrants and second-generation children acquiesce to third-generation assimilation, the numbers will effectively demonstrate fewer Canadians who claim Italian as their Mother tongue. Subsequently, diversity will grow among the Canadian-born population in coming generations regardless of future immigration patterns.

Importantly, the cultural footprint former generations leave does not necessarily determine the interest third and fourth-generation Canadian-Italians (Canadian-born) evidence in maintaining their original cultural identity. First and second-generation immigrants tend to race towards assimilation in an effort to achieve success in the larger community. A distinctive characteristic of the Canadian mosaic, however, is that many third-generation youths want to "take back" their heritage.[11]

The recent resurgence of interest in Italian cultural identity in Canadian cities (which follows a similar and earlier resurgence in many major cities in the U.S.A.) fits squarely into the notion of Canadian multiculturalism. While donning their Italian culture makes them distinct, being Canadian-Italian also makes them part of a larger country made up of small immigrant groups. Wanting to cook like grandma, or speak Italian, visit Italy, or follow Italian soccer teams, becomes a means towards proudly affirming the legacy of their ancestors while also making a powerful statement of generational independence. This social-cultural empowerment foments a strong political (and here I intend political, *polis*, as a collection of citizens) collectivity that is indeed the hallmark of Canada.

---

11   Shawn Conner, "Third-generation Italian-Canadians more interested in preserving their heritage than previous generation, SFU study finds," *The Vancouver Sun*, 03 March 2015.

COMMUNITY

Was it ever sustainable?

Every city, every community within the conglomeration of communities that create a metropolitan city, has a projected outward image and a real, inwardly directed, self-sustaining image of its place and importance as a grounded sociocultural space. Beyond the considerable natural beauty of its geographical site, the City of Ottawa has unfortunately lacked the planned grandeur of other world capitals. Vestiges of Commonwealth colonialism (its privileged location somewhere in between the more influential towns of Montreal and Toronto, yet far enough from the American border to avoid invasion), marred by its lumber-laden rough-hewn past, and eventually hamstrung by the short-sighted pettiness of Canadian politicians, it is only now acquiring an appearance commensurate with its stature as a national capital city on a world stage.

The Italian-Canadian community, similarly, has suffered from the same lackluster image and structural malaise. Though it identifies itself with a clearly definable Preston Street area (or areas if we include the Carleton Heights and Fisher Heights residential neighborhoods) and its outward storefront image might portray political unity and cultural cohesion to a non-Italian outsider, the self-image the group generates behind its official group facade betrays an unfortunate and increasing breakdown of traditional socio-cultural and socio-structural patterns.

The purpose of this chapter is to discuss the cultural and structural image of the Ottawa Italian-Canadian community in relation to their perceived self-identity. As a conglomeration of loosely disjointed congregations of regional and often village-specific associations, professional groups, and independently-minded individuals, the community is probably best described as an ethnically inspired ecosystem; sustainable yet precariously balanced upon the slippery slopes of mutual consensus. One of the most telling realities of this group is that it may not be a community at all in the traditional definition of a North American "Little Italy," and that pronouncements of its imminent death through generational attrition are not premature, but rather unnecessary since it never really boasted any undeniable or identifiable life.

The Italians that settled in Ottawa hoped to find a haven that would provide a better life than the one many had left behind in the villages of Italy. In most cases the dream came true. The greater part found immediate work, established families, provided education for their children, achieved professional success, acquired societal recognition. What one generation could not accomplish was left for the next to complete. But becoming an Italian-Canadian also had its price. Apart from the immediate and profound sense of personal dispossession, the loss of family ties and the insufferable distance from one's own personal reality in Italy, the immigrant came to lose a sense of his own selfhood as normally expressed through his Italian culture.

Hospitable as it may have seemed, the new land demanded a cost usually exacted in back-breaking labor, substandard living conditions, ethnic rivalry, senseless daily caricature, and often visciously overreaching stereotypes. In reaction to the daily *fatica* (toil) of providing for oneself and family, the immigrant formed a loose aggregate that eventually developed into more defined social groups that together helped engender a sense of local community and cultural continuity. Many of these groups endure to this day and form an integral part of the Italian-Canadian's urban experience in the city of Ottawa. All too often, however, this notion of collaborative social continuity leads to a false and romanticized retrospect about the actual history of the Italian migrant group where present and past are conflated into a simplified single story of enduring and shared solidarity.

No great North American city can be understood without exploring it as a destination for newcomers, for myriad groups with their parents, for children and their dreams, each with folkways and values that butt-up against each other to form indigenous survival networks. The codes to measure the acculturation of these evolving groups are many and based on a variety of factors that range from the economic to the spiritual. The broad categories of social history, often based solely upon the perceived upward success of a group, are conveniences that do not often account for the truly complicated nature of man, of individual immigration projects, and of the differing beliefs and mores of the world's ethno-cultures. A common denominator of any judgement, however, must be the baseline value of a sense of shared community.

Before the Industrial Revolution, three frames of reference constructed life around humans: the nuclear family, the extended family, the local community. With few exceptions, personal relationships rarely extended beyond this tightly-knit health, welfare, educational, political, business, and information network. All this changed dramatically over the last several centuries as tradition became convention, spirituality became self-fulfilling righteousness, and fortifying groups became lonely individuals. Most importantly, commodity became struggle. It is not that family and sense of community disappeared completely; they were instead partially, sometimes effectively, replaced by the laws of the state and the needs of the marketplace. Enter the Imagined (call it virtual in contemporary terminology) community.

In recent decades, pseudo-identification with the habits and interests of vegetarians, environmentalists, unionists, and other ideologically based realities, has eclipsed the romantic notions of one people, one nation and one religion in favor of tribal associations that shatter the collective into shards of dissimalar interest groups. The most insidious and pervasive tribal identification overcome smaller group identification and reimagines everyone as part of a great consumer cosmos eagerly purchasing and consuming in order to maintain some imagined global status quo.

The ethnic community has become just such an imagined state of overarching consumer beings. The history of ethnic enclaves is often told as a series of evolving events and positive social structures that provide the displaced individual with a sense of both cultural unity and social identity. There is truth here, but simply enumerating a familiar list of yearly feasts or the personal achievements of a community leader can be misleading. Most members of an ethnic community never appreciate or even appraise the relative calm and well-being a united ethnic neighborhood affords. Most never comprehend the political and economic strength that an ethnic community wields; these communities are the true lifesaver buoying many sinking cities in North America. It's really a matter of timing. Once the perceived relative comfort and security of a community is dissipated, it is often too late to turn back the clock of presumed progress.

In Ottawa, the term *Italian community* is a politically loaded and mine-filled topic. Is the community real or willfully imagined; centered on common goals or dispersed in myriad associations; united politically or merely an aggregate?

J.P. Fitzpatrick, to my mind, ably sums the traditional definition of an ethnic community. For Fitzpatrick a community is: "a group of people who follow a way of life or patterns of behavior which mark them out as different from people of another society, or from other people in the larger society in which they live or to which they have come. They . . . have generally come from the same place . . . they speak the same language, probably have the same religious beliefs. They tend to 'stick together,' to help and support each other. They have expectations of loyalty one to the other and methods of control."[12]

According to this definition, the term community expresses a certain sense of dynamic purpose. It suggests a measure of "institutional completeness", of "available" services, of common cultural currency, of unity of spirit, indeed of inviolable community pride.

An ethnic community does not arise in a vacuum. It is not *ethnic* simply because people from a similar linguistic background have decided to live there. It is instead part of a larger socio-historical process that very often produces disunity. Any attempt to understand the cultural bonding (or lack of) within the Italian-Canadian community of Ottawa must take into account the historical differences firstly between the peoples that emigrated from Italy and secondly, the disunity these inbred historical biases engendered. The specific context for the greater population of this community (Abruzzese and Calabrese) need not be traced back further than the villages from whence most came. Isolated

---

12 J.P. Fitzpatrick, "The Importance of Community in the Process of Immigrant Assimilation," in W. E. Mann, ed., *The Underside of Toronto*, (Toronto: McClelland, 1970): 183.

for centuries within mountainous ravines, governed by numerous faceless rulers from different tribes, dynasties, nation-states, and countries, isolationism became a specific manifestation of village life. This sense of distrust, if not disdain, for the Other, (especially from northern climes) transcends continental shores. It caused the early migrants to seek others of their own kind, to live together in a space of relative security and familiarity, to form associations that provided mutual support and unspoken understanding.

Indeed, the migration pattern for the Italian-Canadian community of Ottawa follows the following traditional template. The first pioneer migrants established a space that was foremost a migration from a familiar place to one of unknown destiny. The first immigrants then beckoned others from the same village and thus began the process of familiarization; their new space was acclimatized with known traditions, kindred mores, similar aspirations, but above all, shared difficulties.

The result is that the Italian-Canadian community of Ottawa, as many others in Canada enjoying the political privileges of multiculturalism, has become a socio-political entity characterized primarily by village ties. By wilfully organizing themselves as disparate groups, the newly arrived immigrants retained their old-world views and traditional social structural hierarchies, as well as their specific village dialects and cultural heritage. Although it can be argued that this is a common feature of many migrant communities, no where is the phenomenon more pronounced than in Canada. This trait persists, to some extent, to the present day in Ottawa and is the major contributing factor to the lack of real economic, political, and social cohesion in its Italian-Canadian community.

Yet, while these factors have laid the groundwork for the *campanilismo* (localism) attitude prevalent in this community, they alone are not responsible for the often negative situational attitude that surrounds many of the social events, public demonstrations, the local associations, and the fund-raising attempts that pepper the yearly social calendar. The intensity of participation and support for any outreaching event has remained contingent upon acute need (i.e., around specific issues) surrounding any one situation, rather than community solidarity.

Whereas many (usually the same minority of the Italian-Canadian community) normally participate in the copius activities that grace the yearly social calendar, most members of the community have resisted joining formal associations that embrace community-wide issues. A latent *campanilismo* replaces genuine concern and mass participation with studied indifference. The result is that activities never really take hold, they too often dwindle; formal organizations languish, and the general community returns to its traditional modes of introverted behavior relevant to restricted self-interests. This is so because the most intense spheres of interaction within the community infrastructure continue to be based on kinship and village ties. Traditional ascription and adhesion to these individual groups is the organizational factor that breeds negativity of spirit in the Ottawa Italian-Canadian community.

The most obvious basis of perceived disunity is to be found, not surprisingly, in the nature of the very organizations meant to unite them. Some of these organizations consider themselves pan-Italian-Canadian. CIBPA (Canadian Italian Business and Professional Association), and the NCIC (National Congress of Italian-Canadians: National Capital District) for example, are not selectively limited to serving people from exclusive regions, small towns, or villages. This pan-Italian-Canadianism is often accompanied with an open policy towards Canadians in general, the motivating factor the recruitment of second and third generation non-Italian speakers and their growing families. The languages of exchange in these organizations includes English, often French, thus avoiding regional and cultural differences thereby promoting a broader spectrum of interest and participation.

The great majority of the associations and groups have much in common with each other in that they promote the local and intra-regional historical differences of their membership. This, however, does not unite them in their cause nor is there any true cooperation between these larger associative organizations and the smaller clubs that feed them their potential membership. On the contrary, the larger organizations are often looked upon as divisive; they may also be viewed as competitors for a dwindling pie of prospective ethnic recruits. The small clubs see themselves as providing a need for sociability among people of similar dialect and background, something the larger organizations cannot do because they cater to a more open and liberal spirit of cooperation amongst equals. This widespread basis of disunity renders the achievement of real community-based goals difficult if not impossible to achieve since the individual contending groups see themselves as incompatible.

An example of this disunity, generally speaking, is based on the differences in the tasks the two distinct groups set for themselves. The larger organizations, for the most part, often have a political and/or cultural goal in mind. They are interested in socio-political survival. The smaller clubs mostly seem very disinterested in any such endeavors, content to *arrangiarsi* (make due) with accommodating fortunate opportunities, directed by improvised strategies that may resolve an immediate crisis but that merely guarantee the perpetuation of controlling cliques.

In addition to these two bases of disunity, others must be noted. Clubs and organizations compete for the same facilities for their social activities. They often solicit participation from the same people for their fund raising and social events. Also, some groups, which had operated under one roof at one time, no longer feel the need to remain with former members and form their own, new social clubs. As these groups pursue different strategies and aims, they tend to accentuate differences, discontinuity, and petty rivalries. Over the years, all this has helped foster a regretful climate of unfortunate pessimism, while perpetuating a situation of ongoing and unprofitable cliquish separation.

The question of whether the Italian-Canadian community of Ottawa is divided into cliques or myopically motivated social groups is impossible to answer by statistical data. Yet, in addition to the natural clannishness that an ethnic group normally exhibits, it seems that one may logically distill the group into three categories: old pioneer immigrants, the newly arrived immigrants, and both of these versus second and subsequently, third generation Italian-Canadians.

The older immigrants, original emigrees, may be divided into two subgroups: those that arrived in the early 1900s and those that arrived from the 1950s onwards. This portion of the community can be broken down further according to age and the relative number of foreign and native born that make-up the two groups.

Very few of the original, pre-1950s immigrants remain but their names still resonate in the community. The familiar names of these pioneer families include: Adamo, Bortolotti, Chiarelli, Costantini, Disipio, Guzzo, Imbros, Pantalone, Tiezzi, Zappa, and Zito.

The Canadian-reared offspring of these early immigrants eventually became leaders and entrepreneurs of the future community. As sons and daughters of the pioneers, they rubbed shoulders, often, with elders from the group that arrived after 1950. This has posed some interesting consequences for the community since second-generation Canadian born Italian-Canadians (children of the early immigrants) have often competed for leadership roles within the community with first generation Italian emigrees from the 1950s of similar age.

Differences of lifestyle and cultures produced rifts between the generally less educated, more conservative Italian immigrants from the 1950s and their contemporary, better educated, Canadian-born age group. While the immigrating group was primarily motivated by economic necessity, the Canadian-born Italians, sometimes of the same age, exhibited patterns of economic mobility that included greater social interaction with the English and French Canadian community. Thus, notwithstanding often similar ages, these two groups display markedly different attitudes and outlooks towards community life that have often and unfortunately impacted negatively upon the community, if only due to the stalemate that the jockeying for social status incurred.

A brief, but telling, example of this type of dysfunctional standoff is the birth of the Madonna della Risurrezione Parish in the mid-1980s. Though St. Anthony's Church had served the entire community since its inception in 1913, the post 1950s immigrants felt it incumbent upon themselves to construct a church of their own, and in their own newer neighborhood. Many of the Italian families that surrounded the old church no longer lived in the Preston Street area but had relocated to the Fisher and Carleton Heights district. Now, while growth and expansion in a community must always be viewed as a positive generational accomplishment, the creation of a new parish in the smallish Italian community of Ottawa caused considerable consternation. The notion underlying this then controversial achievement of a second parish in the *New Italy* as it was often disparagingly called, implied that the needs of the newer community (prospering new immigrants) were not being met by the older one (children of the pioneer immigrants). A new "independent mission" was needed.[13] To be clear, while the immigrant's response to a North American environment is adaptation, the expansion of socio-cultural horizons (especially the building of a new church) that sees the immigrant as protagonist, can destabalize the community and shape the direction of transformation within the community that no one can neither foresee, control or (as happened), in many instances accept. But eventually accept everyone did. The new church brought a wealth of energy to the community; inspiring many to form new social groups, create new social events, and establish new religious celebrations. Rather than separate the *New Italy* from the older Preston Street reality, the two parishes today function to form a more cosmopolitan Italian-Canadian Catholic community.

Returning to our argument, now let us imagine the offspring of these two groups. In other words, the third-generation grandchildren of the pioneer group on one hand and the second-generation children of the 1950s immigrants on the other. How do they relate? They too exhibit considerable differences. Though often of similar age, the former group, because they are third-generation) feels more removed from their Italian origins. Many, after having finished their education and having begun to raise families, attempt to rediscover their roots. This third generation is traditionally an inquisitive lot, interested in Italian culture and the mainland, but more concerned, too often, with ego issues such as memory and family genealogy.

The second-generation youth of the 1950s group, on the other hand, lived an experience much closer to their parents' travails though they faced fewer economic difficulties. Sheltered by a limiting though nurturing social network, they found the Italian community fairly well established, a few associations already formed, the church already constructed. As a result, they have had to spend less time organizing the community and have found time for personal pursuits that move beyond the walls of their homes and the limiting effects of traditional associations. This has caused a rift between these two generations and

---

13 The Archdiocesan Decree of 13 April 1984 officially established the Church of The Madonna della Risurrezione.

has led to a distancing of both from traditional community affairs. Since both groups are normally better educated, they do not intermingle with the Italian-Canadian community as frequently as their parents.

This ideological difference between the multi-layered generations of the community is publically manifested when visiting the old neighborhood. For the third-generation grandchildren of the original immigrants, Preston Street serves as a focus for cultural identification, while for the second generation of children from the 50s immigration, it is and remains a place of commerce and entertainment.

These groups: the elders, the 1950s group, the troubled second and third-generation midlings (and eventual offspring) hardly ever intermingle beyond family occasions. Subsequently, the perceived alienation between the groups of older and younger, hyphenated and non-hyphenated individuals, and the subsequent attachment to or detachment from traditions and customs, is continually widening. Differences in income and occupational patterns, cultural pursuits, daily professional obligations, and expanding kinship structures beyond the Italian community, also proscribe amenable interaction. Divisions are inevitable. The first-generation immigrants, both pre and post 1950s, remain the most clannish, affiliating with associations that offer regional identification. The second generation of Italian-Canadians with parents from the original immigrants are mostly involved with benevolent organizations. The younger second and third generation grandchildren of all groups are usually absent from all organized association life.

Upstart groups sporadically entertain the notion of creating a youth inspired association that promotes *Italianicity* and a more contemporary mindset. One well-meaning group, the Giovani 84, had attempted to rally Italian-Canadian youth with a politically inspired sports agenda but with little real or lasting success. Others have included the Circolo Giovanile, St. Anthony Soccer Club youth teams, as well as youth groups associated with Italian Schools. Beyond the St. Anthony teams, these groups were sporadic at best. Initial enthusiasm is normally squelched once the founder's energy dissipates into community indifference and neglect.

More recently, The Sons of Carpineto Romano, a group of second-generation (1950s parents) business professionals with childhood ties leading back to their parents' Club Carpineto Romano, founded a benevolent society in 2014 dedicated to fundraising endeavors that include golf tournaments and dinner dances for local cancer relief. They are truly unique in the empty firmament of clubs engendered by second or third-generation Italian-Canadian youth. Perhaps their focus on non-Italian activities and apolitical stance allows the best of their inbred Italian character to shine.

Conclusions

When writing about the phenomenon of immigration and the immediate identification of the Italian immigrant in Ottawa as an ethnic, one must come to terms with the sincere attempts of hard working and honest people to form communities in which their merits and sacrifices are both known and appreciated. Building communities in which each individual constituent can learn, share, collaborate, and ultimately survive is critical for a community's growth and relevancy. A social network functions best when interactions are relatively easy, make sense, are secured by shared traditions, and allow for intuitive and positive growth.

But it is not easy; especially when individuals habitually reserve different perspectives, public expectations, and personal ambitions as the backdrop of neighborly activities. People are unpredictable, often creative, usually diverse; bringing them together in spaces where they can interact and socially engage can often become overwhelming. But most communities survive, some even thrive amidst the normal chaos, despite the people that are a part of them.

The sense of an Italian community in Ottawa is, to my mind, a fleeting phenomenon, a studied and crafted stance that has been cultivated over a few generations, nurtured in the young and polished by the old in an attempt to ensure a lasting heritage. But no community can remain fixated on its origins or ponder its future incessantly without succumbing to eventual malaise and protracted demise.

The Ottawa Italian-Canadian community, similar to the plight of any beleaguered immigrant, too often wandered between two worlds. One effectively dead or moribund, belonging to a distant Italian past, essentially unknown in its vital cultural aspects and therefore redressed in vintage, often stereotypical nostalgia. The other world is a present and immediate reality that is estranged from contemporary Italian peninsular mores and trends, rooted in Canadian sensibilities, but willed into fragile existence by the tenacity, volition, and determination of community leaders.

The strength of this community has always been its people. Strong willed, competent, often petulant, but never able to confront an unknown and uncertain future with steadiness, resolve, and with an enduring and endearing sense of community spirit and unbridled devotion to the dream of Canadian progress mixed with Italian pride.

The relatively small Italian-Canadian community of Ottawa, when compared to Toronto or Montreal, has witnessed the disappearance of significant immigration from Italy. Indeed, despite ranking fifth among Canada's five largest urban centers as a destination for immigrants, very few, if any Italian immigrants, have settled in Ottawa since 1980. This would account for the dwindling number of mother tongue speakers and the subsequent integration of a relatively spiritless Italian community into an amorphous Canadian landscape.

Statistically, the history of Italian immigration had not achieved a relative impact on Ottawa if compared to the impact Italians have had on the larger urban centers of Montreal and Toronto. In 1911, for example, 1% of the population of Ottawa, or 643 persons, identified themselves of Italian origin. By 1961, that percentage had meagerly grown to 2%, or 4976 persons. In 2004, Italy was no longer listed as a top source immigration country. In 2011, immigrants comprised 20.6% of Canada's population; though approximately one in five persons were immigrants, the number of immigrants from Italy decreased 19% from 315,455 in 2001 to 256,825 in 2011, ranking Italian nationals as the 6th largest foreign-born group in Canada in 2011. This is an important factor when considering the assimilation and integration of Italians into Canadian society. The trend reflects the changing nature of the group's cultural self-image and ripening identity no longer as

Italian-Canadians but as Canadian-Italians.

NEW PERMANENT RESIDENTS FROM ITALY LANDED IN CANADA

Landing Year	Total
2006	325
2007	316
2008	370
2009	429
2010	434
2011	374
2012	438
2013	545
2014	652
2015	831
2006-2015	4,714

Source: Government of Canada

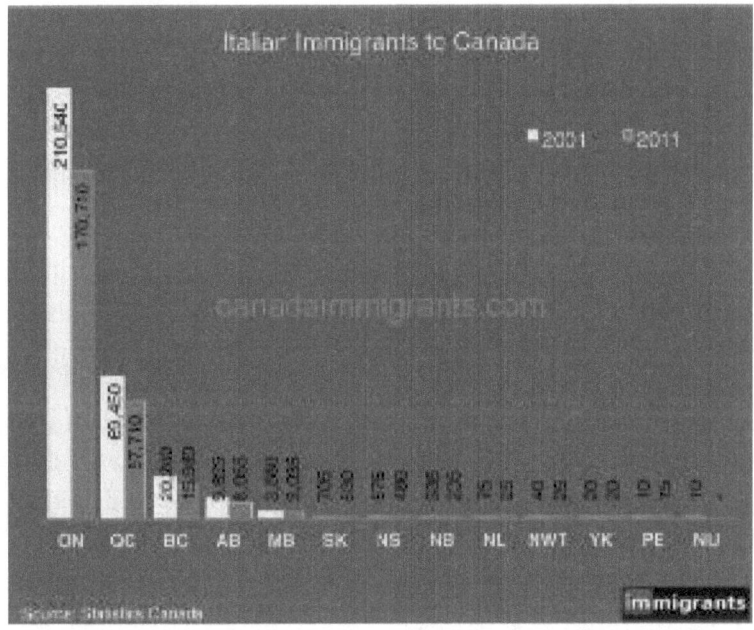

Future Migration

To meet its demands for workers and to fill the vast expanses of interminable land, Canada has relied on immigration as its primary source of population growth. New immigrants, for example, accounted for almost half of the increase in the Canadian workforce between 1950 and 1960. Economic prosperity, political freedom compared with many parts of the world, expanding manufacturing, resource, and construction sectors, quality and security of life gave ample reasons for new waves of immigrants to seek Canadian shores as an attractive haven.

To this day, a large and increasingly sizeable fraction of Canadian residents remains foreign-born. This means that ethnic heterogeneity, linguistic disparity, and cultural dissimilarity remain high. This mosaic, as it is called by Canadians, is indeed the hallmark of Canadian identity.

While tolerance for newcomers rises or ebbs with each sensationalist newspaper headline or fluctuation in the labor market, the notion that the nation of Canada is an accepting mosaic of demographic diversity is more than a truism. In 1962, Canada eliminated racial policies discriminating the ethnic background of its immigrants in favor of a democratic merit system accepting healthy immigrants with the necessary qualifications. Regardless of race, color, or origin, immigrants were allowed entry provided they had the means to support themselves until they became employed.

In 1967, a rating system, radical for its time, was introduced that awarded points based on age, education, fluency in both official languages, and specific work qualifications as necessary tenets to permanent entry into Canada. This merit system, with some recent variation, remains in effect.[14]

But migration is a fluid social phenomenon. The constant movement of peoples across the globe through our known history on the planet has allowed the transmission of tools, knowledge, ideas, cultures, and beliefs that have had a profound impact on the history

---

14 Also called a Comprehensive Ranking System (CRS), a profile of the applicant is ranked according to points that assess language ability, education, professional skills, and experience.

of our species and its civilization upon the planet. From Silk Roads to Tea Routes, from Amber, to Tin, to Salt, to Spice Roads, from trans-oceanic shipping lanes to airline flight corridors, from dusy dirt roads to speedy multilane expressways, the movement of peoples has been unrestrainable.

The mixing and mingling of populations around the globe is the province of humanity. It has produced the world we know, it has engendered the lost tribe.

Just as emigration reshaped the face of the Italian peninsula[15] emptying its poorer villages, collapsing local economies, separating families, and otherwise creating permanent emotional loss, continuing immigration into Canada is the most distinctive and perhaps the most constructive feature of Canadian history. Immigrants and the succeeding generations of their children have integrated well into the Canadian landscape, filling its empty spaces with vibrancy and creating permanent emotional gain. They have established enduring communities and made valuable cultural, political, scientific, and economic contributions to their adopted land. Their labor has formed and reshaped the Canadian landscape, their knowledge has reconstructed established institutions in ways that have paved the road for complete inclusion in a new and constantly evolving society.

But in Canada, as in Ottawa, future immigration will not merely continue old established migrant patterns, especially with respect to Italian immigration. Statistics Canada's population projections and future population trends, according to Barry Edmonston, include three possible immigration scenarios: 1) a low rate of 6.0 annual immigrants per 1,000 population (implying 245,000 immigrants in 2036); 2) a medium rate of 7.5 annual immigrants per 1,000 population (implying 334,000 immigrants in 2036); 3) a high rate of 9.0 annual immigrants

---

15   The variegated peoples on the Italian peninsula began emigrating between villages, cities, city states, and eventually regions, at the end of the 1500s. The great diaspora that left the newly formed United Kingdom of Italy, began in the late 1800s when over 60,000 Italian immigrants came to Canada between 1900 and 1913. Between the period of 1880 and 1976, including emigration to Europe, Australia, North and South America, the total figure of Italians leaving the country permanently reached 13 million.

per 1,000 population (implying 435,000 immigrants in 2036).[16]

While immigration from European countries has waned significantly in recent years, the effect of the ever-increasing entry of immigrant cohorts of Arab, Chinese, South and East Asian, Caribbean, and Latin America origin will have an increasing impact on the Canadian demographic, reshaping and redefining its population. Determining the effects, both positive and negative of this trend, can only be estimated.

Library and Archives Canada lists as many as 1.4 million Canadians of Italian descent in 2017. Many of these immigrants entered Canada between 1946 and 1967, the highpoint of Italian immigration, and were sponsored by relatives, descendants of the early pioneers of immigration that clustered together in the enclaves of Toronto, Montreal and Ottawa and formed the communities we know today.

Most recently, the dire political and economic crisis in Italy may have prompted a new round of emigration, especially among the young. According to the Public Register of Italian Residents Abroad (*AIRE*), figures of Italians abroad rose from 3,106,251 in 2006 to 4,636,647 in 2015, growing by 49.3% in 10 years.[17] What effect these new Italian immigrants will have on the landscape of Ottawa remains to be seen; but it most likely will be marginal. New migration from Italy is primarily from young professionals seeking professional opportunities that have little resonance within the traditional landscape of Italian-Canadiana. Although their numbers have increased marginally across Canada recently they have not impacted an affective change in the Italian-Canadian population, especially that of Ottawa.

For the moment, we return to the past to discuss the original pioneers of Preston Street and present-day *Little Italy* in an effort to better understand how the community grew and prospered.

---

16   See Barry Edmonston, "Canada's Immigration Trends and Patterns," *Canadian Studies in Population* 43, no. 1-2 (2016): 78-116.

17   For an interesting and wide-ranging contemporary view of Italian immigration, see Ruth Ben-Ghiat and Stephanie Malia Hom, eds., *Introduction to Italian Mobilities* (New York; Routledge, 2016).

EARLY MIGRATION TO OTTAWA

In those early days of the 1900s, many of the temporary migrant laborers, having found work and relatively acceptable social conditions, chose to remain in Canada. In Ottawa, dreadful weather conditions, culture shock, and poor working choices made adapting to life in a northern Canadian city more difficult than for those whose fortune led them to warmer southern climes. But the Italian immigrant persisted, establishing thriving Italian-Canadian communities throughout the northern reaches of America. These communities continue to be an important part of the fabric of the Canadian social, political, cultural, and urban landscape.

In Ottawa, many of the first Italian immigrants settled in the Lowertown and Sandy Hill districts. The ranks of these early professionals (normally teachers and musicians from northern Italy) were soon swelled by newly arriving tradesmen and merchants eager to make their mark in the expanding Italian communities across the nation. Business enterprises that were taking their place in the growing Italian community of Ottawa included a string of fruit and vegetable stores owned by Paul Bossio, John and James Mandia, Paul Bova, and Nicola Surdo. The Rollari family grew vegetables on the outskirts of town and created a distribution network for their products at these fresh produce markets.

A particularly enterprising individual was Frank Imbro. He opened a store in the Sandy Hill district in 1909 located at 41S Rideau Street, between Friel and Chapel Streets. The crowded market served an appreciative English and French clientele eager for the feel of an European style experience. Imbros became an important cog in the realization of a nascent Italian presence in Ottawa. Indeed, when the store was renovated in 1935, *The Ottawa Journal* reported the expansion with city-wide fanfare.[18]

---

18   *The Ottawa Journal*, Ottawa, Wednesday 3 July 1935, p.10.

The highly popular and successful business was eventually transformed into an equally thriving restaurant in 1922. *Imbros* advertised itself as Ottawa's first Italian restaurant (although the Madame DiNardo Spaghetti House on the corner of Bank Street and Albert contested the claim). *Imbros* moved to nearby Nelson Street in the 1970s when the original store and restaurant location was replaced by a high-rise building.

Detail of a CMHC photograph taken from the corner of Rideau and Friel, April 1968 showing the *Imbros* restaurant.

It was Giorgio Calderone, however, appointed as "Dean of Ottawa Merchants" by *The Ottawa Journal* in 1960, who left an indelible mark on the local business scene. Giorgio arrived in Canada at the age of 9. A precocious lad, he learned food retailing alongside his father who opened a fruit store first in Toronto and later in Ottawa. At the age of 16, he ventured on his own and opened his own general produce store. But the investment failed, and he soon rejoined his father. A simmering and restless character, he returned to Italy to complete his required army service in 1900, married Antonina Carioto (with whom he had 10 children) and returned to Ottawa in 1902 where he inherited his father's business. Giorgio proved to be an avid entrepreneur. He soon began importing fresh fruit and vegetables in bulk from Chicago and New York in order to maintain a steady winter supply for his growing coterie of local customers eventually becoming a wholesale fruit and vegetable distributor. He was ambitious enough to also support territorial producers; his store was the first in the city to specialize in regional maple products and locally produced honey.

But perhaps the most successful and enduring early business enterprise belonged to Francesco Guzzo and Pasquale Adamo. Arriving in Ottawa in 1895, the family toiled and saved their money, eventually opening one of the first Italian groceries stores in Ottawa that featured Italian products directly imported from Italy in 1912. Unlike many of his compatriots, Pasquale Adamo was fluent in both Italian and English. His store thus became a popular point of contact for the growing Italian community as he provided translations, interpretation services, wrote and read letters for the illiterate. He was also an agent for the Bank of Naples and helped many new Canadians routinely send money to their families in Italy.

The store prospered for decades under the carful and caring tutelage of the Adamo children, Joseph and Pasqualina. They continued his dedication to community service and faithfully provided of their time and assistance to members of the Italian-Canadian community long after their father died in 1927. Pasqualina (Pat) especially, remained a central figure and community stalwart and has been repeatedly recognized and awarded for her humanitarian work both within her community and in the Ottawa community at large.

Pasqualina's energy was and remains seemingly boundless. She has served on all the major committees and executive boards of community importance, has tirelessly given countless volunteer hours to social, political, and cultural causes. She is a past-President of the community television program Tele-30, a past member of the National Arts Center Bursary Committee[19] amongst other charitable foundations, and, like her father, has helped countless compatriots with their legal issues as Official Translator for the Supreme Court of Canada. For her service to the community and achievements, Pasqualina was awarded Knighthood in the Order of Merit of the Italian Republic.

One of the earliest, and perhaps most distinguished, gentlemen to

---

19 Pasqualina has donated not only hours of her time but has also financially supported initiatives to foster community, and especially youth, initiatives. Among her achievements is the National Arts Center *Piccolo Prix* of $1,000, created in 2001 to aid music students who are studying in or are from the Ottawa area and are planning careers as professional orchestral musicians.

grace Ottawa was Rocco Antonio Graziadei, an accomplished musician who landed in Canada in 1883 at the age of twenty-five. His Graziadei Orchestra was a fixture at all local events, and renowned enough to perform on Parliament Hill as well as for the Governor General at Rideau Hall. Due to his high profile and indefatigable activity, Rocco Graziadei was appointed the official agent for the Italian community by the then Italian Consul General. He remained in the position until his death in 1935. Graziadei's offspring followed their father's path into music and became notable musicians in their own right. Sons Sylvio, Domenic, and Joe all played in the Ottawa Philharmonic Orchestra.[20]

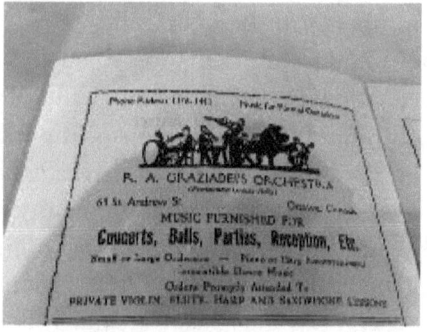

Photograph courtesy of Trina Costantina Powell.

From this small sampling, it is noteworthy that a cadre of prominent, hard-working, able-bodied and courageous men and women graced the early landscape of the Italian community of Ottawa. In his fairly comprehensive but mostly undetailed study, *The Italians in Canada*, A.V. Spada dedicates very few pages to the community in Ottawa.[21] Though superficially listing hundreds of names of persons that had settled in the nation's capital, he offers no biographies and gives even fewer insights. A select few names of note that receive scant attention include: Anselmo Bortolotti, indefatigable community activist, founder of the Order of Italian

---

20 "A business card printed in 1907 . . . shows the pronunciation of the name as 'Grazzy-Addy.'" A.V. Spada, *The Italians in Canada* (Montreal: Riviera Printers and Publishers, 1969) 304.

21 Spada, *The Italians in Canada,* 303-315.

Canadians; Joseph Capogreco, distinguished musician and founder of the first Italian event center in Ottawa, Cabot Hall; Rudolph (Rudy) Capogreco, son of Joseph, was the very first Italian elected city alderman; Tullio Locatelli, a cobbler who began the first shoe-repair shop on Preston Street but eventually moved uptown to Elgin Street where he specialized in orthopedic shoes for war veterans; and Giuseppe Costantini and Antonio Disipio, the original proprietors of The Prescott Hotel, whose story will soon be told.

The Village

What came to be known as *The Village* lies at the bottom of the escarpment that is Parliament Hill. This rock promontory creates a defining eastern boundary that forms a natural geographical barrier. The western edge is marked by the CNN railroad ravine; to the north we find Lebreton Flats and the Ottawa River; to the south Dow's Lake.

"The Dalhousie Ward or Little Italy: Bounded by the Lebreton Flats along the Ottawa River, moving north to Carling Avenue/Dow's Lake, to the west the Bayswater area including the St. Lawrence and Ottawa Railway (now the O-Train), and delimited on the east by Bronson Avenue." From: John H. Taylor, *Ottawa: An Illustrated History*.

Preston Street, the main road, is thus visibly bordered on all its cardinal points by geographically determined physical boundaries. The resulting circumscribed area feels surrounded, confined, even cramped; it has the look of a transitory buffer, a colony almost, that sits between the ever-sprawling and loopy western suburbs and the more formal gridiron patterned downtown core.[22]

When walking on Preston Street from its northern beginnings on Wellington Street and ambling south towards Carling Avenue, even the casual observer is struck by the apparent physical and material separateness of the district from the more traditional eastern Ottawa neighborhoods immediately beyond Parliament Hill. The buildings seem deteriorated, tired and worn. The side streets boast some of the city's crumbiest houses; tall and narrow clapboard clad structures that were shabby at best even in their better days.

Yet, the neighborhood, now officially rebaptized and culturally designated as a *Little Italy*, suggests that while social discrimination and local resistance to assimilation played their part in the relative impoverishment of the area, positive attitudes of mind, shared tradition, social necessity, and the inherent vocation to sacrifice that the local inhabitants carried over from a poverty-stricken Italian village setting, fostered a spirit of self-sufficiency and pride that remains vibrant to this day.

Preston Street itself was and remains the traffic canal of the first western suburban settlements of the newly amalgamated City of Ottawa. The road is a thoroughfare that connects two important waterways, the Ottawa River and the Rideau Canal via the shallow body of water known as Dow's Lake. It is also the *defacto* northernmost extension of Highway 16 which, until the recent opening of Highway 416, was the only direct and fastest link between Ottawa and the

---

22 A distinguishing feature of the area are its street names. During the time of urbanization and industrialization in Ottawa, the Dalhousie Ward was known as the "Tree Street Neighbourhood" because successive streets bore the names of trees: Maple Street, Elm Street, Spruce Street, Cedar Street, Poplar Street, Willow Street, Oak Street, and Balsam Street. See: *Ottawa in Maps, 1825-1974*, Library and Archives, Canada, 1974. No ISBN, p. 35.

modern lifeline to the city of Toronto and beyond, Highway 401.

Though the Preston streetscape has produced very few, if any, memorable visual landmarks, the many family-run locales that animate the street reinforce each other by repetition. Store fronts, restaurants, caffes and pubs not only structure the street visually but also intensify the identity of the district by deepening its pseudo-ethnic character. This outward, visual image, however, lacks any sense of homogeneity or endearing character. The street front structures of partially refurbished houses are of different shapes and sizes, use different construction materials; the old and often derelict is mixed with the brashly new and often modish. The common feature is a general sense of dilapidation and confusion. Despite recent attempts to beautify the streetscape with statuary, benches, and neon logos proclaiming the area as *Little Italy*, the principal visual impression of Preston Street is not of a homogeneous Italian-Canadian space, but of spatial shapelessness.

The architecture of the neighborhood contains houses of no special architectural quality and devoid of historical significance. As seen in period photographs, the buildings are typical of first quarter 20th century wood construction. The dwellings that populate the side streets possess a relative charm but display obvious lower income characteristics: small stoops, narrow shot-gun structuring, clapboard cladding. The property lots are sometimes only 30 feet in width meaning shared driveways or none at all. Nevertheless, the virtues of the area outweighed even these (from an historical point of view) shortcomings.

The area was and remains (although there is a movement towards childless couples and empty nesters, more on this point later) family oriented. The population once consisted of large families whose children now have grown up. Some of these children, now adults and frequently elderly, have remained in the area. Others return frequently to visit parents and relatives, to shop at the local businesses, or to frequent old drinking haunts. Some have set-up shop along the business spine of the area which, at this writing, is restlessly feeling the spill-over effects of urban gentrification.

In the past, however, gentrification was the farthest thing from the minds of the first colony of Italian immigrants as they planted warm roots in their new, often frozen, Preston Street soil. This is a mostly vanished world; formed by the classic 1900 turn-of-the-century Italian diaspora that spread throughout the Americas. It was a space identified through its sweat and labor, with little time for rights or privileges or the niceties of life that extended beyond bountiful Sunday dinners. It was, and in many respects remains, neither fully Canadian, never really fully Italian. The great majority of arriving Italian immigrants at the beginning of the 1900s headed towards the multicultural mosaic of Dalhousie Ward. The environs surrounding Preston Street was composed of a potpourri of European immigrants that included Irishmen, Englishmen, Poles, Ukrainians, a small number of Greek origin, and newly arriving Italians.[23]

The general area was divided into traditional, ethnically inspired parishes, each pastor in friendly competition with the others of the same faith. These included a Polish parish located at the corner of Rochester Street and Balsam Street; a Greek church on Gladstone Street; St. Mary's Irish church on Bayswater Avenue; St. Gerard with its French congregation on Beech Street, and the Saint-Jean-Baptiste Parish located north of Booth Street on Empress Avenue. In the 20s and 30s the neighborhood was referred to as "Stovepipe Village" because most of the homes did not have furnaces and were heated by stoves whose pipes dotted the area's roofscape.

A typical street like Rochester, according to Nola Ferguson who lived on the short block, "consisted on our side of the street of two Jewish families (a tailor and a grocer), a Lebanese (pie and donut maker), two French (a butcher and a livery stable), one Italian, three English plus the Jewish grocer also being a shoe repairman. On the corner was a blacksmith, next to him another shoe repair, a Ukrainian church . . . ."[24]

The increasing concentration of immigrants of Italian origin in this particular area was due to a number of factors, the strongest being

---

23 While today relatively few of these original Italians and their descendants remain, the community maintains a demographic mix composed of more recent immigrants arriving from Vietnam, Thailand, and Indonesia.

24 Quoted in Jeff Johnson, "Battle of LeBreton Flats (?) Warms Up," *The Citizen*, 19 December 1979.

chain migration, or the desire to live near relatives and individuals of similar cultural background who had already settled in the immigrant friendly community.

There was no real factory or other heavy industry in the immediate area. However, many immigrants found work at the Carling O'Keefe Brewery (formerly Bradings Brewery) on Albert Street, and the Pure Spring Company Ltd. Plant located on Aberdeen Street. Smith Transport on Beech beside the Pure Spring Plant provided further employment as did the Esso Depot located at the present Sala San Marco site, as did Hall Fuel Ltd., a former coal yard with a coal shed and exterior coal storage located at 402 Preston Street.

A good many men of working-age were employed as unskilled laborers in a variety of enterprises, none moreso than the construction industry. The work was difficult and, given the times, usually dangerous. But given the demographic characteristics of many arriving immigrants (low education level and low-end skills) the backbreaking work was acceptable and appreciated. Some eventually honed their newly acquired skills and cunningly began their own successful activities.[25] Some created business opportunities and became store owners.

One of the more popular stores in the area belonged to the Chiarelli family. Frank Chiarelli, the first of the Chiarelli clan born in Canada, recalls the village feel of living in the area. "All the action seemed to take place in a six-block area around our store. That was my neighborhood, my Little Italy."

The store he is referring to belonged to his father and was named *Eug. Chiarelli and Son*. It was both a grocery and butcher shop and was located on the corner of Rochester and Pamilla Streets. The area in front of the store was a hang-out for neighborhood youth, like Frank, who played hockey on the street, baseball in a nearby field, and dropped snowballs into the smokestacks of passing trains from the railway overpass on Preston Street for fun.

Frank and the gang grew-up watching crap shooters in front of his father's store. He remembers that he was fascinated with all the paper money lying on the street as the men played. At the age of two

---

25 Some of these daunting pioneers began companies that are still prospering today. See Chapter 7.

he tried to take a few bills and remembers a protracted tirade from one of the gamblers who was more than likely having a bad run. Despite being an octogenarian, the memories are all still fresh, the flavor of the streets still present. "There was a sense of being different from the rest of the city," he states. "The corner crowd comprised of guys from the area gave us a feeling of solidarity in poverty. We seemed to live on a movie set where destiny privileged the quick and the bold. We were always getting into trouble; but then again, who wasn't?"

His father, Eugenio, was born in Cleto, Calabria. As a young man he had survived the trenches of WWI and soon afterwards married his life-long companion, Antonia Lorella. A restless spirit nudged him to escape the poverty of southern Italy to seek his fortune in North America. He immigrated to Canada, landing in Montreal in mid-winter, with forged documents. A local priest found him employment shoveling the interminable snow. Ambition soon drove him to the gold mines of Timmins, Ontario where he worked 2500 ft. underground for 5 years. In the meanwhile, he learned English and remained a voracious reader, especially of newspapers, all his life. Arriving in Ottawa in the late 1920s, he decided it was time to fetch his young wife and family from Calabria and bring them to Canada. Shortly thereafter, and with the help of a newfound friend, a lawyer named McAlley, he was reunited with this wife, two children, as well as his mother and father.

Eugenio Chiarelli soon bought a butcher shop; then learned the trade of butchery. He added groceries; it was his way. The family, eventually numbering seven children and two adults, furnished the upstairs apartment and lived above the bustling store. He soon expanded the business to include a full-fledged dairy operation in the back of the store (another trade he acquired after the fact) and began a popular ice cream business. He delighted in giving neighborhood children free ice cream but was also known to give ongoing credit to his struggling customers during the depression to help them survive. In the meanwhile, he also became a restaurant supplier and plied his skills as a self-made entrepreneur throughout the city.

The Chiarelli family became a well-know fixture in the area and the name Chiarelli synonymous not only with honest hard work and success but also with ambitious children who earned scholarships, went to college (a true feat in those days), became sports figures, lawyers, prosperous businessmen, and politicians. One, Robert Chiarelli, served as a Liberal member in the Legislative Assembly of Ontario from 1987 to 1997 and again from 2010 to 2018. In the interregnum, he became the first mayor of the newly amalgamated City of Ottawa in 2000 after having served as Regional Chair of the Regional Municipality of Ottawa Carleton from 1997-2001. He has held important ministerial portfolios in successive provincial Liberal governments at Queens Park including those of Infrastructure, Energy, Transportation, Municipal Affairs and Housing, as well as a member of the Standing Committees on Administration and Justice, and on General Government.

Still other members of the increasingly visible Italian community pursued a broad range of professional callings while others joined the service industry. Some became cooks and opened restaurants. One such daunting individual was Albert Caramanico. He was son to Antonio Caramanico and his wife Maria Napolitano. They had emigrated from the small dwellings of Ripa Teatina (Abruzzo) to life in Camden, New Jersey in 1902. Albert was their second child; born American. Fortune and desire soon moved the growing family from Camden to Ottawa several years later. Albert was in his teens. Nicknamed Chappie in an age where everyone seemed to carry a diminutive moniker, the young man was an avid sports enthusiast and well-known among his peers.[26]

---

26 A few nicknamed individuals Chappie would have called friends included: Lefty Barbaro, Skipper Disipio, Patsy Guzzo. But Village life, like most small village settings, was animated by the myriad of colorful nicknames attached to individuals. The following list is courtesy of Jim McCauley. In some cases, the given name was never known. No one could ever recall using anything but the nickname to address the following villagers, thus the question marks:

NICKNAME	GIVEN NAME
Aggie	Lucien Lafleur
Babes	? Blondin
Banan	Walter Chapman
Bats	Phil Bianco
Bean	Leonard Mulligan

Beetle	Jimmy Mac Millan
Bib	Alex Calagoure
Bidou	Armand Couvrette
Birdie	Eric Mulligan
Booms / Piano Box	Dow's Lake Swimming Hole
Buck	Gerry Renaud
Bull	Jimmy Cesare
Butchie	Al Carmanico
Cammy	Carmen Defalco
Cement	Ray Dinardo
Chaboo	Art Ciavaglia
Chappy	Albert Carmanico
Checko	Francesco Defalco
Cheech	Anyone named Frank
Chick	Frank and Rocco (Rocky) Cecchini
Cobra	Ed Nicholson
Cootsie	Frank Chiarelli
Costy	Nick and Joe Costantini
Cougar	Fred Disipio
Curly	Joe Licari
Dizzy	Harold Rockburn
Doodles	Wally Swords
Frankie with the Long Pants	Frank Domenico
Goofer	Ken Burrows
Gus	Len Wara
Herbie	Roy Lafleur (McNabb Park)
Hoostick	Karl Calagoure
Hubie	Hubert Garneau
Jesse	Anthony (Tony) Menchini
Jo Jo	Joe Licari
Johnny Red	John Mc Cadden
Knob	Frank Costantini
Kong	Frank Concordia
Lally	Jean-Paul Lalonde
Lanny	Lance Steele
Last Chance	Prescott Hotel
Lefty	Domenic Barbaro
Max	John Mastrangelo
Moe	Maurice Barbeau

Mizzy	Bob Misericordia
Moon	Georgie Mullins
Newsy	Des Dubroy Sr.
Nice Girl	Kay Calagoure
Nooky	Louis Pilon
Onion	Len Tremblay
Pacy's Palace	Palef's Confectionary
Patsy	Pasquale Guzzo
Pepper	Guido Siriani
Petsie	Gord Ventura
Pinky	Fred Mitchell
Pit	Lucien Boyer
Pop	Doug Thompson
Punchy	Ron Gervais
Pye	Paul Provost
Rab / Zeke	Earl Calagoure
Red	Pete Gorman, Don Wellington or Gerry Menchini
Rip	Any Riopelle
Sal	Salvatore Pantalone
Scratch	Richard Calagoure
Shag	? Shaughnessy
Six	Roger Boyer
Skip	Des Dubroy Jr.
Sonco	Santo Imbesi
Sonny	Wilfred Calagoure
Spike	Anthony Girotte
Steam Shovel	Angelo Domenico
Storm	Frank Pantalone
Syke	Orville Mac Millan
T.J.	Tom Donnelly
Tarpot	Frank Pugliese
The Barber / Facci	Tony Ierullo
Ticker	Jimmy Bossio
Timber	Jimmy Patafie
Tippy	Don Philippe
Toby	Frank Defalco
Toe	? Renaud
Tomato	Harding Dawe
Tuggy	? Pilon

An amateur boxer, wrestler, and student of ju-jitsu, Chappie was also a member of *The Indians*, the Norman and Preston Street baseball team. His passion for sport led him to form one of Ottawa's first sport clubs, the Preston Athletic Club, with good friend Harry Menchini in 1919.

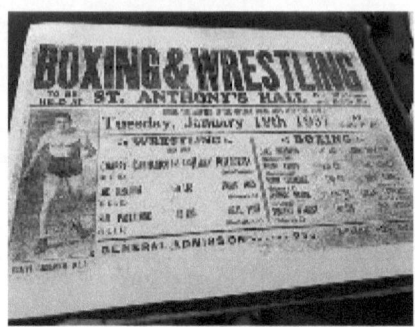

Photograph courtesy of Trina Costantini Powell.

When young Canadians were called to serve in WWII, Chappie acquired citizenship, joined the Army and, given his experience in sport, became a trainer for new recruits. Injured while serving in Europe, war's end found him injured in a veteran's hospital with few employment prospects. But fortune and desire again intervened. Mary Cianci, Chappie's wife, was an excellent cook. Although pregnant with their seventh child, the couple decided to take a chance and convert the store beneath their second-floor apartment into a restaurant. The family lived at 438 ½ Preston Street, a prime location on the evolving streetscape.

As luck would have it, on their opening day in July of 1945, The Orange Order in Canada held their annual parade.[27] The neighborhood

Uncle Jr.	John Licari
V.J. / Fritz	Viger Gendron
Whitey	Len Ventura
Wiggy	Ray Kealey
Willie	William Stewart
Wimpy	Wilmott Moloughney
Woody	Walter Latimer
Zook	Ray Zuccala

27 The Loyal Orange Institution, more commonly known as the Orange

was packed with spectators eager to view the always impressive display of marchers and bands. Many dined at the newly opened restaurant where Chappie, Mary, and children Mary, Tony, Kay, and Theresa, cooked and served. The opening was a rousing success.

Chappie's Lunch was the first restaurant on Preston Street. The family business became a landmark in the neighborhood, known to all and visited by young and old. People still recall mother Mary's famous spaghetti and meatballs. It closed in 1956.

Chappie's Lunch circa 1945-1956.
Photograph courtesy of Al Carmanico.

There has always been economic mobility, genuine ingenuity, youthful enthusiasm and social mobility in the Preston Street neighborhood. Places like Chappie's Lunch consolidated the area as a rising social and economic focal point in the new Canadian reality. These meeting places coalesced these first Italian migrants and the myriad influences of their experiences into what can be defined as the heart of the growing Italian community or, as they preferred to call it, *The Village*.

Order, is powerful world-wide Protestant fraternal organization begun in 1688, to defend "the liberties of Englishmen and the Protestant Religion." Named after Prince William of Orange, these Societies were formed to support and maintain those principles and concepts of democracy. The annual parade commemorates the "Glorious 12th," the victory of Protestant William III over his Catholic father-in-law James II at the Battle of the Boyne near Dublin in 1690. Such parades have caused controversy and violence in Northern Ireland for years, where Protestant militants insist on marching through Catholic neighborhoods. Interestingly, when The Orange Order reached its peak in the 1920s, 60 per cent of the world's Orangemen lived in Canada. For more information see: http://grandorangelodge.ca/history/.

The Village People: Just Hangin' Out

Once a year, a robust assortment of old friends come together to revel, rejoice, remember, and share a few beers. Their sole link is their neighborhood; their sole purpose is to retell their memories, renew their friendship, their past, their ongoing legacy; or as they themselves put it, "to just hang-out." These men both preserve and transmit the memory and lasting heritage of *The Village*.

The yearly event known as *The Village Reunion* began in 1978 at the Recreational Association Center located on Riverside Drive. This initial gathering saw over 200 people pay a $12.00 fee to attend an uncertain and hastily programmed evening. As Sonny Calogoure recalls, "Most of them came because they thought there was going to be a crap game that night."

But the ongoing and increasingly successful event had a more colorful birth than Calogoure's anecdote suggests. The Village Sports Club group had already been gathering informally at The Prescott Hotel for years. At one of these occasions, members of the Calogoure family suggested the group officialize these regular encounters and find a larger venue. Their idea was to gather as many friends as they could find from their youthful days in *The Village* and hold an official reunion. And so in 1976, several of these long-time friends met in the basement (*a small 5 or 6 foot high dugout* as it was described to me) of Ierullo's Barger Shop at 432 ½ Preston Street to hatch their plan. Present at the meeting were Karl, Richard, and Sonny Calagoure, Nick Costantini, Kenny Creppin, Tony Ierullo, Leo Riopelle, and Gerry Tremblay.

This *bunch of guys* (again, all colloquialisms are willfully authentic) formed the first Village Reunion Committee. Some already had had experience with The Village Sports Club group that had been meeting at The Prescott Hotel. One of the guys, Gerry Tremblay, had already unofficially organized a similar reunion with a Centre Town organization in McNabb Park a handful of years earlier. He was appointed The Village Reunion's first unofficial coordinator. This amicable and purposefully informal group worked with no Chair, no Secretary, and no Directors. It was decided, however, that if they were to make any headway, a treasurer was needed to manage eventual funds. They agreed that Nick Costantini act as Treasurer, a position he held for over 25 years until his death in 2004.

And thus, The Village Reunion was born. The initially all-male event gathered neighborhood friends to officially celebrate bygone days with the secondary effect of preserving life-long friendships.

The event normally takes place in October and, according to Michael Whalen, one of the original members, "these days any old guy can get in. Some never had a whiff of *The Village*." The popular yearly dinner normally attracts over 500 people and is limited only by the size of its venue. Awards are normally bestowed to honor notable individuals of families from the community. These include The Community Contribution Award, given to the individual who gives of himself towards the betterment of *The Village*; The Villager Award, given to a high profile and well-known personality (or *bonefide character*) from *The Village*; The Special Presentation Award, normally given to a person or family considered a mainstay of the local community; The Sportsman Award, given for outstanding athletic achievement; and a recently added The Village Athletic Award, given in recognition of athletic achievement and demonstration of high Village ideals. The following is a list of Past Award Recipients:

COMMUNITY CONTRIBUTION AWARD

1979 Hugh Riopelle Sr.
1979 Sam Macli
1980 Charles Ladas
1980 Walter Strelbisky
1981 Ed Daugherty
1981 Ev Tremblay
1982 Les Newman
1984 Ernie Leighton
1986 Tom Coughlan
1986 Jack Snow
1987 John Mangione
1988 George Maxwell
1989 Joe Sandulo
1990 Roy Lafleur
1991 Jim McAuley
1992 Ottawa-Nepean Canadians Sports Club
1993 John Denofrio
1994 Chris Finnerty
1995 Howard Danruin
1996 Keith Brown
1997 Italo Tiezzi
1998 Jim Durrell
1999 George Drummond
2000 Ottawa St. Anthony Italia Soccer Club
2001 Garry Guzzo
2002 Nello Bortolotti
2003 Max Keeping
2044 Ed Champagne
2005 Al Albania
2006 Glen Richardson
2007 Tom Cavanagh

2008 Dave Smith
2009 Joe Cama
2010 Ken Grant
2011 Moe Atallah
2012 Mario Giannetti
2013 Bob Scaini
2014 Larry O'Brien
2415 John Timpson
2016 The Cooper Brothers

2007 Saro Panuccio
2008 Sam Pugliese
2009 Joe Bozzi
2010 Jim McConnery
2011 Joe Cotroneo
2012 Len Cregan
2013 Tony Lofaro
2014 Roger Casagrande
2015 Jimmy Nasso
2016 Bill Duncan

VILLAGER AWARD

1979 Sam Palef
1980 Aggie Lafleur
1981 Frank Concordia
1982 Bill Chinkiwsky
1982 Skipper Disipio
1983 Jimmy MacMillan
1984 Mike Andrusek
1984 Ralph Cameron
1985 Alex Sauve'
1986 Len Concordia
1987 Frank Costantini
1988 Chappie Carmanico
1989 Alex Cameron
1990 Joe Pilon
1991 Andy Lombardo
1992 PeterAndrusek
1993 Joe Pugliese
1994 Alex Lafleur
1995 Joe Adamo
1996 Spike Girotte
1997 Red Gorman
1998 Red Wellington
1999 John Licari
2000 Don Romani
2001 Oliver Medaglia
2002 Joe Guzzo
2003 Ron Gervais
2004 Ken Burrows
2005 John Mastrangelo
2006 Dominic Delle Palme

VILLAGE ATHLETIC AWARD

1982 Edgar Blondin
1983 Nooky Pilon
1983 Toby Dinardo
1985 Andy Nezan
1986 Fred Hughes
1987 Joe Asquini
1988 Leo Blondin
1989 Les Pilon
1990 John Kozak
1991 Harvey Creppin
1992 Rudy Costantini
1993 Paul Ventura
1994 Wally Swords
1995 Gord Pantalone
1996 Santo Imbesi
1997 Roydon Kealey
1998 Art Dinardo
1999 Ed Nicholson
2000 Hubie Garneau
2001 Gord Ventura
2000 Hubie Garneau
2001 Gord Ventura
2002 Pinky Mitchell
2003 Wayne Hughes
2004 Bobby Ransom
2005 Joe (JoJo) Licari
2006 Dom Disipio
2001 Eddie Rose
2008 George House
2009 Conrad Kozak

2010 Roger Hunter
2011 Danny Monk
2012 Roger Provost
2013 Ken Evraire
2014 Randy Blondin
2015 Dick Chiarelli
2016 Barry Hughes

SPORTSMAN AWARD
1981 Patsy Guzzo
1984 Tony Licari
1986 Bill Cowley
1987 Howard Riopelle
1988 Conny Brown
1989 Bill Dineen
1990 Lorne Watters
1990 Frank Chiarelli
1991 Lally Lalonde
1992 Bob Simpson
1993 Billy Watson
1994 Jake Dunlap

1995 Ed Hatoum
1996 Larry Regan
1997 Eddie MacCabe
1998 Hugh Riopelle, Sr.
1999 Lude Check
2000 Ab Renaud
2001 Don Holtby
2002 D'Arcy Boucher
2003 Bobby Copp
2004 Billy Russell
2005 Cliff Neill
2006 John Fripp
2007 Marcel LegrisBo
2008 Greg Fagan
2009 Brian Kilrea
2010 Clayton Kenny
2011 Denis Potvin
2012 Jim Chiarelli
2013 Bob Abelson
2014 Gord Montagano
2015 John McDonald
2016 Whit Tucker

In addition to these individual citations, the group awards bursaries to meritorious students in Italian studies who require funding to continue their university education. The awards initially ranged between $100-$200 but have generously increased over the years to $1000 per student.

But *The Villagers*, as they define themselves. are also proud of their enduring legacy in the world of sport. In its heyday, the streets and alleys and fields of *The Village* were alive with organized sport and sporting events that drew crowds from the entire neighborhood regardless of ethnic background. It would be a flawed and stereotyped generalization to assume that these young men eventually entered sport in order to improve their socio-economic standing. For this hypothesis to be valid, a preponderance of them would have had to have lived in abject poverty. At the very least, some of these future athletes did indeed come from difficult backgrounds, but upward social mobility out of the lower-class was not the driving force behind their success.

I am assured by these men that sport was instead a passion, a rite of passage, a proving ground of their individual worth. A convivial aspect of living in *The Village* was participating with friends in sport. It should not surprise that an extraordinary number of well-known sports figures came from this relatively small area and that some went on to become highly respected figures in their chosen sports. Among them we name only a few and include: Joe Asquini, Grey Cup Champion; Frank Chiarelli, U.S. College Hockey record holder; Peter Chiarelli, General Manager and NHL Executive; Rudy Costantini, RA Hall of Fame member; Bill Dineen, Two-time Stanley Cup Winner; Patsy Guzzo, Olympic Hockey Gold Medalist; Fred "Pinky" Mitchell, Canadian Boxing Champion; Howard Riopelli, Montreal Canadiens player and QSHL leading scorer.

But the list hardly exhausts the names of the many tough guys who played semiprofessional hockey or baseball, or those who became professional boxers and wrestlers. Guys like Fred "Pinky" Mitchell and Gale Kerwin, for example, went on to become professional boxers *because the ring*, it is reputed they mused, *was safer than the streets*.[28]

Whatever the reason, whatever the means, *The Villagers* left their mark in their chosen fields, sports or otherwise, and continue to revel in their legacy today.

Over the years *The Village Reunion* has grown in popularity and tradition. It is difficult, if not impossible, to obtain tickets to the event that is normally highlighted by well-known, often comedic but always eloquent, guest speakers. Gord Bunke, Jake Dunlap, Garry Guzzo, Lally Lalonde, Fred "Pinky" Mitchell, Hughie Riopelle, Royden Kealey, J.J. Clark, Brian Kilrea, as well as many other celebrities, politicians, and local entrepreneurs, have graced the dais and entertained the loyal villagers.

At this writing, we are sad to learn that there are rumblings that the 2018 edition of *The Village Reunion* may indeed be it's last. Dwindling attendance (down from 600), an aging demographic, and indifference from the younger villagers may be the formerly greatly anticipated event's death knell.

---

28 Cited in Dave Brown, "Old Gang," in "Brown's Beat," *The Citizen*, 19 January 1980.

But *The Village Reunion* is only part of continuing Village lore. Every Sunday morning a group of life-long friends meet at Joe Calabro's Pasticceria Gelateria Italiana on Preston Street to maintain friendships and just shoot the breeze. Joe too is a Village boy and shares the group's enthusiasm and eagerly supports their continuity. A larger group of old boys meets every Wednesday morning at the Local Heroes Sports Bar on Merivale Road. Stories are exchanged, memories are relived, insults are cast, and a good time, and breakfast, is had by all.

These ongoing groups, these wonderfully amusing and spry pensioners instruct me, serve as a second family, a sounding board, and a mutual aid association. Bloodlines and friendship ties run deep, all the way back to hanging-out on the streets. Most of them have known each other since adolescence and have proudly shared life in *The Village* in good times and bad.[29]

Preston Street Streetscape: Visiting the Past

The first buildings along Preston Street included small groceries, confectionaries, restaurants, coffee houses, and cobbler shops. Most of these were situated in converted homes or on the ground floor of two-story box-like structures. A good number of families lived in the homes on Preston Street, very few of them of Italian origin. Newly arriving immigrants normally inhabited the dwellings on the side-streets.

The following stroll down Preston Street was provided by Sam Pantalone[30] during my interview with him many years ago.

---

29 Stories of lost loves, missed opportunities, and present-day maladies are the norm when these friends meet. Their happiest memories revolve around the end of WWII and celebrations in the streets of the neighborhood. Their most sorrowful tale, by consensus, regards the tragic death in 1950 of three of their friends: Tony Zito, Silvio Tiezzi, and Loren Smirle. Their car was hit by a train in Bells Corners. There were four other friends on-board. All were returning from a softball game in Stittsville. The funeral embraced the entire community.

30 Salvatore Pantalone was born in Ottawa in 1924. He is the fourth

It represents a personal memoryscape of *The Village* area between Gladstone Avenue and the former railway right-of-way now present-day Queensway overpass.

The words and following map are Sal's. They are unaltered and reflect a purposeful and truly remarkable recollection process that extends back to his youth. His virtual (as we would term it today) walk through his old neighborhood and observations are supremely personal. At times only a name is provided without details; in others the memory is crisp and steeped in past interactions with the person and the locale. I am truly grateful for his meditated contribution to the evolving face of Preston Street.

1. The Whelan family lived upstairs. They were related to another Whelan family that lived in an apartment facing Gladstone.
2. Family related to the Tiezzi's who owned the Tiezzi grocery store.

---

child of Rocco (Fred) from Pretoro, Abruzzo and Antonietta Locatelli from the Region of Lazio. Sal's father, Fred, was a Lieutenant in the Ottawa Fire Department. He was part of the crew that worked to contain the February 1916 fire that ravaged the Canadian Parliament buildings. An unfortunate victim of Italian Canadian internment, Sal recalls that his father was demoralized and embarrassed when arrested and handcuffed in front of his men in June of 1940. He was interned at camp Petawawa for seven months before returning home to find that his long and proud career with the Fire Department had vanished. But his most traumatizing event after his release was the look on his children's faces after seeing that their father's hair had changed from black to grey. The family faced financial difficulty with the loss of their father's job, so Sal joined the Canadian navy at 16 in order to help provide support.

Despite the hardship, Sal maintains that his father was not a victim of the actions of the Canadian government, but rather "a victim of Italy declaring war against us." His father eventually received a letter of apology from James Hyndman, the Wartime Rental and Salaries Controller, and eventually as deputy judge of the Exchequer Court of Canada, explaining that he was an innocent man and that he never should have been interned.

Fred Pantalone was eventually given a position with the Navy which led to a career after the war with the Canadian Joint Staff in Washington where he spent many happy years with his wife.

3. Property owned by the two Paquette brothers who lived in unit #3 and rented out unit #4.
4. The Olivieri family. Despite the Italian sounding name, they were Francophone.
5. Duplex owned by Frank Cotroneo. He lived on the ground floor and rented the upstairs space to Hey and Mary Lamba.
6. Home of Frank Saro'.
7. Property owned by the Chiarelli family.
   A – Butcher Shop
   B – Shipman Realty
   C – the Chiarelli residence
   D – the Chiarelli garage had an external stairway access to a second-floor apartment.
8. Owned by Giuseppe Palermo. An Italian couple with two children lived there.
9. Property owned by Giuseppe Palermo.
10. The Tenori home.
11. Duplex owned by the Locatelli family; former owners of Preston Hardware.
12. Gino Tiezzi's store.
13. Mike Morgan's Barber Shop.

14. An old apartment tenement that burned down and was replaced by a 3-story building.
15. Alex's Barber Shop.
16. Someone named Crupi. Did not really know him.
17. Someone named Sgorboso. Another simple acquaintance.
18 and 19. Three families lined here: The Pantuso, Boschetti, and Barone families.
20. Kelly's Restaurant, later became John's Restaurant.
21. The Cuccaro family home. Son Tony owned Capones Restaurant on Carling Avenue.
22. Lisa, the owner of Giovanni Restaurant, lived here.
23. Ralph and Kay Domenico, owners of the property. It was a large old house with 5 units. When we (the Pantalone family) lived there the other families included Ralph and Kay, Frank Fatia, and Pat Larkin.
24. Mike Ventura, his brother and sister-in-law lived here. Mike was the owner of the Ace Sports Club on Rochester Street.
25. Sbaballoni (or something to that nature).
26. The Leone family.

Sal Pantalone also graciously provided a list of Names of Preston Street inhabitants according to Year and Address. The list is severely incomplete but rigorous, again, in its portrayal of his personal memories of knowing or remembering and perhaps interacting with these people on Preston Street. It is to be noted, again, that the numbers range between Gladstone Avenue and the present Queensway overpass. All street numbers refer to buildings located on Preston Street.

1906
274 Luigi Buccino
295 Luciano Antonio Grocery Store

1908
224 Angelo Ambroser

1909
226 Giovanni Rizzo Grocery Store

1910
226 D. Sciarroni, Baker
432 G. Guzzo

1911
360 F. DiNardi

1912
98   Louis Rossino Confectionary
114   Vincent Cosenzo Fruit

1913
364   Guzzo and Adamo Grocery Store

1914
360   Giuseppe Coppolios
489   Arthur Ventura
432½   Louis Scarcella
434   Domenic Bianco
438   Palif Italian Fruits

1915
295   Angelo Luciano Grocery Store
362   Guzzo and Adamo Grocery Store
462   Domenic Pantalone
438   Palif Italian Fruits
488   Giuseppe Cianci
487   Rocco Pantalone
489   Arthur Ventura

1916
277   Angelo Locatelli, Shoemaker

1917
438   Brethren Sunday School
438 ½   Anthony Mendola Fruit
440   Frank Rossi

1918
291   Salvatore Locatelli

1919
120   Joe Gargano
420   Pasquale Zito
422   Pietro Lombardo
438   St. Roch Separate School

1920
354 ½   Anthony Buccino
438 ½   Anthony Mendola Fruit
488   Kathleen Cianci

1921
287   Palombo Confectionary

1922
276   Tullio Locatelli Shoes
438½   Giuseppe Palermo, Tobacconist

The list now jumps to the late 40s.

1949
438 ½   Chappy's Lunch

1950
440   Anthony Mendola

1951
271   Maria Calabrese
440   Albert and Mary Caramanico

1954
271   Frank Cotroneo

Who lived on Preston Street, Ottawa in 1958?

The following list of Names and Addresses on Preston Street is borrowed from *Il Postino,* November 2009:5. I thank Angelo Filoso for permission to publish. One notes a lack of Italian names for two reasons. First and foremost, the late 50s early 60s wave of Italian immigration to Ottawa had not fully developed. The prevalence of English and French names also indicates the street was never truly an Italian enclave as is popular lore. Though the perennially depressed working neighborhood became an economic magnet for arriving immigrants, arriving Italians normally rented space, often purchased homes, on neighborhood side streets.

EAST SIDE OF PRESTON STREET

47 Viau, Bouchard, and Minch
49 Mangone
51 Balestra
53 Riva
57 Truglia
59 L'Orfano, Carlo
61 Puccio, Randanoves, and Habole
63 Mitchell
65 Patry, Robert
67 De Carlo
69 Mc Court, Leduc
71 Preston Food Market
73 Schlitter Shoe Repair
75 Zinni and Picard
77 Ray
79 Dea and Dea
81 Mason
83 Brule
85 Plante
87 Turpin and Zito
89 De Millo and Kelly
91 Basso
93 Ritano
95 Peruzzo and Taffalo
97 Ledvinka and Mineau
99 Iacovetti
105-107 The Hinkman Apartments: Hewitt, Holmes, Stewart, Fraser, Purcell, Kelley, Laroque, Rodier
109 Azar Signs
121 Dufoe
123 Helmer
125 Joe's Coffee Shop and Nesrallah
129 Joynt
131 Kerrigan
133 Chenier
135 Benoit
137 Jackson Taxi
139 Campbell Apartments: Akeson, Ellwitz, Findlay, Trunderung, Seltitz, Hrassnig
141 Campbell Apartments
181 Apartments: Lavergne, Paluso, Martin, Lacroix, Grozelle, Witt
183 Lavergne
185 Lacelle
187 Orr
187 ½ Dinelle
189 Casagrande and Mc Connery
191 Legault
193 John's Place and Cuccaro
197 Rockburne
225 Malmberg Auto Service Ltd.
241 Forti
243 Harris
247 Nolan
249 Zidichouski and Bradshaw
251 Zidichouski, Berry, Walton, Muscoli, Cody
253 Preston Lunch
257 Whalen (Variety and Sports)
259 Whalen
261 Brandonio and Arnone
265 Paquette, Paquette and Sincennes
287 Jacques
271 Cotroneo and Lamla

273 Loyer and Robson
275 Chiarelli (Alfredo) Butcher and Grocer
277 Morgan Barber Shop
297 Emery and Larkin, Draper and Rowan
301 Brewer's Retail Store
309 Tavern
311 Mc Cullough
333 Hall Fuel Ltd.
339 Motorways Ltd. And Capital Storage Co.
355 Christie Brown and Co. Ltd.
357 Adamo
359 Bova
361 Ranieri
363 Cameron
367 Germain and Curry
369 Licari
371 Guzzo and Albanio
379-381 Prescott Hotekl
381 Frank's Taxi Service
399-401 National Printers Ltd.
409 Charbonneau
411 Pantalone
435 Kostenuk, Peterkin, Romaniuk, Richard
437 Toth
439 Kozak and Valois
447 Cianci
449 Lefebvre
451 Elford
453 Clint's Barber Shop
453 ½ Gauthier
455 Meadow's Grocery
455 ½ Collins
481 Vallillee
483 Moloughney
483 Lachapelle and Lachapelle
487 Mullen
489 Patafie and Marks
491 Leroux Electrical
499 Parson Memorial Baptist Mission
501 Sherman
505 Cardillo Service Station

WEST SIDE OF PRESTON STREET

32 Law and Ottawa Window Cleaning
34 Morin
36 Boucher
38 Perrault
40 Carrigan
50 Panetta
52 Mc Kale
54 Lane
56 Appotive and Rozon
58 Jessiman
60 Diotte
70 D'Onofrio
72 Parrington and Gamiro
74 Faucher
76 Gaugreau
80 Giofuocoro and Zinni
82 Jubi and Sgarbossa
86 Riopelle
90 Migas
92 White
94 Flaviani
96 Bennie's Confectionary
98 Bennie's Grocery
100 Marcusm Link and Lanoue
104 La Flamme and Connolly
104 ½ Beaupre and Mitchell
106 Finateri
112 Schlitter
114 Truglia Bakery
116 Sanitary Barber Shop
118 Bisson and Stewart
122 Rainbow Grill
___ Plouffe Park
130 The Plant Baths and Scott
160 Barresi and DiMisi

162 Disipio
164 Dodge
166A Lafleur
166B Gallincer
166C Lafleur
168D Akeson
168E Demers
170F Bradley
188 Kelly and Duschesneau
190 Montuoro
192 Montuoro
194 Lemay
196 Holt
198 Maxwell
200 Strang
224 Macrillo and Saunders
226 Macrillo and Casey
228 Pietro's Lunch and page
230 Vena Shoe Repair
232 Breadner
234 DeFalco and Villeneauve
246 Locatelli and Germain, Kaptein and Spicer
248 Preston Self-Serve Hardware
250 Sicily Barber Shop and Gail's Beauty
252 Spagano and Graziano
254 Clover Farm Store
256 Landreville
258 Lester and Reid
260 Paquette
262 Philippe
266 Blais
268 Ferrone and De Felice
270 Locatelli and Sullivan
270A Di Filippi
274 Tiezzi Groceteria
276 Phyl's Beauty Salon
280 Baggio's Clothing Store
282 Little
284 Paquette
286 Lee

288 Halpenny Oil Burners and Fusi
298 Fusi and Williams
300 Cusenbury and Whitehead
302 Bachinski Shoe Repair
302 ½ Macintyre
304 Testa Grocery and Testa
306 Dellavalle
___ CNR Railroad Crossing
330 Defalco Confectionary and Defalco
338 Bisson
340 Bisson General Store
344 Lanthier
348 Pack
348A Riopelle
350 Ferrone
352 Chinkiwsky
354 Purcell
354 ½ Scereino and Shorrock
356 Schbobb
358 Robillard and Michaud
360 Pantalone
362 Guzzo and Adamo Grocery
402 Scott's Service Station
406 Peloso
408 Caloia
410 Iogna
410 ½ Del Zotto
412 Lebrun
414 Di Giuseppe
416 Delle Palme
418 Nick's Lunch Bar
420 Preston Meat Market and Zito
422 Mulligan
424 Hunphrey
424 ½ De micheli
428 Pantalone
430 Prospereine and Nasso
430B Prospereine Real Estate
432 Filosa and D'Alosio
432 ½ Ierullo Barber Shop and Ierullo

434 Bianco
434 ½ Caccamo
436 Palef Confectionary
438 Carling Croceteria and Chinkiwsky
438 ½ Chappie's Lunch and Caramanico
440 Costello, Suave, and Robinson
442 Rossi
444 Trocino
450 Buntin Rien paper Ltd.
482 Lamoureux, Goudie, and Haagenson
484 Dixon and Holness
484 ½ Cook and Patafie
486 Dabene
486 ½ Trottier
488 Cianci
488 ½ Crozier
490 Barbera

Expropriations

Life in *The Village*, for the most part, was good. People were content. Upward mobility seemed assured. Yet two events, unrelated and separated by time, would change the homey feel of *The Village*. In the process, the Preston Street area would undergo a drastic and debilitating transformation as the face and heartbeat of the Italian-Canadian community would be changed forever.

Between 1958 and 1961 the Department of Planning and Urban Renewal set its sights on the widening gap in infrastructure between the populace and the environment in the growing City of Ottawa. The study was mostly concerned with the physical condition of dwellings and particular attention was paid to the deterioration of property in the areas of Lower Town East, Hurdman Bridge, and Preston Street. The Urban Renewal study was undertaken concurrently with the preparation of an Official Plan for the entire city. Wishing to improve the quality of life of residents in the urban districts, the Department identified almost thirty distinct areas reported to be substandard in living conditions. One of the cited districts contained eight square blocks bounded by Balsam, Booth, Preston Streets and the CNN train tracks. Officially known as The Preston Street Urban Renewal Study (1962) over 1,200 individual dwellings would be condemned, promptly expropriated, and eventually demolished. The following photographs display the Preston Street neighborhood.

A document prepared by Central Mortgage and Housing Corporation: *Architectural and Planning Division* titled *Urban Renewal in Ottawa and Hull*, dated February 1971 presented the following facts:

- Total area - 2008 acres, including streets
- Predominantly residential land use with spot industrial and commercial
- Many households derive income from business on residential properties
- Residential density higher than the city average
- Buildings crowded together with little useable open space
- Serious need for public open space
- Road system on grid with all streets open to through traffic
- Population mainly Roman Catholic with 27% of Italian origin
- Total of 335 houses with more than half as tenants
- 248 houses show signs of structural deficiency
- 26 houses show signs of extreme deficiency
- 58 families qualify for public housing
- The neighborhood is considered in urgent need of renewal though immigrant families have made a substantial effort to improve their properties
- A strong desire expressed by the residents to remain in the area. Scheme proposals included:
    - Total clearance of the area

- The closing of streets
- Public housing
- Clear-cut road patterns
- The provision of a site for a Commercial High School including an Auditorium and Library with Playing Field for public use
- The provision of commercial sites, primarily for persons displaced from business within the site.
- The provision of sites for public and private housing expected to re-house families displaced from the Scheme area.
- The provision of a site for a Nun's residence and Day Care Centre to replace land already owned within the area. This residence would form an important and integral part of the neighbourhood institutional complex.

Progress to date (1971) is as follows:
- The total clearance of 16.7 acres and the closure of streets has been completed.
- A public housing project on 6.8 acres and containing 125 row housing units with provision for public and private open space, car parking and play areas has been completed and occupied.
- The Commercial High School complex and the playing fields are now complete and in use.
- The Nun's residence and Day Care Centre is complete.
- In lieu of the commercial site at the south-west corner of Gladstone and Booth, a public park has been provided.
- 2.5 acres of the site, bounded by Preston, Balsam, Rochester and Gladstone remain to be developed. Originally intended for private multiple residential buildings and commercial development, this area has been approved by the Province and the Corporation for construction of a 24-unit senior citizen apartment tower. The City believes the remainder of the site will be required for a second and similar building. The question of commercial development is in abeyance.[31]

---

31 See *Urban Renewal in Ottawa and Hull, Central Mortgage and Housing*

The 1971 report presented a positive outcome of the renewal project. A derelict neighborhood had been refurbished to include public housing, a high school complex, a nun's residence, and a senior citizen's apartment tower. The overall political scheme boasted a heartening and successful civic accomplishment: an urban eyesore had been opportunely revitalized with significant affirmatory impact on the community. The enhanced property values would instill a sense of civic pride, stimulate the local economy, help established businesses and attract new ones. The overall local reaction was another matter altogether.

An article in *The Ottawa Journal*, dated Saturday 14 February 1970, asked the rhetorical question: "Preston Street Renewal: Physical Success But Social Failure?"[32] The article featured "New Look" photos of nondescript low-rise rent-to-housing public units contrasted with the "Old Look" of "wooden buildings constructed circa 1900 by the British Lumber Company to accommodate employees after a fire raged through part of the city." The short description of the photos concluded by stating that "about 55 per cent of the buildings in the renewal area were owner-occupied, half of them by Italians."

But it was not only those Italians homeowners who suffered the distress of forced relocation. The Preston Street neighborhood also suffered the loss of a substantial portion of its population. In the same article, Father Ferraro, the outspoken and caring Pastor of St. Anthony's Church felt, at the time, that "planners should have come up with a scheme that would have kept some of the long-established families, used to owning their own homes, in the area." From his office window that looked down towards the area once known as Rochester Heights, where some of those people had lived, he continues: "I am not against urban renewal. Buildings get old the same as bodies and the city has to develop. But it should try to retain the people in the area." The popular and amicable priest believed that a "real vacuum" was created when the neighborhood was gutted of its inhabitants who took with them "community spirit, tradition and friendship." Those,

---

Corporation: Architectural and Planning Division, February 1971: 3-4.

32 Carroll Holland, "Departed Families Left 'Real Vacuum' – Father Ferraro," *The Ottawa Journal*, 14 February 1970.

like Mrs. Frank Licari who were forced to move to the non-Italian areas of the city where neighbors hardly spoke to each other, felt lost and abandoned. "It was an awful shock to us."

A less sanguine popular view classified the scheme as a political ploy by then Mayor Charlotte Whitton to derail an increasingly important Italian community from gaining economic or political influence in her city. Indeed, though the renewal scheme promised and delivered a new school and affordable housing, the nine-block area had a depressing effect on the adjacent neighborhoods. Values declined; properties deteriorated.

The expropriation initiated a downward social, economic, spiritual, and cultural spiral in the Italian-Canadian community. Bitter accounts of the event, as well as heartfelt antipathy towards the municipal administration, still rumble amongst older community members. Yet, their protests and discomfort appeared small in scale and unremarkable compared to the power of the institutional structures that enabled and enforced neighborhood redevelopment (i.e. destruction). Frank Chiarelli, who grew-up in the area, felt the brunt of the hurt. "It felt like the heart had been pulled out of the community. Longtime friends, neighbors, hangouts . . . suddenly disappeared."

In the aftermath of the unpopular expropriation, rumors abounded of impeding further developments spreading fear and uncertainty in an already fragile community. Instead of bettering the area, the dream of ongoing spot renewal, as it was called, became a latent and debilitating social worry that the Italian-Canadian community, and especially the Preston Street area, carried for years to come. The neighborhood remained relatively stagnant; devoid of genuine economic hope, reduced to upstart caffes and backroom gambling havens that served a dwindling local clientele.

Arriving on Preston Street in the 70s and 80s, one was struck by the grayness and uninspiring view of tired storefronts and weather-worn homes. The limp landscape had succumbed to time, sentimental neglect, and upscale indifference. Many families had moved away; and those that remained had little energy to renew businesses that seemed headed towards a deadend future. Like many broken urban centers in North America, the neighborhood pathway towards communal depression seemed a natural descent fueled by its own weight.

What indeed, if anything, could a tired Italian-Canadian community do to renew its own increasingly irrelevant past on Preston Street when that past had been torn from its roots, when its neighborhoods were succumbing to the geographic infusion of Asians, especially Vietnamese, and when newer, more upscale enclaves of Italian-Canadians where sprouting in the Carleton Heights and Alta Vista neighborhoods?

ETHNICITY AND INSTITUTIONS

Ethnic is a Greek word meaning people or peoples. Though the term has suffered some confusing meanings in history, it usually refers to a given group of people linked primarily by kin ties and a common set of historical experiences. Values, behavior patterns, customs and culture arise from these basic bonds and relationships. The attachment to prevalent outward signs (such as modes of dress, language, food), the commonality of place (such as bars, caffes, clubs), may help identify one ethnic group from another but are not usually the key to group survival.

Contrary to popular belief (and political convenience), ethnic communities are not static; they don't simply live or die, but instead evolve, normally adapting long-held and inherent traditions to embrace new environments, while remaining actively conscious of former roots. In this sense, ethnicity is thus not limited to foreigners but is applicable to any community that shares concomitant experience (signs and places) over succeeding generations.

Given these defining parameters, most people who live in a world of personal and professional relations are part of a delimited ethnic group. These types of relations are sustained by modes of ancestral identification, normally to a village, but can also ascribed to a city, or better, a neighborhood. This personal identification with a group need not be conscious to be effective, often working at an intuitive level. Social scientists thus generally agree that individual personality is formed in the context of specific public and private relations that lie both within and without our conscious efforts. Fully mature and ethically responsible individual selves can only develop if social institutions are constructed that permit these vital public and private shared cultural experiences. Community is that social environment that permits healthy growth. It is the place where the individual perceives his personal experiences as part of a larger human and meaningful context. The community permits adaptation, cooperation, interaction, indeed survival. In the process of using traditional inter-personal bonds, the community can foster an evolutionary process that guarantees the growth and continuation of itself over future generations. It does so by creating institutions.

Beyond the family, institutions are primary ties to the external social environment that form the basic organizing principle of society. While the concept of belonging to a clan had a definite territorial basis in the old world, in the newly hatched world of the migrant, institutions reinforce the incorporation of the self within the larger, often more foreboding, cityscape. Institutions transform sojourners into established immigrants. Formal institutions also initiate a cycle of distinctiveness - tapping into the unique qualities of community members allowing them to influence others and, by doing so, refashioning the direction of the community.

When given the occasion to remain successful and useful, community institutions can provide the base for effective social functioning. In order to remain useful to the evolution of the community, however, institutions must regularly renew their ideological mandate, and subsequently their membership ranks, through the recruitment of new and younger members; a difficult process at best and often rendered impossible by generational conflict. Indeed, and unfortunately, in many instances this turnover process is actually discouraged or frustrated by myopic practices, preclusive policies, the forces of vested local interests that favor the semblance of power while relinquishing legitimate social responsibility. It is thus often assumed that it is natural for ethnic institutions to die-off in second and third-generation offspring. The argument goes that as the young become assimilated, the old traditions are lopped-off for fear of identification with community elders and with an ethnic past of poverty and depression, argument and conflict.

Prosperity (and familiarity, though it can be argued that the youth or any ethnic group have very little knowledge of their own traditions) it is assumed, breeds comfortable contempt; and coerces youth to reject the very history that would make them strong and effective community members. The result is that the very institutions that once helped strengthen the community are oftentimes debunked and sorely depleted to the point of near extinction. Two types of critical problems arise from the above reality: (1) the community institution dies from lack of physical, systemic, and ideological rejuvenation and, (2) a spiritual demise occurs as second and third-generation youth remain stunted in both their personal and civic growth due to the lack of the continuance and evolution of traditional grassroot institutions.

The consequences of this state of affairs are often apparent in the Italian-Canadian community of Ottawa. Because of its past inability to effectively foster and renew the social networks and social institutions critical for true community development, the ethnic group never fully evolved to attain the sufficient institutional and economic autonomy critical to the control its own political and social existence. This gap in the transformation process has resulted in the further alienation of those very elements of the community that would have otherwise helped to ensure ethnic continuity, if not survival. The community thus remains mired in a state of ineffectual lethargy.

The lack of an initial core of fixed community principles that still leave room for divergent desires, differing intellectual and economic capabilities, youthful enthusiasm, and an effective transmission of tradition, only produces an unrelenting loss of forward momentum with troubling implications for the future. It is apparent, then, that a sense of community can be lost, or better, squandered, by the ineffectual maintenance of its institutions.

This occurs when the group is either unable or unwilling to identify long-term problems and therefore does not devise strategies that establish new community goals.

This occurs because too often community leaders use ethnic institutions (such as recurring mudane festivals) to bring tourists to town while allowing ethnic neighborhoods to disintegrate.

This occurs because the group mistakenly believes that the destruction of the old is a natural process of migration that cannot be thwarted.

This occurs when the group itself is unable, if not incapable, of engendering the necessary synergy to instill natural pride in its community members.

If we add to the mix advancing trends in real estate, land use and gentrification, population distribution, generational aging, widespread cultural apathy, political indifference, and other sundry sociological items, then the disappearance of ethnicity and ethnic institutions in Ottawa seems inevitable.

Yet, the importance of an ethnic dimension in city development is critical to the life of the City of Ottawa if not the Italian-Canadian community at large. It is paramount for the growth of mature and responsible individuals, for nurturing morality and social consciousness, and for ensuring the survival of those institutions that will allow the group to deal with its own sociocultural problems while safeguarding those values that have defined its growth and characterized its imprint on society at large. Conclusively, it is not about the importance of maintaining the *ethnicity* of ethnic communities but how any ethnic community defines itself and guarantees its properly willed survival through the nurturing of its institutions.

Institutions

In this section, I attempt a profile of the Italian-Canadian community of Ottawa's *de facto* grassroot institutions; the ones normally associated with a thriving community. These include mutual aid, religious formation, social instruction, and political fixtures that cement people together.

The coming and going of people that form, inform, or transform these institutions is, by its very dynamic, a disruptive social force and a source of authentic and substantial tension. The ancient Romans recognized the unease that exists between valuing the old ways and accepting the new, between the stability of tradition and the function of change in the polyglot and cosmopolitan city of Rome. Peaceful homogeneity is not the salt of multiculturalism, nor is it the sum of the collection of disparate regional villages that comprise the patchwork fabric of Ottawa's Italian-Canadian community. Local institutions always present a polyphony of diverse voices and a hierarchy of discourses that contest the same limited terrain. There may be reason for caution in attempting a survey of their dappled histories while speculating upon their uncertain futures. But, notwithstanding the innately asperous nature of the immigrant personality, the landscape of these enduring institutions, though often problematic, remains surprisingly solid.

I am consoled also by the fact that, at any given moment, the institution encountered by an objective observer is not the institution itself but a rich and multi-layered text comprised of a mass of signals that though often dense, obscure, and sometimes indecipherable, invariably lead to a swarm of interesting and well-meaning individuals dedicated to socially significant causes. Social environment, specifically immediate family, lifelong friends and the old neighborhood, influence personal behavior and most often determine quality of life both for the individual and for the community. Social institutions are determinants of those patterns of behavior that forge who we are, what we become, and regulate the rise and fall of a community. The early Italian migrants quickly developed those socioeconomic and sociocultural institutions, those familiar and comfortable niches that permitted them to transmit inherently shared traditional values while forming a unique Italian-Canadian genetic heritage for succeeding generations.

Mythopoeia, or myth making, are narratives that create reliable genetic explanations for ontic stability. They are stories that interplay archetypes and stereotypes, roam between past and present experience, facilitate socialization, actualizes spiritual or non-secular belief systems that, when held by a group of adherents, express traditions that explain man place in the universe and relationship with the infinite. The adherence to these beliefs and practices consolidated, beyond the daily labor, the immigrant dream of success and notions of individual identity and worth within the group.

The influx of relatively poor foreign migrants poses problems to any host country. Bureaucratic and social services need to be invented to resolve basic, though vital, issues. Where and how would these new arrivals live? How would the skilled and unskilled find employment? Who would provide for the sick, for the education of youth? What of language training?

Given the general postwar climate in Canada, these potentially explosive problems were easily ignored, if not dismissed, by local government for a variety of reasons. The process of moving through

Pier One in Halifax, though daunting and always frightening, was mitigated by a Canadian cultural climate that accepted immigration as a necessary, and welcome, asset necessary for national economic prosperity.

The dependence of arriving Italians on their own kinship network for social support, the relative ease of finding some sort of temporary employment, and the location of Italians in tight-knit enclaves of people from the same region or village, softened the struggle immigrant counterparts had suffered in the United States. Furthermore, Italians arriving in Canada seemed self-sufficient, politically innocuous, socially untroubled and willing to sacrifice personal dignity for economic survival.

Reassured that these immigrants would not fundamentally change the social landscape and that the new arrivals were of good character and could be easily absorbed, public opinion remained generally undaunted and indifferent. In an age where social difference was not ethnic but primarily economic, migrants settled in overpopulated immigrant quarters reminiscent of the colonies of Europe's rural towns. As a lower class, they lived in conditions different from the more affluent citizens of Ottawa.

Furthermore, the English and French politicos considered their ethnic ghettos relatively safe, their networks (migratory, economic, social, and political) were not really peninsular Italian but specific to each individual's *paese* and therefore not threatening. Most importantly, their acculturation to their Anglo-French surroundings was quick, deliberate, and accommodating. In short, Italian immigrants were just plain folks ready to adapt to the exigencies of survival in the New World.

If we understand the identity of these clusters of colonies throughout North America in local terms rather than in those of a national Italian identity, it is possible to comprehend each individual community's struggle with the rising levels of expectations and other social disruptions pressing down upon the community daily, as a capacity to comply to local power while forging a new way of life.

The age of the ethno-cultural ghetto had begun; it seemed, for all practical purposes, that migration had infused a vigor of adaptability into the immigrant. If it were true that natural laws of selectivity demanded that only the strong sought adventure in the new world, it was also quite evident that while the stagnant and lethargic had remained behind in their homeland, the *paesani* who arrived, once given a modicum of possibility for success, quickly nurtured those customs and traditions that gave meaning to their lives.

While the home, school, and church were, and remain, the primary institutions that guaranteed some degree of uniformity and helped to create and to solidify what may be called the basic personality type of the Italian-Canadian community around patterns of self-organization and self-recognition, once the necessities of home, school, and church are relatively satisfied, communities tend to form social organizations that serve to fill the emotional gaps of suffering and loss that accompany the immigrant throughout his extra-village journey. In this manner, the community shapes the maturing of their members in differing ways, while the individual's basic personality structure is affected by the various subgroups to which one belongs. These groups are normally based upon religion, occupation, social class, age and gender.

These institutions thus augment those interpersonal social relationships that are the chief means by which the sociocultural environment exerts its influence on individual development. People generally tend to identify with those institutions that nurture both their immediate and long-term needs. For an institution to remain solvent over the years, it must provide a moral, social, economic, and cultural conscious the community recognizes as its own thereby sanctioning the cohesion of the community.

Fraternity: The *Order of Italo-Canadians*

The very first pro-Italian society to embody and promote self-esteem, community service, civic education, and provide a moral backbone to the fledgling Italian-Canadian community of Ottawa was the *Società Figli d'Italia di Ottawa*, founded in 1907.[33] The officers of the newly

---

33   *The Order of Sons of Italy* was formed in New York City in 1905 by Dr. Vincenzo Sellaro. It was a society devoted to caring for the Italian immigrant in the early days of the 20th Century. The first lodge in Canada was formed

formed *Società* included: Lorenzo Valentine, President; Vincenzo Rossi, Vice-President; Vincenzo Mari, Secretary; Luigi Demaria, Financial Secretary; Gaetano Defalco, Treasurer; Francesco Guzzo, Sergeant at Arms.[34]

The following year, 1908, the short-lived society *Fratellanza Sant'Antonio* was formed. It eventually merged with the *Figli d'Italia* to create the *Società Figli d'Italia di M.S. Sant'Antonio di Ottawa* in 1919. Officers of new society included: Pasquale Adamo, Chair; Giovanni Palmieri, Vice President; Nicola Storto, Secretary; Vincenzo Macri, Financial Secretary; Francesco Guzzo, Treasurer; Vincenzo Rossi, Sergeant at Arms. Administrators for the society: Angelo Licari, President; Antonio Peca, Vice-President; Sebastiano Polverigiani, Secretary; Orazio Amato, Vice-Secretary; Basilio Ferraro, Financial Secretary; Sam Macli, Accountant; Dr. Vittorio Sabetta and Paul Dioguardi, Counsellors; Rev. P. Girolamo Ferraro, Chaplain.[35]

In 1924, the *Daughters of Italy and Italian Women of Canada* was founded, possibly in response to the growing number of immigrant woman entering the workforce and gaining a voice outside the home. This particular group, as well as the *Società Educativa Italiana*, founded in 1926, are called protective or reference groups because they officially point towards the norms, values, and goals that model the behavior of the individual that chooses to participate. As subgroups, they tend to foster behavior patterns which may be subject to the restrictions

---

in 1915 in Sault Ste. Marie, Ontario, as a mutual benefit society dedicated to providing financial help and protection to Italian immigrants. It played a crucial role in the lives of many immigrants by contributing material and spiritual support in times of illness, accident and death. There are 15 lodges in Canada, over 3,000 lodges in the U.S.A, Bermuda and Hawaii. It is the largest fraternal order of Canadians and Americans of Italian origin. At its inception, only persons of Italian origin made up *The Order of Sons of Italy*. Over the years, membership has been opened to persons of Italian birth or descent, or persons married to someone of Italian birth or descent, regardless of religious faith or political affiliations. Its mission and philosophy have remained constant over its history: belief in God; the brotherhood of man; government by law.

34   Spada, 314.
35   Spada, 314.

imposed by society as a whole.[36] They are sheltering associations that tend to nurture those needs that are often neglected by the larger community.

In 1930, an Ottawa branch of just such a protective group, the *Independent Order of Sons of Italy*, was established under the guidance of Raffaele Lallo of Montreal. The Ottawa branch was baptized *Lodge Colombo no. 10* and was followed soon afterwards by the *Ladies Lodge Venezia no. 12*. They remain the most prosperous and long-standing lodges of the Order. These two Ottawa lodges, the *Lodge Colombo no. 10* and *Lodge Venezia no. 12*, enjoyed considerable success in the growing Italian-Canadian community. The two lodges were relatively non-political; more interested in the social and economic welfare of their members in Canada rather that the political climate brewing in Europe. For these reasons, in 1927, they along with several Québec lodges who were also opposed to the *Independent Order of Sons of Italy's* openly pro-fascist leanings, broke away from the larger, more politicized Order.

The Ottawa and Quebec lodges founded instead a parallel national society, eventually renamed *The Order of Italo-Canadians* (*L'Ordre des Italo-Canadiens*), incorporated by an Act of Parliament in 1936. The founding members included: Angelo Spada, Enrico Perazzo, Raffaele Rossi, Vincenzo Martello, Franceso l'Oddo, Salvatore Murano, Sabino Bozzer, Raffaele Lallo, Giuseppe Mastropaolo, Frank de Martinis, Domenico Lapiana, Fortunato Talevi, Mario Marchionni, Giovanni D'Onofrio, Mauro Orefice, Antonio Sabetta, Nidata Vigilante.

An extract from the Dominion Charter stipulates that the Powers of *The Order* include:

    a)   to institute, organize, establish, and carry on local branches of the Society, which branches shall be called lodges;

    b)   to propagate and develop among the members of the Society a mutual and fraternal spirit;

    c)   to enlighten the members of the society in the history, constitution and legislation of their foster land, the Dominion of Canada, with the object of making them good Canadian citizens conscious of their rights and duties as such;

---

36   For more information about these groups, again See Spada, 303-15.

d) to promote the intellectual instruction and development of the members of the Society by the reading of newspapers, periodicals, and books, and especially to facilitate the study of the French, English and Italian languages;

e) to facilitate and encourage the study of sciences, music, singing and arts and generally to enhance the instruction and education of its members, and for that purpose to establish, help and maintain schools and teaching institutions;

f) to preserve and strengthen, through the practice of physical culture and sports, the health of its members;

g) to protect, help, support and assist such members of the Society as may be in need or afflicted by disease, accident and other misfortune, and in the case of death of one of its members to help his widow, children and dependents;

h) to establish, maintain and support homes and shelters for old disabled members of the Society, and to establish and maintain or assist orphanages to care for the orphan children of the members of the Society;

i) to borrow from time to time such amounts of money as may be required for the purposes of the Society;

j) to solicit, receive and accept, by gift, bequest or otherwise, and to hold and dispose of, for the purposes of the Society, any monies.

As a federally chartered fraternal benefits-insurance society, *The Order of Italo-Canadians* provided mutual aid, benefit, and insurance for instance, to its members. At a time when the community was just beginning to grow, membership in *The Order* (as it came to be known) offered financial security, assistance for education, social aid during periods of unemployment, benefits at the birth of a child, sickness and medical expenses, administered funds for retirement, and eased the costs of funerals. A variety of life insurance plans were offered to adult members while juvenile members could become beneficiaries of endowment insurance certificates. Many members used their growing funds for educational purposes or to provide their children with gifts at marriage.[37] *The Order* provided lifelong security, assured corporate

---

37 Many major financial institutions existing today, especially insurance companies, mutual savings banks, and credit unions, trace their origins

fealty, and *beneficial order* in a land where too often the fortunes of fate quickly turned sour.

While *The Order* hesitated to grow in the rest of Canada, the two Ottawa lodges grew to membership heights of over 500 thanks, in great part, to the indefatigable and unfailing loyalty and drive of Financial Secretary Anello Castrucci. A true believer in the fraternal ideals of *The Order*, Castrucci spent most of his free time marshalling support for the unifying values of the association by recruiting new members citywide.

Past Presidents of *Ottawa Lodge Colombo no. 10* and *Ladies Lodge Venezia no. 12* have included: Rosina Ranieri, Angelina Carpenti, Assunta Zuana, Palmira Coletti, Paola Ladelpa, Giuseppe Capogreco, Sam Guzzo, Giuseppe Regalbuto, Paolo Ruffo, Luigi Gianetti, Mimmo Idone, Antonio Toscano, Ruggero Nicoletti, Giuseppe Castrucci, Wilma Bianco.

The Ottawa Lodges, energized by the work of Anello Castrucci, eventually founded a youth group or *Comitato Giovanile* in 1977 in the hope of sponsoring recreational and cultural activities among the younger members of the *The Order*. In 1987, the group was instrumental in establishing a $5000.00 scholarship fund in Italian Studies at the University of Ottawa. Past Presidents of the youth group have included: Giuseppe Castrucci, Anna Di Rienzo, Fabio Leggeri, Mariano Ranallo, and Raffaele Castrucci.

Though its beginnings are clothed with the politics of the times, and the present is burdened with the general public antipathy towards these types of institutions, *The Order* was an early safe shelter and benevolent society for immigrants seeking haven or help amongst their own kind.

One, if not the main, driving force of *The Order* was the Bortolotti family. Born in Friuli in 1897 and immigrant to Canada in 1920, Anselmo Bortolotti was an active and untiring supporter of community associations and a member of the national "Canadian Aid to Italy" committee in support of relief for families in war-torn Italy. He was an original founder of *The Order of Italo-Canadians* and remained one of its most dedicated promoters his entire life.

---

back to these types of benefit fraternal societies.

His son, Nello Bortolotti, continued his father's philanthropic legacy. A long-time President of the Supreme Council of *The Order*, Bortolotti began community work as a young man when he participated in a YMCA advisory committee that assisted new immigrants to Ottawa. Since those early beginnings, he has served on countless boards and executive councils including: the Council on Aging; the Somerset West Community Health Centre; the National Congress of Italian Canadian (National and District); the NCIC's Eastern Ontario and Outaouais District Foundation; the Italian Canadian Community Centre; the Ottawa Festival Network. He has served on the Multicultural Advisory Committee of the (former) Ottawa Board of Education and was involved in Ottawa's Italian Week festivities.

The Villa Marconi Long-Term Care Centre project presented him an intense occasion of community service. An untiring fundraiser from its inception, he was involved in various Board capacities at Villa Marconi and was a major promoter of its success. Frequently acknowledged for his community work, Bortolotti was recognized by the federal Minister of Citizenship and Immigration for his work with newcomers to Canada and by the Province of Ontario for his continuous volunteering service. He was awarded the Millennium 2000 Medal from the (former) City of Nepean for his service as a community builder. At the Village Reunion Annual event of October 2002, Nello received the Community Contribution Award for his dedication to the growth and development of the Italian-Canadian community. Though a humble man, Bortolotti fought exhaustively for the preservation of Italian culture in Canada and looked towards the younger generations to preserve their heritage.

7 September 2018 marked the passing of Nello Bortolotti, a long-time President of *The Order* having succeeded his father, Anselmo Bortolotti. Described by friends as a kind, gentle, knowledgeable, indefatigable man, Nello Bortolotti was a pillar of the Italian-Canadian community nationwide having supported and fought for the implementation of equitable multicultural policies throughout his lifetime. His tenure as National President of the Canadian Fraternal Association helped render *The Order of Italo-Canadians* one of the

most prestigious, most respected, most enduring and longstanding organizations in Canada.

Faith
Sant'Antonio di Padova
Madonna della Risurezzione Parish

For the arriving immigrant, religion often served as a filter for examining, understanding, and ultimately accepting the daily societal issues, working conditions, loneliness, and other unfamiliar and stressful components of the new culture. It became the expression of social cohesion. Emile Durkheim contended that religion is the celebration, if not self-worship of human society. He proposed that religion has three major functions in society: it initiates social cohesion by fostering solidarity through shared rituals and beliefs; it maintains social control by enforcing religious-based morals and norms that shape conformity and control in society; finally, it offers meaning and purpose to existential questions.[38] While the traditional social institutions play an important role in community dynamics, it is essential not to overlook the singular importance of the institution of religion as an icon for the arriving immigrant. By guiding the immigrant to accept his place in the universe, the church allowed him to better understand his situation within the throes of the modern and often obscure society churning around him.

The adaptability of the Italian to these extreme conditions not only eased social tensions in the adopted Canadian landscape but created a space for the growth of those institutions that provided for the material and spiritual welfare of the growing number of Italians in Ottawa. By permitting an immigrant ambience, government also inadvertently reinforced the role of those same institutions that usually helped wayward and troubled souls in the immigrant's native villages. Primary of these was The Roman Catholic Church.

---

38 Emile Durkheim, *The Elementary Forms of Religious Life (1912)*, Translated by Carol Cosman and edited by Mark S. Cladis (Oxford: Oxford Classic, 2008).

The Italian-Canadian community of Ottawa is Roman Catholic by tradition. In the historical development of the community, the church of *Sant'Antonio di Padova* (or St. Anthony) helped restore meaning and gave stability to the uprooted lives of the growing immigrant population. The Church not only reinforced deeply set faith but also consolidated an evolving cultural identity. In the absence of physicians and lawyers, who were most often at least competent in the immigrant's language, the role of the local priest was infinitely much wider than today and embraced many professions. How Italians regarded one another, how they were treated in their everyday lives, often stemmed from the sense of solidarity that was given them via the church and its parish priest.

Sunday mass thus became a community focal point, providing space not only for worship and religious services, but also secured the secular, material, and social well-being of parishioners. Religious processions, the veneration of saints, parades in honor of important Italians began and ended at the Church. Religion was used as a mechanism that facilitated greater involvement in community causes and it was a decisive instrument for the development of a cohesive immigrant experience. The Church became the collective unconscious and served to define the physical location, the cultural potential, and the political limits of the Italian community.

The first mass for the newly arrived Italians was celebrated in the month of April 1908 in the Capuchin Church of Saint Francis by the Reverend Father Fortunato Mizzi da Valletta of the Capuchin Order. A pioneer preacher of sorts in the early days of Ottawa, Father Fortunato took it upon himself to nurture and grow his small flock and, with the help of devoted parishioner Domenico Nasso, rented a small chapel on Murray Street near Dalhousie Street for religious services and celebration of the sacraments from May 1908 to October 1913. The location was close to the small Italian immigrant community assembling in the Preston Street area.

By 1913, the original group of 150 worshipers had grown to include most of the burgeoning community. The small Murray Street chapel could no longer sustain the increasing number of parishioners. It was time to build a larger church. Father Fortunato received permission from the Archbishop of Ottawa, Monseigneur Carlo Ugo Gauthier, to launch a new Mission, or parish, close to the Italian immigrant population of Dalhousie. The cornerstone of the church was laid by the Monseigneur on the bright and sunny Spring day of 18 May 1913.

No sooner had construction begun, however, when the house immediately adjacent to the church was fortuitously available for purchase. Father Fortunato promptly set about to find the necessary money to purchase the property as he felt it was a perfect location for a future monastery. The Capuchin Order was unwilling to assume the debt for acquiring the building nor, he was told, were they willing to assume responsibility for maintaining the new Church once it was completed.

What to do? Never one to accept defeat, the good Father spoke to Brother Tommaso Ciofini O.S.M., and convinced him to speak to his confraternity in Montreal regarding both the purchase of the nearby property and the future funding of his church. Shortly thereafter, the Order of the Servants of Mary agreed to purchase the property that was Up for Sale. On 31 July 1913 the land became a church holding. The future of St. Anthony's was also secured as the Servants of Mary officially assumed responsibility for its financial well-being.

Construction of a rather primitive building was rapid. It was not very large, measuring only 19 by 12 meters. "Quattro muri per non dire tre," Father A. M. Prosperi, O.S.M. and first Pastor of St. Anthony's Church would often say. Indeed, the church was small. Three walls were of brick; the wall behind the altar was constructed of wood in order to facilitate anticipated future expansion. A typically Canadian sloping roof and two large but simple windows graced the plain brick facade. A large basement ensured space for parochial events, social gatherings, and provided a first meeting place for the nascent community associations. The building's most striking feature was a long steep wooden staircase that led up to the chapel.

Monseigneur Pellegrino M. Stagni, Apostolic Delegate to Ottawa, blessed the church on 2 November 1913. The congregation was officially placed in the hands of the Servite Order as Father Aurelio M. Prosperi was named Pastor on 16 March 1914. Father Fortunato presented the new pastor to his congregation in a moving and heartfelt homily on Sunday 22 March. Father Prosperi guided the parish for sixteen years. That same month, construction of the monastery began and was completed and blessed by the Apostolic Delegate His Excellency Monseigneur Stagni, on 22 November 1914. The first Prior of the new house was the Reverend P. Prospero M. Bernardi. Other priests followed to fill the ranks of St. Anthony and included M.R. P. Stefano M. Cheli, and Father Giovannangelo M. Bertsche.

The church stood at the corner of Division and Pine Streets, current day Booth Street and Gladstone Avenue. This site was chosen, after much discussion, because of its proximity to the flourishing Italian immigrant population in the area. Not only Italians, however, but the local French and English neighbors enjoyed the hospitableness and generosity of the Servite fathers.

On 26 March 1917, four years after its construction, the church fell victim to a ruinous fire, probably from candles on the main altar. The flames completely engulfed the rear wooden wall of the church and spread so quickly that little of the structure remained standing. A painting by the artist Guido Nincheri, representing the Sacred Heart of Jesus with St. Giuliana Falconieri and St. Margherita Maria Alacoque, was lost to the flames. Nevertheless, despite the obvious confusion, inconvenience, and general dismay, the customary Passion Week devotions were carried out on the night of the fire.

Not prone to despair, the community set about to reconstruct the church, this time under the guidance and supervision of Guido Nincheri, an architect and painter from Montreal. The building was inaugurated in November 1925 with a solemn mass celebrated by the then Apostolic Delegate Monseigneur Pietro di Maria. The new church was heavily influenced by Nincheri's Gothic vision. The high-vaulted ceiling, lateral chapels, tall stained glass, the imposing belfry, and the long exterior staircase, are from this period.

Yet, fate once again intervened in the storied history of St. Anthony's. On 21 April 1929, another disastrous fire raged through the building, just four fateful years after its reconstruction, gutting its interior and rising as high as the belfry. Cause of the fire remains a mystery, but the blaze spread with such rapidity that the assembled crowd outside feared the building doomed. But the church, like its parishioners, survived. In June 1930, Father Prosperi was succeeded by Father Cheli. He too remained shepherd of his flock for sixteen years, leaving in 1946.

Reconstruction began immediately, this time with less wood, more steel and mortar, again under the guidance of Nincheri. Well-known in his native Montreal where is honored as one of its builders, Guido Nincheri arrived in Canada in 1914. He was originally from Prato, in Tuscany, and completed his education in classical design and architecture at the prestigious Academy of Fine Arts in Florence. Here he would succumb to the influence of his master mentors Michelangelo and Botticelli. Baptized Canada's Michelangelo by art critics and public alike, the prolific and seemingly inexhaustible artist was truly a Renaissance man of many passions. From drawing to painting, sculpture to architecture, and ultimately stained-glass tableau of sparkling inspiration, the diminutive Tuscan born artist became Quebec's most important liturgical artist.[39]

Photograph courtesy of Trina Costantini Powell.

It is estimated that Nincheri created over 5000 stained glass windows in Canada and the United States. His style is bold, realistic, extraordinarily three-dimensional; his color palette is exceptionally vast and blessed with subtleties that bring his biblical scenes to life. The stained-glass windows that adorn St. Anthony's Church are a

---

39   Nincheri was part of a hallowed group of only three artists to develop the fresco technique in North America, the other two being the Mexican mural artists Diego Rivera and José Orozco. Their work adorns the walls of museums, atriums, railway stations, and churches across the continent. Nincheri painted more and larger murals than any other Canadian artist.

true tour de force of historical, symbolic, realistic, and archeological accuracy. Their illuminating thrust is breath-taking, while their artistic importance and relevance is as lofty as those of the Gothic cathedrals of Europe. For an exhaustively comprehensive and detailed description of these marvelous and inspiring visions of faith, please see *A Journey of Faith — A History of St. Anthony of Padua Church: 1913 – 2013* (See Note 3). The description is lovingly written by Roger Boccini Nincheri, edited by Melanie Grondin, with photographs by Roger Boccini Nincheri.

Under Nincheri's artistic direction, the belfry, turrets, and roof were completely replaced, the interior gutted. Appropriately, the church ceiling and walls were finished in stucco, the floor in terrazzo tile, and galleries were constructed to support a choir loft for the organ. In May 1938, the church was consecrated as an Italian-English parish by order of the Archbishop.

In 1946 Father Girolamo M. Ferraro (known as Father Jerome), born in Montreal and completely fluent in Italian, became parish Pastor at age 27. He would remain attached to the church for 40 years, eventually retiring in 1972. Devoted, caring, dedicated to the community, Father Ferraro was an indefatigable servant of his flock. Stories abound regarding his kindness, his humor, his formidable character, his strength and resolve. The 1950s witnessed a surge of Italian immigration to Ottawa; under his supervision the church became a clearing house for social woes. No problem was too great, no issue too small. A new arrival needed a job, talk to Father Ferraro; problems with a child at school, talk to Father Ferraro; relatives abroad need a local sponsor for immigration, again, see Father Ferraro. During his tenure as Pastor the Italian population of the parish ward swelled and prospered. When he died in 1972 at age 55, the parish lost an heroic servant of God; "The soul," as is commemorated on the bust dedicated to him near the church, "of the Italian community."

Father Ferraro has been ably served by a string of pastors to the present day. Among them: Reverend Gaston Venne, who immediately succeeded Father Ferraro, Reverend Andrew Carrier, Reverend Marcel Brodeur and the smiling Irishman (although born in Quebec of French Canadian stock on his mother's side), Reverend Paul McKeown.

The church and its ministry have been the focal point of the Italian community of Ottawa for over 100 years and is still very much part of life in the community. The church's importance to the Preston Street neighborhood in the 20th century was and remains immeasurable as it not only met residents' spiritual needs, but the church also served political, civic, social, and educational functions.

St. Anthony's was instrumental in establishing the first school located in the Italian community that was built by the Separate School Board after protracted solicitation by Father Prosperi. The pioneering priest felt that a proper parish school was an absolute necessity towards preserving both the language and culture of the Italian immigrant community. Located adjacent to the St. Anthony's Church on Booth Street, work was complete in May of 1925. The school was officially christened *Accademia Dante* and blessed on 7 June, Feast of the Holy Trinity, by Monseigneur P. A. Campeau. That same day a monument to Dante Alighieri was dedicated adjacent to the school.

Documented facts surrounding the *Accademia Dante*, or Dante Academy, are scarce. It seems that unfortunate archival problems occurred during the city mergers of the late 1980s causing havoc with school board records. Many important documents were lost. Nevertheless, St. Anthony's School, whatever its name, was both a haven for the wayward and a center for community learning since it opened its doors. It provided the *common unity* for the Italian-Canadian community, a true anchor institution providing quality education for its children and, eventually, opportunities for students of all economic and cultural backgrounds and walks of life. Today, the school teaches over 200 students per year and is a cultural microcosm of the larger Ottawa community, a true blessing in the mosaic of cultures that now inhabit the Preston Street area.

It is a truism that in order for any community to truly flourish and maintain prosperity, there must be top-quality public education, a place where youngsters develop life-long friendships. The relationships developed in school create family ties that bind the neighborhood and ultimately lead to an environment of communal cohesion, neighborly trust, and community longevity. But we must not forget the social wealth bequeathed to the community by the religious pillar of St.

Anthony's catholic mission. Beyond The Order of Servants of Mary, The Servite Sisters of the Addolorata, the vital chapters of the Ladies Auxiliary and Knights of Columbus, and St. Anthony's School, the church was also home base to Italian-Canadian associations, sports teams, and social groups young and old.

The many social clubs, each dedicated to a village, city, region, or activity, have supported the church with donations of work, time, and love. They also contributed to the cultural wealth of the parish with their own celebrations of local saints and feast days. As immigrants transplanted their local religious traditions to the Canadian capital, they brought their patron saints, home altars, folk art and annual street processions to fill the yearly calendar of St. Anthony's Church. Just as village feasts marked the rituality of life for Italians in Italy, recurring celebrations of saints and patrons lent a sense of continuity to immigrant life that perseveres to this day.

St. Anthony's Church has thus both dutifully enriched and has graciously benefited from the local mutual benefit societies that have collected funds to purchase and house statues in their local parish while devotees engaged in convivial socializing have fostered a rich mixture of the sacred and the secular. Over the years, many of the early religious feasts have disappeared, others have been replaced by secular festivities that invite suburban residents to feast on Preston Street as they sample sausage and peppers. Attitudes toward ethnic celebrations have become more commercial, attracting larger crowds, overshadowing the penitential practices of the original feasts, while summer picnics and winter dinners promote the social over the religious.

Nevertheless, the establishment of St. Anthony's Church, the lasting heritage of its school, the many social clubs that create a rosary of annual social and religious events, are testament that religion as a formal institution still provides the Italian-Canadian population with a sense of community. The Church is not merely a center of religious services but undoubtedly embraces the larger role of secular and material benefactor for the well-being of its congregation. While the Church of Rome may struggle with ecclesiastical and political issues that bear international implications, the daily lived and heartfelt religion of the local faithful remains a locus of Mediterranean piety and the backbone of the Italian-Canadian community.[40]

Madonna della Risurrezione Parish

If the Church of St. Anthony of Padua helped restore meaning and gave stability to the uprooted lives of arriving Italian immigrants in mid-20th century, the movement of the founding community from its urban ethnic enclave to suburban homes in the more southern environs, made those neighborhoods more economically prosperous and in turn attractive for new businesses and amenities. The influx of Italian-Canadian residents in the Carleton/Fisher Heights area of the city brought a congregation in search of a place of worship that was closer to home.

Since the narrative surrounding the new community of Italian-Canadians had changed, evolved beyond its village-laden roots, a new church would not only reinforce and reinvigorate deeply-set faith but also consolidate a maturing cultural identity. Yet, how could a new church remain relevant in a newly forged neighborhood where most of its congregants were still members of the old parish? It is simply not enough for anyone to want newcomers and accept diversity; they must effectively communicate that message and gently, yet forcefully, shepherd it through. Enter Father Antonio and a commitment to serve.

On any given Sunday, Father Antonio can be seen standing outside his parish greeting the parishioners of the *Madonna della Risurrezione* Parish. Located in Carleton Heights, in the heart of what has come to be known as the "New Italy," the founding and construction of a new Italian church was the result of a positive investment in the Italian-Canadian Christian community of Ottawa. The parish's continuing

---

[40] For a more complete history of the Church of St. Anthony of Padua, see the wonderfully informative coffee table book, *A Journey of Faith — A History of St. Anthony of Padua Church: 1913 - 2013* (Montreal: Cusmano Books, 2015). The work commemorates the church's centennial year and is replete with a detailed history of events, people, anecdotes, and many wonderful photographs chronicling St. Anthony's ministry and role in the community.

growth and success is the result of it taking personal ownership of an area where the community can express its unique set of gifts and talents.

Father Antonio Pannunzi views his parish as a mission. And indeed, his missional view of church evangelism is not merely an add-on to church activities, but instead a recognition that both God and the church are intrinsically and principally missionary in nature. The purpose of the church, then, is derived from its very nature as a place of communal sending, a place that seeks to reach out to the community that surrounds it and draw people into its fold.

Towards this end, *Madonna della Risurrezione* views its primary function as actively moving to embody and enflesh the word, deed, and life of Jesus into every nook and cranny of the community. In effect, the church is not the starting point but instead the result of God's mission. This focus is apparent from its almost anecdotal beginnings.

Father Toni Ostan OMI, a former missionary to Inuit peoples, and Father Barry McGrory, pastor of Holy Cross Church in Ottawa, met for the first time in the month of March 1978, while visiting inmates at Burritt's Rapids Correctional Institution. On that occasion, the Irish Father McGrory asked the Italian Father Ostan for advice regarding the pleas of his Italian parishioners for services given in Italian. The conversation led to a greatly attended first Italian mass celebrated in the gymnasium of St. Victor's School for what would become the pioneer parishioners of the future church on Sunday 5 November 1978. Subsequently masses followed and were so popular that they were eventually moved to the Archbishop's chapel on Kilborn Avenue and to St. Rita's School.

The growth of the Italian-Canadian community in the Carleton Heights and Carleton Heights-Rideauview area of the city in the 1970s warranted, according to Archbishop Plourde, "the need for two Italian parishes." And so, given the continuing success of the church's outreach to the members of the Italian-Canadian community, on 15 May 1980 the *Madonna della Risurrezione* Christian Community was removed from the jurisdiction of The Holy Cross parish and established as an independent mission. On 13 April 1984, official church status was afforded the Community and the *Madonna della Risurrezione* Parish was born. Soon afterward, the Parish purchased a modest home at 1621 Fisher Avenue that served as a temporary rectory until the current structure, the inspiration of local Italian architect Filippo Piazza, became a reality in 1990.

The church has become a hub of activity for neighborhood residents. Beyond the traditional religious celebrations, parishioners enjoy a senior citizen group, a bowling club, an adult choir, and regular pilgrimages to religious shrines. Periodically scheduled events include a yearly summer picnic, an end of Spring festival, as well as an annual social gala.

Construction of church began in 1988-89. Completed under the direction of Gino Nicolini, and architect Filippo Piazza, the project was supervised by Nicolini Construction. The magnificent bell tower that welcomes parishioners are a later addition to the church structure. They were designed by architect Angelo Mattia Spadola. The three-tiered structure holds three bells and appears as spires reaching towards heaven.

With two churches, the community can boast a consolidated and stable Ottawa presence. It remains to future parishioners to connect to their home parish and play a role in shaping the future of the changing community.

The Prescott

The Prescott shares a reputation with The Lafayette House in the Byward Market as the oldest licensed drinking establishment in Ottawa. Originally called The Preston Hotel (it stopped renting rooms in 1978), the establishment was re-baptized The Prescott in 1941 most likely, it is held, in recognition of its status as the last watering hole between Ottawa and the town of Prescott, 100 km down the Prescott Highway. This fact also earned it the moniker "The Last Chance."

Most agree that the building, located at the corner of Beech and Preston Street, is it is one of the area's oldest structures, probably the most stable anchor and visible point of orientation in the hierarchy of the Preston streetscape. Founded in 1934 by partners Giuseppe Costantini and Antonio Disipio, the hotel was the result of a local petition to City Hall for a bar license. But securing such a license required rentable rooms for eventual stayovers; and so the Prescott Hotel was born. Once the government charter permitting liquor in the hotel was acquired, the location quickly established itself a cornerstone of the community, a favorite spot for the locals as both Costantini and Disipio proved themselves able hosts and entrepreneurs. Business was good, the future seemed secure; little did they suspect that life on Preston Street was soon to change forever.

The 1930s witnessed the height of the wave of Fascism in Europe; a world war loomed on the horizon. The political repercussions of a war with Europe were beginning to affect the growing migrant communities across North America who were targeted as possible fascist sympathizers. Governments reacted to the perceived internal threat of sedition by placing sanctions on those immigrants, German, Japanese, and Italian, they had previously welcomed. While the United States applied detention only to German, Japanese, and Italian nationals, not to US citizens, or long-term US residents, conditions in Canada, because of its membership in the British Commonwealth, were different.

Internment of Canada's undesirable foreigners began almost immediately; German-Canadians, Japanese-Canadians, and Italian-Canadians were interned at different times during World War II because they were considered a threat to national security by the Canadian RCMP. There were 26 internment camps in Canada during World War II. Those individuals deemed dangerous or otherwise sympathetic to foreign nations from central Canada were sent to Petawawa, Ontario.

Following Italy's 10 June 1940 declaration of war against the United Kingdom, Minister of Justice, Ernest Lapointe, signed the order that designated Italian nationals and Italian-Canadians naturalized after 1922, as "enemy aliens."[41]

Across Canada, 6000 men and 5 women, between the ages of

---

41   Individuals were rounded-up by the R.C.M.P. or the police pursuant to a federal Order-in-Council what called for "the registration of enemy aliens and the prohibition against the possession of use of firearms to all persons of German or Italian racial origins who have become naturalized British subjects since September 1, 1929." Commons Debates, Vol.1, 1940: 658.

16 and 70, were arrested without charges. Their numbers included doctors, lawyers, carpenters, bakers, pressers, cab drivers, priests, candy-makers, postmen. 5300 were eventually released on condition they report monthly to local authorities, approximately 700 Italians were interned in camps across the country. The average length of internment lasted 15.8 months; some held for periods ranging up to three years. Oswald Giacomelli of Hamilton, born in Canada, was held under arrest for over 5 years.[42]

To be sure, many honest, hardworking laborers, law-abiding and otherwise innocuous citizens became enemy aliens overnight but for the spelling of their surname. The "reasonable grounds" required for internment usually consisted of membership in Italian associations or hearsay from informers of dubious credibility.[43] Although many Italian-Canadians managed to carry on a somewhat normal life under the transparent umbrella of "enemy alien," existence became much more difficult for those whose families were officially branded with the traitorous mark.

In Ottawa, as in every single other branded community, the cost was tremendous and marked it for decades both financially and psychologically. Households were disrupted, properties confiscated, jobs lost, friends separated, suspicion planted. Individuals were arrested, fingerprinted, photographed, and interrogated. Relatives who remained at home suffered physical and verbal abuse, public discrimination, and personal humiliation.

When an individual was released, a denigrating admission of guilt form required signature. The form attested possible and potential crimes for which the individual had never been officially prosecuted.

I undertake and promise that I will carefully observe and obey the laws of Canada and such rules and regulations as may especially be prescribed for my conduct by competent authorities, and that I will do no act nor will I encourage the doing of any act which might be of injury to the Dominion

---

42 Redress Committee Public Hearings, Toronto, 24 March 1991.

43 A Toronto Globe and Mail article entitled "All Italians and Germans Required to Register" and dated June 15, 1940 summed that: "it is the law and not a request that all persons more than sixteen years old who are of German or Italian racial origin must register."

of Canada, the United Kingdom or any of his majesty's Dominions of any of the allied or the associated powers. (Internment Operations, Canadian Internees, Releases, 1939-1942)

The formula is a lasting blight that echoes in many families and individuals to this day.[44]

In Ottawa, five men found themselves in a similar predicament and were taken from their homes and workplaces by officers who offered no explanation and acted with disdainful impunity. Made to feel like prisoners in their own country, these men were detached from the warmth of their families and deprived of their self-esteem as men and honest wage earners.

On 10 June 1940, Mussolini declared war on France and Great Britain, officially joining the Germans in their quest to conquer Europe. In Ottawa, the following men were arrested.

Gino Tiezzi (arrested and interned 10 June 1940; released 17 February 1941; re-interned 21 August 1941, released 20 September 1943); Frederick Rocco Pantalone (arrested and interned 10 June 1940, released 17 February 1941); Dr. Vittorio Sabetta, a naturalized British subject (arrested and interned 12 June 1940, released 15 February 1943); Carlo Scarabelli, a naturalized British subject (arrested and interned 2 July 1940, released 12 August 1940); and Giuseppe Costantini, a naturalized British subject.

When Costantini was interned, he, like all the others who suffered the unexpected humiliation of seizure, was forced to surrender his

---

44   On a personal note, Julius Molinaro, a personal friend and mentor during my years as a student at the University of Toronto, was arrested with his father and brother and escorted by the police to a large automotive building in Toronto. There they joined many other men of Italian origin. During the day, the men were taken outside for exercise where they were ridiculed and insulted by passersby. At night, mattresses were laid on the floor side by side. They were never told why they had been arrested, nor how long they would remain in preventative custody. Their families were not informed of their internment or whereabouts until much later.

Julius would later serve as an intelligence officer with the Canadian Army and after his distinguished service to the very institutions that had interred him, become a respected teacher, scholar and Professor Emeritus of Italian Studies at the University of Toronto.

freedom in front of his bewildered family and children. Arrested on 10 June 1940, he was taken to Carleton County Jail, eventually placed on a train for Petawawa, and released eight months later, on 7 February 1941.

Because of internment, Costantini lost his job as Baggage Master with the CNR, a job he would eventually regain after his release, ultimately working his way up to Assistant Station Master. But he also was prohibited from any dealings with the Preston Hotel.

His partner in the Preston Hotel, Antonio Disipio, was also seized in the round of arrests that fateful week, but he was released following an eight-hour interrogation. Like Costantini, however, Disipio was not permitted to return to work. Ordered to either leave the country or close the business, The Preston Hotel was managed by a City Hall appointee and eventually closed by the RCMP until war's end. All this occurred while Disipio's son, fought in England as a member of the Canadian Armed Forces.

This period of Italian community history is murky at best given the highly volatile circumstances of internment, the painful memories of charged recollections, the passage of time and its healing aftermath. Suffice it to say that the best of intentions are sometimes misplaced and resulting events unintentionally cruel.

Given Costantini's internment, the hotel was no longer permitted to hold a liquor license; the property, after all, was half-owned by a politically marked Italian. Yet, though deemed a dangerous enemy, Costantini was unwilling to give up his partnership and claim to the hotel. In order to safeguard his share in the business while interned, he surrendered his share of the business to his lawyer, John Ebbs Senior who then approached Disipio. Being Canadian, the lawyer was able to reacquire the hotel's liquor license and keep the business afloat during those murky days of government oppression.

The lasting effects of internment, however, scarred everyone involved and cut the community profoundly. The fact remains that both partners were removed from the business because of the war. Both families were victims of the Canadian government. Yet, having come face to face with the reality of unexpected prejudice and unwarranted discrimination, like many men who had been branded, but never actually charged as traitors, Costantini, as many others who continued to fear reprisal, refused to challenge the injustice of internment in a court of law. The silence of these men was purchased on the altar of self-abnegation in a land that had promised much but eventually exacted unexpected subjection.[45]

The Preston, now Prescott Hotel, continued under the sole ownership of Disipio; John Ebbs Senior remained a silent partner of the business up to 1979 when his share was purchased by grandson Tony Disipio. The Prescott has progressed steadily through the years has and become an established Preston Street icon. It has been home to family celebrations, weddings, baptisms, and confirmations. It has served the community well in its sponsorships of sports teams and community events. It boasts a hardcore clientele, dedicated to its meatball sandwiches, sworn to its homestyle pizza; it is a destination place on most Friday nights for revelers young and old. It is indeed an institution, a relevant fixture not only in the Italian community but on the city's entertainment scene.

At this writing, the news on Preston Street is that the legendary tavern has been sold to The Properties Group, an Ottawa-based real estate investment and management firm. The handover date is scheduled for April 2020.

Tony Scipioni, third-generation owner, will remain an establishment quantity and continue to manage daily operations. Now a senior and 69 years old, Tony admits the decision to sell the family business was labored but necessary. Nothing will probably change for at least 10 years. Square pizza, meatball sandwiches, tables of eager sports teams sharing pints, and regular patrons enjoying the atmosphere, will continue to congregate on a regular basis at the Preston Street mainstay.

Whatever its short-term circumstance, The Prescott will remain a purposefully retro greasy spoon; an iconic throwback to its days as a public house. What is certain is that its checkered history, and now uncertain future, are forever a part of disappearing *Village* lore.

---

45 See also *A National Shame: The Case for Redress*. A brief to the Government of Canada on the violation of rights and freedoms to Canadian citizens of Italian origin during World War II. National Congress of Italian Canadians, February 1992; Franca Iacovetta, Roberto Perin, Angelo Principe, Eds., *Enemies Within: Italian and Other Internees in Canada and Abroad* (Toronto: Toronto UP, 2000).

L'Ora di Ottawa

The process of building an Italian community in Ottawa began in the early 20th Century and continues to this day through socialization in clubs, family celebrations both public and private, annually scheduled community events, and recurring religious feasts and festivals. As the community and its members re-elaborated their self-images, they slowly moved away from an inbred *campanilismo*, the tendency to confine one's attachments to one's respective town and townspeople (in Italian the word implies that people live within earshot of the bells of their villages) and looked outwards towards the community at large, new formal structures emerged that served as venues for the conscious expression of a growing Italian, and eventually Italian-Canadian, sense of pride. The most enduring, and probably one of the most important of these institutions, is the community newspaper, *L'Ora di Ottawa*.

The origins of the newspaper are bathed in family memories. Renata Coppola recalls that the usual Sunday afternoon card game of *scopone* between father-in-law Mario Colonnese and son-in-law Elio Coppola, Renata and her mother, normally escalated into an animated discussion concerning the lack of real-time news from Italy. Both men were avid newshounds and regularly satisfied their need for Italian printed media at Giovanni's Snack Bar, a local caffè where men gathered daily to share coffee amidst animated discussions with friends. The bar's newsstand featured the major newspapers and magazines from Italy. Mario and Elio, however, sensed the need for an Italian community publication that featured local news and events as well as news from the homeland presented in a more accessible format.

The men brought some experience to their dream. Mario Colonnese's grandfather had worked for a Neapolitan newspaper, *La Mezz'Ora*. Mario was a typographer who, in the early 1950s, had managed his own typography shop in Naples. Elio Coppola, on the other hand, was a Medical Technologist in the Bacteriology Laboratory at the Civic Hospital. Yet he too was no stranger to the printed word. An avid writer, he had experimented writing his own fictional works. And so, after months of what seemed interminable Sunday debates about the need of a local newspaper, their efforts became a reality when Elio and Mario decided to take matters into their own capable hands.

To ensure professionality and local input, Elio recruited respected community leaders (and friends) as associates. These included: Piero Canesso (a printer), Franco De Carlo, and Steno Rossanese. Renata Coppola (who years later became the paper's defacto Business Manager) helped with subscriptions and advertising. The newly formed Editorial Group held its first meeting at the Coppola home on 92 Hamilton Street. It was decided that a facsimile of a possible newspaper was to be created for immediate distribution and feedback. The letters for the title *L'Ora di Ottawa*, Renata recalls, husband Elio scissor-cut from the Italian weekly magazine *L'Espresso*. The title was a family tribute to Mario's grandfather's work on *La Mezz'Ora*.

The facsimile newspaper was first distributed amongst friends at Giovanni's Snack Bar and was received with great enthusiasm. But resounding approval and initial enthusiasm was one thing; selling subscriptions was another. The community was composed primarily of workers, not a demographic known as avid newspaper readers. Renata recalls countless miles of canvassing door-to-door as well as many hours of phone solicitation. Her father Mario, on the other hand, sold subscriptions to his many friends and acquaintances.

The first issue of the tabloid style newspaper appeared on Monday 18 November 1968 with a circulation of 5000 copies and the following *Lettera al Lettore* signed by Elio Coppola:

The letter began: *Cari amici lettori, come vedete, è giunta anche per Ottawa l'ora di avere il proprio giornale in lingua italiana (Dear friends, as you can see, the time has come for Ottawa to have its own Italian newspaper).*[46]

---

46 The letter continued: *Siamo arrivati a questo punto di regolare pubblicazione e distribuzione, solo attraverso la seria ed impegnata collaborazione di vostri giovani connazionali che hanno sentito da anni la necessità di tale pubblicazione. Siamo giovani, e ben sappiamo, viviamo in un mondo che sorride ironicamente ogni qualvolta tentiamo di dire o di fare qualcosa. Ma benvenuta sia anche la nostra eventuale ironia. Sarebbe del tutto inutile volersi soffermare sulle difficoltà che abbiamo incontrato nella fase organizzativa; nè sarebbe permesso volere usare tali difficoltà da giustifica per le sicure pecche ed imperfezioni di carattere letterario, giornalistico e tecnico, dalle quali riconosciamo di essere tutt'altro che immune.*

Ma cercando di dimenticare le ore di lavoro, le accalorate discussioni, i dubbi e le incertezze che ci hanno perseguitato nelle scorse settimane, vi presentiamo questo modesto giornale, che sarà poi il vostro giornale. Vostro perchè rappresenterà tra l'altro, un mezzo di contatto, di intercomunicazione in questa comunità una volta concentrata all'ombra del campanile della nostra chiesa di S. Antonio, oggi sparsa un po' dappertutto in Ottawa; vostro perchè sarete voi lettori a decidere della sua sorte. Starà a voi innalzarlo con incoraggiamenti e benevole accoglienza, o inabissarlo con l'indifferenza che specie in questa fase iniziale, va vista come il pericolo numero uno. Sarà vostro il diritto ed il dovere di guidarci e di criticarci per trarne poi delle conclusioni di assenzo o di dissenso. Siamo ora come in seguito, esposti e predisposti ad ogni critica, ogni giudizio, valido o meno che possa risultare. Ci venga però concesso di aggiungere che, in definitive, ciascuno di noi realizzatori di questo, ripetiamo, modesto giornale, divide una parte della comune ambizione di tentare di espandere le forze positive che operano tra noi italiani e di respingere invece, nei limiti del possibile, l'azione delle forze negative. Crediamo in cio', senza alcuna presunzione. Riteniamo, in conclusione, di meritare un minimo di considerazione; non fosse altro che per aver tentato un qualcosa che, speriamo, potrà risultare di vantaggio a tutti noi.

We have reached this point of regular publication and distribution, only through the serious and committed collaboration of your young compatriots who have felt the need for such publication for years. We are young, and we all know, we live in a way that smiles ironically whenever we try to say or do something. But our eventual irony is also welcome. It would be totally useless to want to dwell on the difficulties we encountered in the organizational phase; nor would it be permitted to use such difficulties as to justify the certain flaws and imperfections of a literary, journalistic and technical nature, from which we recognize that we are far from immune. But trying to forget the hours of work, the heated discussions, the doubts and uncertainties that have haunted us in recent weeks, we present this modest newspaper, which will then be your newspaper. Yours because it will represent, among other things, a means of contact, of intercommunication in this community once concentrated in the shadow of the bell tower of our church of S. Antonio, now spread all over Ottawa; yours because you will be the readers who decide its fate. It will be up to you to raise it with encouragement and benevolent reception, or to sink it with the indifference which, especially in this initial phase, must be seen as the number one danger. It will be your right and duty to guide and criticize us to then draw conclusions of assent or dissent. We are now as then, exposed and predisposed to any criticism, any judgment, valid or not that may result. However, we are allowed to add that, ultimately, each of us realizing this, we repeat, modest newspaper, divides a part of the

The open letter would begin an inimitable editorial style that would characterize the newspaper for years to come. Smart, intelligent, permeated with ironic wit and subtle sarcasm, Elio spoke of the *modesto giornale* (modest newspaper) as un *mezzo di contatto, di intercomunicazione* (a means of contact and intercommunication). The paper's fate, according to Elio, was in the hands of its readers who could sustain its presence: *starà a voi innalzarlo con incoraggiamenti e benevole accoglienza* (it is up to you to raise the paper with encouragement and benevolent welcome) or condemn its efforts and *inabissarlo con l'indifferenza che specie in questa fase iniziale, va vista come il pericolo numero uno* (and drown it with an indifference that, especially in this initial phase, must be seen as the number one danger).

A recurrent theme of the open letter was that the paper belonged to the community and that he hoped that the paper would *tentare di espandere le forze positive che operano tra noi italiani e di respingere ... l'azione delle forze negative* (try to expand the positive forces that operate amongst we Italians and to reject ... the action of negative forces).

And so, after months of pondering and deliberation, Mario and Elio's dream, to their joy and surprise, had seen the light of day. It was an immediate success.

The Editorial Board for that first auspicious issue listed: Mario Colonnese, *Redattore-Editore* (Editor-Publisher); Elio Coppola, *Direttore Responsabile* (General Manager); Piero Canesso, *Capo Servizi Tecnici* (Head of Technical Services); Steno Rossanese and Franco De Carlo, *Pubbliche Relazioni e Pubblicità* (Public Relations and Advertising); Prof. essa Claudia Persi and Antonio Ferrante, *Collaboratori* (Contributing Collaborators); Renato Lapalorcia, *Corrispondente dall'Italia* (Italian Foreign Corrispondent).

The paper had a modest subscription rate of $5.00 per year; $8.00 for two years. The newspaper office was listed at 542 Booth Street, in the heart of the community. But several other locations

---

common ambition to try to expand the positive forces that operate among us Italians and to reject instead, within the limits of possible, the action of negative forces. We believe in this, without any presumption. We believe, in conclusion, to deserve a minimum of consideration; if only for having tried something that, hopefully, can be beneficial to all of us.

became the wayward paper's home including a brief stint in a small office next to Giovanni's Snack Bar, then a house at 43 Eccles Street, eventually landing at its permanent home, 18 Louise Street. All were near Preston Street.

Newspaper publishing was obviously very different in those early days of the tabloid. In those pre-digital days, the newspaper needed long hours of dedicated work and tiring determination since, without computers or convenient mobile platforms, the team assembled the entire newspaper by cutting and pasting all articles and advertisements. Nevertheless, despite the often mundane drudgery and growing pains any such new endeavor faces, *L'Ora di Ottawa* quickly became the official community organ for local news as well as news from the Italian mainland.

Slowly, the newspaper was eradicating the inter/intra village-regional-social rivalries latent to the community. The disparate dialects, fears, beliefs, and traditions that normally estranged Italian immigrants both from each other and from the community at large were lessened in the melting pot of information that arrived on one's doorstep.

By providing useful information to all members of the community the regional exclusivity and restricted group ethic that often stifled dialogue and progress gave way to a better informed populace and a growing understanding and tolerance for all members of the community, regardless of village or regional origin. Whatsmore, the community could take pride in the many events and newsworthy information that bound them as a community and affirmed their place in the City of Ottawa.

At first a bi-weekly newspaper, *L'Ora di Ottawa* eventually shed its tabloid shape and became a weekly broadsheet that presented political, cultural, and the always coveted sports news from Italy at a time when the only news sources were late-arriving Italian publications or shortwave radio. But the mainstay of *L'Ora di Ottawa* was local news. Often criticized (Elio's weekly *Punto di Vista* a pointed lightening rod) but never imitated, the paper was widely circulated and provided coverage of community happenings, promoted local businesses, discussed national and international news, proffered opinion, shared family recipes, published authored fiction, fed the local voracious sports fan, and in short became the mainstay and gateway of information for the Italian community.

At its heyday, it was considered among the top 10 Italian newspapers published abroad.[47] Mario and Elio were also bestowed the highest honor given to civilians by the Italian government when they received the prestigious title of *Cavaliere al Merito della Repubblica Italiana* (Knight of Merit of the Italian Republic); Mario on 4 December 1984 and Elio 4 November 2010.

Like most community editors, Mario, Elio and Renata were also a part of the neighborhood fabric. They attended the same church as their readers, shopped at the same grocery stores they advertised, were always there to volunteer at community functions, or to simply shake hands with passing friends and readers. Renata recalls the pain of writing and publishing necrologies of friends, the tedious and relentless task of soliciting advertising to stay afloat, the heartbreak of unfounded and usually unjustified criticism. But she also recalls the joy of friendships garnered through the newspaper and its many community sponsorships, the memory of meeting celebrities including the daughters of Gugliermo Marconi, as well as Umberto Agnelli, Renato Balestra, Giulietta Masina, Gina Lolobrigida, and Francesco Cossiga.

Indeed, *L'Ora di Ottawa*, under the Colonnese-Coppola proprietorship, was a community plus family affair. Brother Mario Colonnese lent his services as a bookkeeper along with sister Vittoria Colonnese Benni who lent her skills as copy editor amongst many other tasks. Mother Maria Colonnese also participated in a supporting role, providing unfailing guidance and strength. A true labor of unending love, political passion, social engagement, and dispassionate observation.

L'Ora di Ottawa published its last issue (Anno XXXII – N. 1386) with Elio Coppola as Editor in Chief on 30 October 2000. The original 10 cent tabloid then listed an annual subscription rate of $85.00 for 47 issues. The paper was also mailed to numerous subscribers in Italy at an annual rate of $150.00. The final issue printed two open letters: one by Renata, the other by Elio.

---

47 See the website Giornalisti Italiani nel Mondo. www.giornalistiitalianinelmondo.net.

"Oggi è il primo giorno del resto della mia vita . . . dopo L'Ora di Ottawa" (*Today is the first day of the rest of my life . . . after L'Ora di Ottawa)* began Renata. Elio's opening line was just as definitive, equally saturated with the fatigue of years of labor, justifiably inspired by the prospect of future leisure: *"E anche per me, che con mia moglie ho diretto questo giornale per tanti anni, è giunto il momento di dire . . . statevi bene;"* (*And for me too who, alongside my wife have directed this paper for so many years, it is now time to say . . . stay well).*

Almost 32 years to the day that their *baby,* as they referred to the newspaper, was conceived, the couple decided to abandon the hectic rhythm and routine of deadlines, public relations, pressing deadlines, undless administration, and more deadlines, in order to enjoy the freedom of personal and unrestricted time. But their letters are also replete with nostalgia and heartfelt memories of the good times, the good people, the many successes and blessings one secures when working honestly and for the good of the community.

The couple remained co-owners of the newspaper as the editorial responsibilities were passed on to Rolando Del Rio and his wife Rosita. They maintained ties with the printed page, however, as occasional commentators. Elio continued his opinion piece, continued writing to his *"tredici lettori (erano 14 fino a poco fa*[48]*)"*; (*thirteen readers (there were 14 until recently),* and continued to rail against the *"cinquantina di persone"* (*50-odd persons*) responsible for all sorts of calamity within the Italian community.

Rolando Del Rio's short two-year tenure as Editor was marked with relative calm. As the former *Editore Sportivo* (Sports Editor) of the newspaper, he was familiar with both the rigors of publication and with the community at large. The paper, however, suffered a noticeable subscription downturn and measures were taken to shore-up

---

48 The reference to 13 readers is an allusion to Alessandro Manzoni's sarcastic remark about the fictitious 25 readers he imagined reading his novel, *I promessi sposi* (*The Bethrothed*): "Pensino ora i miei venticinque lettori che impressione dovesse fare sull'animo del poveretto, quello che s'è raccontato." (Now think, my dear 25 readers, the sort of impression this makes upon the state of that poor soul to whom the story is told).

the sluggish enterprise. Ownership was expanded to include to seven business partners, whose silent role was to keep the paper solvent. They included: Joe Nicastro, Delio D'Angelo, Corrado Nicastro, Pat Nicastro, Tony Ferrante, Franco Giammaria, and Luciano Gonella (an original owner, soon to become Editor and Publisher).[49]

Luciano Gonella's tenure is best remembered for his polemical stance on many and all issues affecting the community. A well-read, well-informed, and firmly opinionated individual, *Vox populi, vox Dei* (*The voice of the people is the voice of God*) subtended the populist spirit of his editorials and guided his hand in publishing. He used his public voice to effectively berate and disapprove of measures that he felt stifled the community or rendered it servant to larger political ends. The shackles of his biting editorials may officially remain around his ankles, but the courage and all-too-often veracity of his stances overshadow the discomfort he may have installed in the search for truth and honesty amidst adversity. To quote the poet, "No legacy is so rich as honesty."[50]

Paolo Siraco became Director and Editor of *L'Ora di Ottawa* in the summer of 2008. A long-time friend of Elio and Renata Coppola, Siraco followed on the wake of Luciano Gonella who had been released from his responsibilities by the Board of Owners. Upon becoming Editor, Siraco's stated intent was to return the newspaper to its Mission Statement as a *modesto giornale* in service of the Italian community. That mission, and the community, had changed over the years. The community, along with the rest of the world, was now digitally informed of world news. As a result, *L'Ora di Ottawa* filled its pages with community events instead of real news. Siraco wished to refocus the paper towards the important elements of local and regional news, culture, the arts, and a smattering of international news thereby returning the paper to its roots. A teacher by profession, Siraco brought a new energy to the *news* reported in the newspaper. He updated all technical aspects of the paper's production, upgraded outdated computers and printers, and oversaw the internal reorganization of personnel; all with a view towards creating a professional and economically sustainable operation.

---

49   Carmelo Marchese was involved briefly as caretaker between editors.
50   William Shakespeare, *All's Well That Ends Well*.

Siraco also brought Enrico Del Castello to the Editorial Staff as a non-paid volunteer weekly contributor and capped his changes with the introduction of Elio Coppola's weekly, and usually salty, editorial *Punto di Vista*.

The paper acquired immediate new life and was thus able to withstand an ever-decreasing subscription base. The most obvious sign that the paper was reviving its founding mandate was a return to its original tabloid form. In its new format, the *L'Ora di Ottawa* again became an important informational and educational portal for the needs of the Italian and Italian-Canadian community. Despite the changes, and continuing success, advertising became increasingly difficult to obtain. Times were tough; old subscribers were dying-off, and new readers were an elusive commodity in an increasingly web-based information age.

The decline of traditional community newspapers is a seemingly permanent trend. Many legacy newspapers have disappeared throughout North America while those that remain have significantly reduced overall news coverage in favor of fluff. But *L'Ora di Ottawa* survived and continued its legacy, even amongst seemingly unsurmountable odds, to serve the community with honesty, respect, and a sense of personal duty on the part of its Board and Editor.

When asked about his tenure as Editor, Paolo Siraco recalls enjoying his eight-year stint and admits to having attained much regarding the publishing world. He describes his eight years as a "huge learning experience" and enjoyed his role as both educator and student of the Italian community. He enjoyed interaction with community leaders, made many new friends, solidified old friendships. An opinionated, honest, and intelligent man, the most difficult part of the job, he confesses, was remaining neutral while reporting the many conundrums that always churn in any community.

Final attempts by Siraco to expand the newspaper's scope and influence by collaborating with Joe Volpe, owner of *Il Corriere Canadese* were met with skepticism by the Business Owners who decided to once again sell the newspaper. Although asked to continue as Editor, immediately upon the sale of the paper to its new owner, Paolo Siraco submitted his resignation to the old Business Owners, citing personal reasons, effective 18 April 2016. What does he think about the newspaper that survives him? The new *L'Ora di Ottawa*, he reproves, "is not faithful to its original mandate; the paper is no longer representative of the community."

The prospective new buyer and eventual new owner was local businessman and well-known community icon, Angelo Filoso. *L'Ora di Ottawa* continues today under the stewardship of Filoso, Its story formats have changed, its focus more commercial. Beyond the printed version, *L'Ora di Ottawa* also boasts an electronic edition and a Facebook page. The new formats reflect Filoso's renewed commitment to local news, community profiles, and broader circulation on social media. "I want to highlight our local heroes, community news," Filoso states; "bring people together on a positive note, as well as spread the news of our community to a wider, extra-Ottawa audience." Unhappy with the paper's overabundance of news from abroad, the new Editor wanted a newspaper that focussed solely on local issues and current community events in order to highlight, acknowledge, and discuss relevant community affairs.

But as a long-serving member of the community, Filoso also wanted the paper to serve as a medium of rediscovery of the community's past and of its local heroes. He began publishing articles recalling past historical events and acclaiming past community leaders. A philanthropist by nature, Filoso's stated intention was to recover the community's history in order to provide the current generation a template for future growth. By moving towards electronic information formats for streaming news he hopes to engage youth and their enthusiasm to sustain and advance community relevance.

Though his initiatives are bold, Angelo Filoso seems to have succeeded in bringing a new stability to *L'Ora di Ottawa* as it boasts a sustainable subscription base as well as continued circulation growth.

Editorial Conclusion

Because a newspaper is more than just published information and always moves beyond the herculean efforts of its editors and writers to produce issues on time, its consequences, outcomes, and ramifications continue to echo long after an issue has been read and discarded. The ultimate magical power of a newspaper, at least before the heyday of electronic information, was that nothing had happened or was believed until it had been read on the printed page.

A community newspaper like *L'Ora di Ottawa* quickly became an institution that administered stabilizing comfort and direction to readers of the Italian-Canadian community; it provided a sense of existential belonging that moved beyond the immediate neighborhood, reached back into collective memory, and forward to future growth and continued stability. It awarded, and indeed created, above all, a sense of community purpose; a feeling of being in the midst of happenings and of flowing with temporal events, whatever they may be.

L'Ora di Ottawa made the community *feel* real. It established common territory. Once a story was told on its pages, it became part of the assembled; a source of pride and of undeniable Italian presence in a growing and expanding Canadian metropolis. That presence was important in the evolving Italian-Canadian community of the 60s and remains important today as the community is pulled into the digital era.

Most importantly, however, *L'Ora di Ottawa* created a collective memory of the community. It promised the continuity the confidence of an unfolding future while resting on the certainty of its past.

L'Ora di Ottawa, the *modesto giornale* (modest newspaper) begun by Mario and Elio with the support of wife Renata, was and is above all a source of pride. As such, it was, and remains, a powerful instrument of good and invariably continues to make a profound difference within the community because, among newspapers that endure and even prosper, there is always a common denominator: a trusting and thankful readership.

Settimana Italiana - Italian Week Inc.

The official registered Letter of Patent incorporating *Settimana Italiana* - Italian Week Inc., dated 15 July 1977 and recorded 26 July 1977, displays the names of founding members Luigi Mion, Angelo Filoso,

Dino Venier, Sebastiano Pagano, Antonino Cuffaro, Saro Panuccio, Angiola Lombardi, Mariano DeMarinis, Frank Piscopo, Gloria Zuana, and Romano Battel. Their mission statement was *"To instill and inculcate in Italian Canadians principles of Canadian citizenship through sponsoring and organizing social, cultural and recreational events of an Italian nature; . . . ."*

For over 40 years the Italian Week Festival has succeeded in providing its participants the feeling of *being Italian* by celebrating all that is Italian in art, culture, music, technology, and food. Founded by Professor Vincenzo Tripodi, a Visiting Professor of Italian at the University of Ottawa, the first Italian Week was held on the university campus 14-20 March 1975. Professor Tripodi's wish was to celebrate the richness of Italian culture with fellow Canadians in the capital city of Canada. According to Enrico del Castello, a student of Tripodi, the professor's mindset was emphatic: "I want Ottawa to have an Italian week! And you students should take the lead!"

The idea was quickly embraced by the local community and endorsed by the Italian Embassy. A modest affair, the first Italian Week as it was quickly baptized, nevertheless attracted a respectable number of participants to the university campus where lectures and academic events showcased the achievements of Italians and Italian-Canadians in Ottawa while also focusing on the heritage of Italy's past.

The event continued to grow and expand over the ensuing years as community leaders began to take a deliberate interest in the yearly success of the blossoming festival. The events were soon moved to Dows Lake where activities grew to recall the pageantry of festive days regularly celebrated in small villages throughout Italy. An open mass at St. Anthony's Church and the raising of the Italian flag in front of Ottawa's City Hall now normally initiated the festivities and opened the festival to broader media attention. Besides food tents and music, participants were treated with cultural events and processions of Patron Saints. A memorable early event was the celebratory 1000 candle flotilla on the waters of Dow's Lake. The spectacular production was followed by fireworks and attracted a crowd of 10,000 people.

In 1986, *Italian Week* was officially moved to Preston Street, the natural and official heart of the Italian-Canadian community, and quickly became a street festival. The closing of the street to auto traffic (an idea proposed by local entrepreneur and then President of *Italian Week* Tony D'Angelo) quickly turned the street into a magnet for Canadians eager to share in the rich cultural and food traditions on display by the local businesses and restaurants. For Italians, closing Preston Street to vehicle traffic made them anxious to stroll the street and meet friends as one would in their home villages in Italy. The move proved so successful that participation figures jumped from 1200-1500 (1985) to over 40,000 (1986) in the first year alone. In 1987, participation figures spiked to 120,000; an impressive number considering that in those early days the festival lasted 3 days.

Today's elaborate festivities maintain their link to St. Anthony's Church and always coincide with the feast of St. Anthony in early June. No longer a weekend affair, *Settimana Italiana* - Italian Week Inc. lasts 11 days and is spread across the entire month of June, officially declared Italian Heritage Month by the House of Commons in 2017. Preston Street becomes an open-air block-party where members of the old neighborhood invite the city at large to celebrate *being Italian*.

Entertainers have included well-known performers such as Louis Prima Jr. from Las Vegas, Gianni Capobianco Super Show Band from Montreal, comedian Joe Cacchione, The Rio & the Rockabilly Revival from Detroit, Michigan, Enrico Capuano and T Rock from Rome, Italy, and international recording artists Pino Gioia and Patrizio Buanni, as well as Opera in Piazza. Not surprisingly, attendance at the festival now include people from as far as Boston and New York, as well as many other locations in Ontario. In 2011 a group of *sbandieratori* from Carpineto Romano entertained crowds of people both on Parliament Hill and during the festivities on Preston Street.

This minestrone of homegrown and imported activities is highlighted by an annual Ferrari Festival, an Italian Car Parade, a Bicycle Race, live bands, soccer and bocce tournaments, gala dinners, an amusement park for children, stand-up comedians, religious processions, and street performers.

The Italian Car Show and Parade

The Italian Car Show and Parade has become a staple of Italian Week festivities and is normally held on the Grand Finale Weekend. The parade was inaugurated in 1976 when 20 Italian cars rumbled down Booth Street. The idea originated with car enthusiast Rinaldo Palanza and friend Mario Simioni. According to Palanza, the idea was "to attract people to Italian Week using the beauty of Italian cars."

In 1978, Franks Auto Centre became the sole sponsor and organizer of the annual event and remained such up to 2012. Since 2013, the car parade is held under the aegis of the Italian Car Club of Ottawa (ICCO) and sponsored by many of the Preston Street car enthusiasts. Recently, the Preston Street BIA has lent its sponsorship to this growing yearly event.

The Car Show and parade has since grown to feature in excess of 140 Italian cars and displays the finest examples of Italian automotive design from roaring Ferraris to diminutive Fiats, to colorful Vespas and Moto Guzzis to fierce and imposing Lamborghinis. Hundreds of spectators line the streets to view the cars as they parade the entire length of Preston Street. A haven for car aficionados and photographers, the cars are also displayed on side streets for closer inspection of engines, retro interiors, and classic styling lines.

Ottawa Ferrari Festival

With more than 200,000 spectators and visitors, the annual Ferrari Festival, sponsored by the Ferrari Club of America Ottawa Chapter, is by far one of the most anticipated events of the Italian Week Festival calendar. More than 50 Ferraris and other rare Italian and exotic sports cars not only rumble through the streets of Little Italy but are displayed along both sides of Preston Street on the final festival weekend.

The Ferrari Festival follows on the heels of the successful, 20-year old, Annual Car Parade, hosted by Franks Auto Centre. The Parade featured vintage Italian cars. These cars normally traveled downtown main streets with highlighted stops at both the Federal Parliament

Buildings and The Governor General's Residence. The parade route was changed to Preston Street in subsequent years due to heightened security measures.

The FCA Ottawa Chapter was established in 2001 by founder Giuseppe Castrucci. As Chair of the Festival he is also its logistical coordinator aided by the expertise of Franks Auto Centre, the Preston Street BIA, and the Italian Car Club of Ottawa.

The main event of the Ferrari Festival sees the Saturday closing of Preston Street and Carling Avenue to create an oval racetrack where the participating Ferraris along with a host of other Italian cars put on an eagerly anticipated demonstration of stylish lines and raw power in a safe environment. This is the highlight of the Ferrari Festival and attracts over 5,000 spectators annually.

Collateral events normally include the Friday/Saturday Preston Street Ferrari Display, the Race Car Display Paddock, a Saturday night Gala Banquet, and the Sunday National Bank Dream Ride where participants can purchase a Ferrari ride where all proceeds go directly to charity. Local partners include: Maserati Ottawa, Dream Zone Racing, Mortimer Racing, and OB Prestige Auto.

From its humble and earnest beginnings, the local Ferrari Club Chapter has grown from 12 eager Ferrari enthusiasts to well over 35 members and 40 associate non-members. Over these years the club has evolved from a track-based club to a social driving club. The Chapter also sponsors numerous activities throughout the calendar year that include BBQs, pleasure drives, and social events that keep the membership connected through the winter months. The eagerly anticipated yearly motorcade alone has raised over $160,000 for The Villa Marconi Center and over $35,000 for The Kidney Foundation, Ottawa Stem Cell Research, and Habitat for Humanity. They are also proud supporters of the local youth soccer program at St. Anthony Soccer Club.

Amongst the many highlights of the local Ferrari Club was the presence, in 2018, of special honored guest, His Royal Highness Prince Emanuele Filiberto of Savoy, a member of the Italian Royal family. A Passion in Red Gala was held in honor of the Prince who welcomed guests to a formal evening featuring a select Italian menu presenting dishes from various regions of Italy.

Interested Ferrari enthusiasts can visit the local club's website at www.ottawaferrarifestival.com. The site maintains a full Calendar of Events including social gatherings, parties, track events, rallies, drives and charitable events.

The Preston Street Criterium Bike Race

In 1973, local cycling legends Alan Large and Peter Tyler decided to celebrate Father's Day on Preston Street. Now in its 47th edition, the race is the longest-running bicycle race in the Ottawa area and has become a popular feature of the Italian Festival.

But regardless of the augmented social activities or more contemporary spectacle events, the focus and aims of the *Settimana Italiana* - Italian Week Inc. festival that arose from much humbler beginnings remain true. And this is the true lure of Italian Week. That focus was and remains food, a foundational element of the festival through the years, with a sprinkling of religion, and the desire to preserve Italian traditions, music, culture, and history while promoting a newly acquired Italian-Canadian heritage. Indeed, from its origins, the festival wished to invite participants to experience Italian heritage and traditions, to take them on a cultural journey that showcased the positive contributions of Italians and Italian-Canadians to the greater Ottawa community.

In this sense it is a community builder, an event firmly entrenched in the region's annual calendar that has an impact that goes well beyond what can be measured in economic terms. Italian Week contributes to the quality of life across the entire region by providing unique activities and events, building awareness of Italian-Canadian culture and identity, diseminating artistic heritage, preserving local history, and acting as a source of local community pride. But it is also like a family reunion; a time when friends and neighbors gather for the same purpose: to enjoy a spirit of camaraderie. Like those family reunions everyone partakes of good food, is entertained, or simply interacts with others.

Settimana Italiana - Italian Week Inc. is therefore a rallying point that strengthens, unites, and indeed encourages members of the community to feel the pride of their heritage while meeting the challenges of an aging community. Towards this end, a new generation of youthful volunteers, both local and from Italy, as well as newcomers from other Canadian cities who are retiring in Ottawa, are taking an active part in diversifying Italian Week to meet the interests of the Ottawa community at large.

For Alessio Monterosso, Italian Week Chair at this writing and a recent arrival to Ottawa from Italy, the festival will continue to build upon its past as it moves towards a city-wide celebration of Italian ethnicity. His youthful organizing committee includes Dylan Burger, Lydia Di Francesco, Masha Klimentyeva, Rachel McDonald, Noor Sunba, and Laura Scaffidi. As the festival moves slowly away from a community-oriented focus to a more global representation of Italian culture, the committee is pledged to maintaining the traditional framework of local activities while initiating a dialogue for positive growth and adaptation. "Coming to Italian Week," says Alessio, "should still feel like going to *nonna's* house for dinner, with a sprinkling of Italian fusion cuisine. We will continue, then, every year in June, to invite everyone in the Ottawa Region, to come and feel Italian with us."

From its humble origins in a university classroom over 45 years ago, Italian Week, as it is called on publicity posters, has evolved to become a month-long, truly collaborative community-wide event that enlists primetime entertainment and activities to create something as simple as a good feeling and a great memory . . . to something as wonderful as a new friendship that can last for years.

Settimana Italiana - Italian Week Inc. List of Presidents:

Dottore Vincenzo Tripodi (1975); Dino Venier (1976); Tony D'Angelo (1977); Massimo Ciavolella (1978); Giovanni Liani (1979); Romano Battel (1980); Angiola Lombardi (1981-82); Enrico Del Castello (1983-84); Tony Cuffaro (1985); Tony D'Angelo (1986-93); Matteo Mancini (1994-95); Raffaela Plastino (1996-99); Giovanni Mazzotta (2000-01); Orazio Rizzi (2002-03); Raffaela Plastino (2004-07); Joe Cama (2008-09); Claudio Pagani* (2010 -15); Tony Mariani (2016-

17); Alessio Monterosso (2018-19). *Claudio Pagani is proud to have been the sole Canadian-born President to date.

St. Anthony Italia Soccer Club

On 25 May 2017, the Ottawa St. Anthony Italia Soccer Club celebrated its 65th anniversary. From modest beginnings in 1952, the Club has grown to become one of the sporting, cultural, and social cornerstones of the community. But it wasn't always so. . . .

As is often the case in ethnic communities, St. Anthony's Church was instrumental in establishing meaningful non-religious and sporting activity for its parish youth. The original soccer team, according to the official story, was founded by Fathers Jerome Ferraro and Domenico Fiore, ably assisted by soccer *aficionados* Saro Panuccio, Frank Porreca, Angelo Ciardella and Armando Cantusci.

These beginnings of the team, however, like most worthwhile and successful community endeavors, are somewhat nebulous. While the idea for a soccer team had migrated for years amongst the more enthusiastic and sports-minded members of the community, the spark that set the proverbial ball in motion apparently arouse spontaneously in May 1952 during an informal gathering between Father Ferraro, Benito Schiffo, Luigi Schiffo and Attilio Rizzi. The ever-enterprising Father Ferraro quickly found a benefactor, a certain ceramic merchant from Hull named Bianchini, whose $100 offering was sufficient to purchase a soccer ball, 13 pairs of shoes, jerseys, pants and socks. The team was baptized St. Anthony Soccer Club. Benito Schiffo became its captain, and an audacious Father Domenico Fiore its first goalie!

In 1959 the Club added a new chapter to its already storied beginnings as Steno Rossanese and Luigi Fasan were appointed official President and Treasurer. The Club immediately set its sights on fielding a more competitive team and merged the St. Anthony team with the local Blue Wings. So was formed the new St. Anthony Italia Senior Men's Soccer Team, part of the Ottawa Soccer League.

The team now needed a clubhouse. Father Ferraro offered the St. Anthony Church hall free of charge on the condition that the players first renovate the room. After the departure of the well-intentioned and generous priest, however, his replacement was not as generous and decided to charge the group a fee for use of the facility. At this juncture, Rossanese decided to begin his own clubhouse. The entire team contributed to the venture and eventually an old home was purchased at 523 Arlington Avenue.

In 1967 the St. Anthony Italia Soccer Club was incorporated as a non-profit organization. Its stated mandate was to provide cultural, social and recreational activities to the community. Once the new clubhouse opened in 1968 the club was finally able to provide a full venue of diverse programs for members of all ages, a mandate it continues to fulfill in full measure. This clubhouse was eventually demolished when the present banquet hall building was inaugurated in 1986. An impressive and welcoming lobby was added to complete the building in 1993. Though it had never neglected its amateur soccer roots and continues to sponsor soccer activities and events for both young and old, the club slowly evolved into a social center for the Italian community. The new building was capable of supplying full banquet facilities, as well as hosting a variety of social, business, and cultural events.

Throughout the years, the success of the St. Anthony Italia Soccer Club was due to the commitment and selfless involvement of the club's pragmatic members, none moreso, however, than Steno Rossanese, longtime president and driving force behind the sport club's progress. Steno was a determined character, honest to a fault, and hard working. He had emigrated to Canada in 1956 from Castelfranco-Veneto, a small town near Venice. He began his immigrant adventure by opening a hair salon in Ottawa but soon found an outlet for his true passion, soccer.

Never far from the sport, Rossanese was among the original founders of the St. Anthony Italia Soccer Club along with Father Jerome Ferraro. Steno was the driving force that moved the club from its cramped house quarters on Arlington to the larger present facility. As President, he was instrumental in maintaining the many soccer teams and numerous sports activities sponsored by the Soccer Club, all while managing an extremely successful banquet hall facility. In 1994, after 35 years of service to the community, members and friends of the club held a dinner in his honor for his dedication to sports in Ottawa. "Steno made a difference in how soccer was perceived in the community not only locally but internationally too," says his cousin Angela Ierullo. His passion for the game was contagious and it spread amongst the many soccer fans in the entire city, some of which accompanied Rossanese to every FIFA World Cup competition since 1970.

Steno Rossanese was known in the community for his love of the game, his unending donation of time and financial support to local soccer teams, and his sponsoring of players from around the world to play in Ottawa. But Rossanese was also aware of his civic responsibility to the community. In 1988, the St. Anthony's Church Choir began an annual fundraiser to raise awareness of the work done by the Canadian Cancer Society. Since 1990, the Ottawa St. Anthony Italia Soccer Club, following suit, launched the Annual Dafodil Gala. In the past 28 years the Gala has raised over $550,000 for Research, over $125,000.00 for the Steno Rossanese Endowment Fund and $30,000.00 for the Family Transportation Assistance Program Society.

Steno Rossanese passed in 2001. He is remembered for his generosity, meticulousness, and hard-headed approach to business. He remains a true community icon whose philanthropic legacy endures in the hearts of Ottawa soccer fans.

The Teams

The early soccer scene in Ottawa saw teams from different nationalities regularly face-off in well-organized local tournaments. There was no lack of competition for avid German, Hungarian, and Italian players. The exceptional skills and competitive level of at least one team, however, led St. Anthony Italia Soccer to routinely play in the Montreal League where they won the O'Keefe Cup twice. Its skill-set was so complete that the team eventually won the Canada Cup. For Masimiliano Moretto, current President of the Club and longtime former associate of Steno Rossanese, "The winning of the Canada

Cup in Vancouver in 2006 was one of the club's best and proudest moments for Ottawa soccer fans."

Though the enthusiasm of those heady days has languished among the older fans in the community, St. Anthony Italia Soccer remains a focal point for youth who enjoy soccer in Ottawa. The Club currently fields 10 teams for youngsters 12 and older and 20 teams for 12 and under players. It remains one of Ottawa's oldest and most prestigious recreational organizations. Named for the Italian-Canadian community's patron saint, St. Anthony of Padua, the club, provides opportunities for interested youth to enjoy the game of soccer. Expert coaches teach the fundamentals of the game, emphasize teamwork, and create a spirit of respectful competition in order to fully develop both individual players and the team.

In 1972 the Ottawa Tigers Soccer Club was founded to compete with St Anthony. It remains a recreational league where players enjoy the game, meet new friends and basically have fun. In 1980 a meeting was held in an attempt to merge these two teams, but unfortunate pettiness and internal dissent rendered the well-intentioned effort unsuccessful. Both teams continue along their respective paths and have remained separate community entities. The home base for St. Anthony Italia Soccer continues to be the St. Anthony Banquet Hall in the heart of Little Italy. The club maintains a soccer room, an office, an equipment room, and the only club-owned turf field in the City of Ottawa.

Società Dante Alighieri - Ottawa

Mention the words *Società Dante Alighieri* and the name Padre Pagano is immediately elicited as sure as morning dew. For better or for worse, Padre Sebastiano Pagano, an Oblate priest stationed at St. Paul's University, administered the Ottawa branch of the Society for over 40 years. Originally from Sicily, Padre Pagano arrived in Ottawa in 1936 and was part of that first influx of immigrants that embraced Preston Street and its burgeoning Italian community. A feisty if not bristly character, Padre Pagano relished the task of teaching the language of

Dante Alighieri, Italy's *sommo poeta*, to the children of immigrants. "These children," the bespectacled priest once mused, "don't try to hide their Italian identity, but at the same time, they are 300% Canadian."

Beyond the symbolic importance of spreading the language of Dante, the practical necessity of maintaining relevant ties with the immigrant's culture of origin was not lost on the socially minded shepherd of souls. The need for an Italian school to teach the language and culture of Italian immigrant parents to their children was a topic of discussion and interest in the growing community and Padre Pagano was at the forefront of the efforts to unite people in the spirit of universal humanism and love for the Italian language.

It is towards these lofty ends that Rosalie Puccio wrote a three-page letter to the then Ambassador Carlo Del Ferrariis Salzano dated 12 April 1964, concerning the need to "Promuovere la cultura italiana in Canada" and specifically in the capital city of Ottawa. The Embassy agreed. A provisional committee was quickly formed composed of Rosalie Puccio, Pasqualina Adamo, Italo Tiezzi, and Angelo Licari. The committee's mission was to help form a *Società Dante Alighieri* in Ottawa that would be affiliated with the *Società Dante Alighieri* of Rome. The Society's first official committee met on 8 December 1965 at the home of Doctor Sal Carioto. Its members were composed of Doctor Aurelio Siriani (President), V. Arnone and Padre G. Grieco (Vice-Presidents), M. Giaccone (Secretary), and V. Giaccone (Treasurer). Counselors included: Doctor Sal Carioto, N. Delabio, A. Licari, G. Saracino, I. Tiezzi, R Vigneron, S. Pantalone, M. Favilla, P. Adamo, J. Bennet, A. Guttadauria, S. Pagano, C. Rivard, P. Ruffo.

The *Società Dante Alighieri* was warmly embraced by the Ottawa community and by 1969 had 84 registered members. The coordination of the Society was initially run from volunteer homes and after work hours. In December 1973, however, the Society established its official office in Room 110 of l'Edifice Deschâtelets where Padre Pagano resided as a Member of the Congregation of the Missionary Oblates of Mary Immaculate.

The Dante Alighieri School was founded in 1967. The School received funding from a number of sources including: the Government of Canada, through the office of the Secretary of State; the Government of Ontario, through the Ontario Ministry of Education; and the Government of Italy, through the Ministry of Foreign Affairs. The classes offered by the School allowed children of elementary school age to study Italian culture, learn the language, and hopefully acquire a better understanding of their origins. The school was very successful. Hundreds of students attended the three-hour lessons every Saturday morning from September to May annually. Padre Pagano was devoted to the school and the children. In his efforts to instill a love for their culture in the students, he created a library of diapositives depicting the architecture, landscape and art of Italy. The collection eventually numbered over 23,000. Plans are currently underway to adequately file and store this material in the Dante archives.

A strong and tireless figure, Padre Pagano served as Secretary of the *Società Dante Alighieri*, Executive Director and Treasurer of the Dante Alighieri School of Italian Language and Culture, Secretary-Treasurer of the Italian Week, Treasurer of the Società Sicula, and collaborator of the Vicentini Club of Ottawa. He passed on 5 December 2003 at the age of 93.

The *Società Dante Alighieri* continues his legacy and cultural mission with cultural events and cinema festivals designed to educate and entertain an increasingly diverse public within the culturally plural landscape of the nation's capital. Their program of events may be visited on-line at: http://www.danteottawa.ca

Past Presidents of the *Società Dante Alighieri* include:

Antonio F. Sirianni	1965-1968
Sebastiano Pagano	1968-1972
Emilio Panarella	1973-1975
Maurizio Bonardi	1976-1977
Massimo Ciavolella	1978-1979
Leonardo Sbrocchi	1980-1981
Pasqualina Adamo	1982-1983
Angelo Spadola	1984-1985
Sal Carioto	1986-1987
Paolo Brun del Re	1988-1989
Giuseppe Monorchio	1990-1991

Between 1992 and 2001 the *Società Dante Alighieri* experienced a period of adverse indifference and unfortunate inattention. The concerted efforts of then Ambassador Marco Colombo and Community Liaison Alessandro Cortese (and myself amongst others) helped revive the once sole link to Italian culture in Ottawa. The following are Presidents of the new *Società Dante Alighieri*.

Antonio F. Sirianni	2001-2003
Orazio Rizzi	2003-2005
Alfredo Mazzanti	2006 -2010
Louise Terrillon-McKay	2011-2013
Francesco Loriggio	2014-2015
Cynthia Nuzzi	2015-2019

The National Congress of Italian-Canadians, National Capital District

The National Congress of Italian-Canadians (NCIC) was founded in 1974 with the purpose of unifying the 1.4 million Italian-Canadians (or Canadians married to, or descendants, of Italians) nationwide by representing local Italian-Canadian community associations. It is thus a federated umbrella organization officially representing the political, social and cultural interests of Italian-Canadians throughout Canada. It is non-profit and non-politically affiliated. At the National level, the Congress is made up of a National Executive Committee, whose headquarters are currently in the City of Ottawa[51], seven affiliated Regions each representing a geographical division of Canada, and a number of Districts in those regions where the concentration of Italian-Canadians is such as to warrant their creation.

The primary focus of the NCIC is to act as a link among Italian-Canadian communities, the promotion of various activities amongst Italian-Canadians, to foster the retention of a shared cultural heritage

---

51 National offices have alternated between Montreal and Toronto. The Ottawa offices were once located a downtown building but that changed in the late 1990s.

and traditions, and the promotion and dissemination of information and news for the benefit of the Italian-Canadian community. It's purpose is to give a sense affiliation, of united strength, and influence to local Italian-Canadian communities across Canada.

The NCIC's main objectives include the safeguarding of the interests of Italian-Canadians; the growth and wellbeing of a viable Italian-Canadian community that maintains Italian values and traditions in the multicultural pattern of Canadian life; fostering the integration of Italians in the Canadian landscape; to vigorously combat discrimination against Canadians of Italian origin when and wherever necessary. As the voice of all Italian-Canadians, the NCIC gives individuals and local organizations in Canada, a greater opportunity of expressing their views within a bonafide and recognized national forum.

The National Capital District was founded in 1984 with the same principles and historical underpinnings of the National organization. It was incorporated in 2000. The NCD represents the interests of the approximately 46,000 Italian-Canadians in the Nation's Capital at the municipal, provincial and federal levels of government. It is a not-for-profit, non-political organization which provides assistance to the local Italian-Canadian community in dealing with civic affairs, provincial, and federal programs. In general, it represents the community and its local associations in projects of common interest and welfare with respect to economic and political issues affecting the Ottawa community.

In 1997, the NCD organized a number of special events to recognize the 500th anniversary of the landing and discovery of Canada by Giovanni Caboto. The group worked closely with the National Capital Commission in the annual Flotilla parade at Dow's Lake where it won second prize in the Canadian Flotilla. Over the years, the NCD has organized special gatherings and welcome ceremonies for high profile government officials from both Canada and Italy, sponsored fundraising for earthquake relief in Italy, organized conferences, honored deserving members of the Italian-Canadian community, and promoted local events that best represent community interests.

As the Italian-Canadian community has matured across Canada, integrating itself into the Canadian fabric, the NCIC has been vigilant to safeguard the principles of honor, dignity, and equality that animate its founding principles.

Past Presidents of the National Capital District:
Italo Tiezzi	1984 - 1989
Giorgio Tavazzi	1989 - 1990
Giorgio Flumian	1990 - 1992
Tony D'Angelo	1992 - 1993
Josephine Palumbo	1993 - 2016

Tele-30 and CHIN Radio Ottawa

A key ingredient that permits a community to grow both within and without itself, and in doing so create a sociocultural footprint of enduring value, is community television and radio.

Contemporary democracy works best when a wide array of voices can be seen and heard, when citizens can freely express opinions and concerns. Television media is that democratic tool that provides residents a platform that creates opportunity for dialogue around issues that address the community. People build a sense of community through media. One of the strongest community builders in the Italian-Canadian community of Ottawa is Tele-30.

Founded in 1982 by Dr. Giovanna Panico to celebrate Ottawa's Italian roots, Tele-30 has ably served the community and provided quality locally produced, locally reflective programming to the National Capital Region. Its one-hour program, done primarily in Italian, has been a staple in community homes for over 40 years and has not simply reflected the Italian-Canadian community, but, through its creative practices, has helped develop stronger social ties, cultural self-awareness, and community cohesion throughout the City of Ottawa. In 1987, Tele-30 was incorporated as a not-for-profit organization under the guidance of Dr. Giovanna Panico, Pasqualina Adamo, and Angiolina Magone. Their perseverance was instrumental in achieving this important milestone and solidified Tele-30 as an anchor for the Italian-Canadian community.

Tele-30 is currently managed by a board of eight volunteers and receives funding from donors and supporters; it is proud to advance its role as a major community stakeholder that collaborates with the many Italian-Canadian organizations and businesses in the region.

Community television everywhere has always lacked the economic resources of the public and private sectors and Tele-30 is no exception. At this writing, Tele-30's programs are carried by Rogers TV Cable 22 (Ottawa) and is aired on a bi-weekly schedule. Nevertheless, through good times and bad, Tele-30 has remained faithful to its principal mission of celebrating the Italian-Canadian community's precious connection with its own culture and traditions by showcasing local events, group activities, as well as personal experiences that link viewers to their shared heritage with their Italian origins. Tele-30 offers content that spans the varied interests of its audience. For example, past shows have featured topics such as Italian-based community art fairs, literature readings, musical festivals, dances, fashion shows, sporting events, children carnivals, food preparation and cooking, as well as health and wellness segments, among many others.

The natural extension of the community programming concept is to make the programming available on the Internet. Aided by this technology, a once linear and static community program becomes available to a world-wide audience potentially increasing both the diversity and content of its programming and, as a consequence, its audience. Towards this end, Tele-30 has actively extended its reach into the community via social media. Unfortunately, in the absence of focussed financial support and the necessary technical resources for this new form of community outreach, this kind of user-generated-content may be more difficult to sustain. The imprint of digital technology, though promising, have not as yet been measured.

Nevertheless, Tele-30 will continue to look towards a bright future as it seeks new and innovative media opportunities to remember, recharge, and renew the community's evolving culture imprint while deepening a shared Italian heritage for future generations.

CHIN Radio Ottawa

Community radio, by its very definition, implies local. This is precisely its strength and firmly locates community media in a framework that promotes participatory approaches and practices. Community radio is an important player in community, especially ethnic community, development. If information dissemination is a manifestation of democratic process and of equitable cultural exchange, then community radio works with the belief that the tools of communication and the rights of communities to be heard are fundamental rights. As a possible response to media globalization and the corporate dominance of politics, the accessibility of local radio guarantees a voice to the sociocultural needs of ethnic communities.

CHIN Radio was the first multicultural/multilingual local radio station established in Ontario. Originating in Toronto, the AM station began broadcasting on 6 June 1966, followed by an FM sister station 1967. It was founded by Johnny Lombardi. CHIN Radio is the pioneer in multicultural radio broadcasting in Canada and has been the consummate leader for similar broadcast operations in communities across Canada.

CHIN Radio Ottawa launched its unique multicultural/multilingual style of broadcasting to the Ottawa/Gatineau region in October 2003. Present for the auspicious occasion held on Preston Street was original founder Johnny Lombardi and son Lenny Lombardi. The frequency call letters of the new station, CJLL (CHIN Ottawa) reflect the Toronto company's long arms as the C stands for Canada, J for Johnny, L for Lenny and L for Lombardi.

The early years of the eagerly anticipated radion station were exciting yet unfortunately plagued with a dearth of possible funding sources as the potential for revenue in the smallish Ottawa market were, and remain, scarce. Yet, while advertising revenue and private donations that would normally help defray operating costs were slow in materializing, the general lack of an aggregate source of sustainable funding from the ethnic communities of Ottawa has not stopped CHIN Radio Ottawa from maintaining and expanding its high-quality content and variety programming.

True to its multicultural mission, General Managers for the station have included a Canadian-Finnish Edward Ylanen and a Lebanese-Canadian Gary Zahab (known professionally as Gary Michaels, a top radio DJ on AM Radio. The General Manager at this writing is Francesco Di Candia, a radio personality with over 30 years of broadcasting experience. Originally from northern Italy, yet boasting southern roots, he spent 13 years in Toronto before transferring to CJLL - CHIN Radio Ottawa in July of 2007. A dynamic personality, since joining the Ottawa radio station he has solidified programming, expanded language content to include Portuguese and Russian, increased the hours of both Latino programs and increasingly popular Arabic programs, and has added new Italian cultural programs to the weekly broadcast schedule. Under his mandate annual revenue has noticeably grown. Most impotantly, he has consolidated the station's position as a major player on the Ottawa ethnic scene through effective community outreach. As a result, CHIN Radio Ottawa was featured in the Top 5 Radio Stations in the Capital based on the *Ottawa Life Magazine* contest held in December 2018.

"My mission and inspiration derive from my favorite mentors Johnny and Lenny Lombardi who have unleashed my passion, channeled my energy, guided my growth and encouraged my success," states Di Candia. "My biggest satisfaction is knowing that my personal goals and the interests of my Company are becoming reality. Additionally, I have a personal love for everything ethnic and international; I myself speak five languages. One of my tasks has been to offer a good variety of professionally produced radio programs in Canada's Capital which are a great service to the many who listen to them. These shows are lifelines to their homelands and it is my responsibility to ensure that the lifeline is authentic."

CHIN Radio Ottawa has grown to become a unique and locally sustained third-language radio station serving the nation's capital. It broadcasts in 20 languages to 37 distinct cultural groups and ethnic communities. The contribution of parent company CHIN Radio International to the cause of multiculturalism, understanding and tolerance between people of diverse national, racial and religious origins has been recognized with countless awards and accolades throughout

Canada. Its role as a community builder has been acknowledged globally. Within that family, CHIN Radio Ottawa has become one of the prime examples of successful local broadcasting.

CHIN Radio International also broadcasts worldwide over the Internet.

SOCIAL GROUPS
CONSERVING A PAST, RESHAPING ETHNIC IDENTITIES

When speaking of Italian-Canadian Social Clubs, the word association is often used. The phenomena of *associazionismo etnico*, or, the coming together of like-minded groups of individuals who separate themselves from the larger community by identifying common village, regional, professional, or arbitrary signatures, is a practice normally related to first generation immigrants. Common roots, similar dialects, nostalgia for familiarity in a strange land, cause the immigrant to create a social space outside the new Canadian home that feels like the old Italian one. The number of associations, or clubs, is often astonishingly in contrast with the paucity of similar voluntary associations, or social clubs, in the immigrant's hometown reality.[52]

If associations tend to proliferate in the first generation of immigration and wane with the limited interest of second-generation offspring, they normally disappear in the third-generation cohort as the traditional clubhouse setting no longer serves as the primary source of social interaction. Indeed, if ethnicity is a social construction that undergoes a continuous process of renegotiation and change, the practice of classifying other members of the larger society as different (according

---

52 "One would not expect to find many volunteer associations in the villages and, in fact, few are found. This is not to suggest that these social groups are non-existent in Italy. Even a cursory view while strolling on the mainstreet of a middletown might reveal the presence of several associations: Pro Loco; Pro Musica; Calcio Club; History and Archeology Club; etc. Somewhat more formalized, but still dependent on local initiative, would be a Camera di Commercio." Leonard Moss, "Voluntary Association in South Italy and Detroit," *The Family and Community Life of Italian Americans*, in Richard N. Juliani ed., Proceedings of the Thirteenth Annual Conference of The Italian American Historical Association 209: 11-22. file:///C:/Users/fricci/Downloads/d61435d4-51bf-47bf-ad26-affd8d85bc12.pdf.

to a criterion of inclusion and exclusion based on allegedly inherited biological or cultural differences[53]) must of necessity portend the demise of local village or regional loyalties and the advent of a broader and borderless pan-nationalism. Immigrants eventually supersede the legacy of their ancestral village and accommodate themselves within their respective countries of adoption within a profile of homogenized Italianicity rather than designated ethnicity. The very notion of self-segregation thus gives sway to an associationism (in its philosophical, psychological sense[54]) that is based on shared behaviors of the group (rather than origins) and normally portends relationships that can be measured in terms of learned common local practices.

The history of social clubs or associations in the Italian-Canadian community of Ottawa follows the same historical pattern of rise and demise of any organized social group regardless of age or cultural background. The early enthusiasm of collectivity, efforts focussed on

---

53   See Werner Sollors, *Beyond Ethnicity: Consent and Descent in American Culture* (New York: Oxford UP, 1986).

54   Associationism is a theory that connects learning to thought based on principles of the organism's causal history. Since its early roots, associationists have sought to use the history of an organism's experience as the main sculptor of cognitive architecture. In its most basic form, associationism has claimed that pairs of thoughts become associated based on the organism's past experience. So, for example, a basic form of associationism might claim that the frequency with which an organism has come into contact with Xs and Ys in one's environment determines the frequency with which thoughts about Xs and thoughts about Ys will arise together in the organism's future.

An associative structure describes the type of bond that connects two distinct mental states. An example of such a structure is the associative pair salt/pepper. The associative structure is defined, in the first instance, functionally: if X and Y form an associative structure, then, *ceteris paribus*, activations of mental state X bring about mental state Y and vice versa without the mediation of any other psychological states (such as an explicitly represented rule telling the system to activate a concept because its associate has been activated). In other words, saying that two concepts are associated amounts to saying that there is a reliable, psychologically basic causal relation that holds between them—the activation of one of the concepts causes the activation of the other. See *Stanford Encyclopedia of Philosophy,* https://plato.stanford.edu/entries/associationist-thought/#AssTheMenProEmpCon.

mutual aid and protection of culture or ideology, typically gave sway to tiredness and indifference. As the community developed extra-community bonds and matured beyond its neighborhood, these voluntary groups changed in nature. Practically speaking, part of the difficulty of describing the history of these groups derives from the same difficulties of researching Italian-Canadians. These problems stem from the perceived image of the group and the actual reality in which they survive. The image conjured in the mind when one speaks of any immigrant group is limited, fraught with misconceptions, highly romanticized notions, and sociopolitical baggage.

At current writing, there are 32 listed social groups in the *Italian Telephone Directory 2017-18 Edition*.[55] Not all of these groups are active; some did not respond to repeated queries regarding their past.[56] Nevertheless, their analogous time spans, the similarity, origin, and stated purpose, as well as their yearly social and cultural calendars that tend to overlap each other's eagerness, create a profile that is both objective and failry accurate. My telescoping of each group's individual history does little to acknowledge the unstinting and relentless work done by many individuals to further the aims and scope of each group, and in turn, that of the community. The point is, though they often worked in competition and cross purposes while catering to the same, limited audience, through these associations, the community has nevertheless succeeded in moving beyond its self-imposed and fractured image of multiple *paesi* and consolidated an image of cultural continuity.

---

55   Published and distributed by *Elenco Telefonico Italiano/Italian Telephone Directory*, Ottawa.

56   Several associations have succumbed to the constraints of human longevity and no longer contribute to the daily life of the community. A few simply did not reply to my repeated and varied solicitations. These include: Associazione Colle D'Anchise; Associazione Marinai; Associazione Piemontesi nel Mondo (Sezione di Ottawa); Associazione Sammartinese di Ottawa (now Associazione Molisana); Giovani-84; Lega di Bowling di Castropignano.

CLUBS
Associazione Culturale Calabrese Savuto-Cleto

The Associazione Culturale Calabrese Savuto-Cleto, renamed the Calabria Cultural Association, boasts a near 50-year presence in the community since its founding in 1972. The original founding members includ Gino Marrello, Corrado Nicastro, Franco Rizzo, and Sam Caputo. It is one of the most active associations remembered for its popular yearly celebration of Miss Calabria. The club suffered a period of inactivity during the 1990s but was rejuvenated in 2001 with a renewed and reenergized local presence. Its most recent accomplishments include the institution of the Community Achievement Award for meritorious persons, the purchase of the statue of the Madonna del Soccorso that resides in St. Anthony's Church, and a popular Christmas party that attracts young and old alike. A weekly radio program moderated by Gino Marello on CHIN Radio maintains and spreads the culture, history and music of the region of Calabria to the community at large.

Associazione Giuliano-Dalmati of Ottawa and Eastern Ontario

Although listed as part of the Associazione Dalmati nel Mondo, the Ottawa section has been moribund since 2008. Outgoing President Dario Zanini cites a lack of energy and interest as reasons for the demise of the club whose charitable activities were always well received in the community. The international association is a mutual aid group created to help immigrants of Italian language, culture and nationality originating from the provinces of Trieste and Gorizia, as well as exiles from Istria, Rijeka, and the Kvarner islands who were forced to abandon their homes following the Yugoslavian occupation of their lands following the First and Second World Wars.

Associazione Emiliani di Ottawa

Founded in 1979, the group is committed to maintaining and promoting the cultural traditions of the Emilia-Romagna region of Italy. Yearly events include a popular golf tournament, summer picnic, card tournament, and an annual and well attended member's dinner.

Associazione Molisani di Ottawa

The Association was founded in 2008 during an event organized by Prof. Giovanna Panico that wished to highlight the customs and cuisine of the regions of Italy represented in the City of Ottawa. Since then, and under the leadership of successive Presidents Paolo Siraco, Giovanni Saracino and Tony Battista, the group has organized many highly successful cultural, social and commercial events including the sponsorship of storytellers, performers, concerts from Molise, as well as artistic and culinary events. In 2018 the association organized a well-attended group excursion to Italy and continues to sponsor annual events aimed at highlighting the history and culture of Molise. The association also manages a website: www.amoottawa.com.

Associazione degli Alpini di Ottawa e Regione

The Associazione Nazionale Alpini A.N.A. was founded in Milan on 8 July 1919. As of December 2017, the ANA proudly boasts 348.956 members worldwide including 80 sections in Italy, 30 sections in the various nations of the world, plus 8 autonomous groups. In Canada there are twelve sections. The Associazione degli Alpini di Ottawa e Regione was founded in 1972. Ex-Alpino Romano Battel had long expressed the idea of creating a local chapter of the corps and often discussed the possibility with good friend and fellow Alpino Albino Pescatore. In winter 1971, he placed newspaper ads in the local *L'Ora di Ottawa* asking interested local alpini to contact him. He received 20 responses. Bolstered by the unexpected but heartening interest, the following 3 May 1972, the local chapter was officially founded with Romano as its first President. Within its first year the group numbered 70 members.

The original founding members include: Romano Battel, Giuseppe Bertorelli, Ermano Bortolotti, Bruno Boselli, Ricccardo Bosselli, Ernesto Capellazzi, Amerigo Cardarelli, Isidoro Casagrande, Adriano Chiappa, Alberto Copelli, Eugenio Dal Cin, Umberto De Pretto, Gioravanti Grappolini, Donato Mariani, Albino Pescatore, Attilio Rizzi, Giuseppt Scaffadi, Rito Visentin, Erminio Zanette, and Dino Zanchettta.

The first executive council counted: Romano Battal, President; Aberigo Cardarelli, VicePresident; Alberto Coppelli, Secretary; Giuseope Scaffardi, Treasurer; Counselors Ernesto Capellazzi, Adriano Chiappa, and Umberto De Pretto; Giusepope Bertorelli, and Attillio Rizzi, Account Reviewers; Luisa Lunelli, Godmother; Albino Pescatore, Public Relations; Vittorino Mazzarolo, Alpine Choir Master.

A very closely-knit group, respectful of military tradition and dedicated to the ethical principles of Duty, Respect, Selfless Service, Honor, Integrity, Personal Courage, and Loyalty, the chapter is justifiably proud to have maintained and fostered the spirit of the Alpine Corps in Ottawa. In the best tradition of their corps, the chapter immediately began a choir, the "Coro Alpini," in order to share their captivating lore and stories in song. The choir quickly became a part of community culture and lent its services to both social and religious events. The group also acts as a social club providing friendship and support to all its members. Beyond recurring celebratory events, social gatherings, picnics, and snow vacations, the group was well connected to its parent international association and members regularly attended congresses and meetings across Canada and in Italy. The chapter also proudly sponsored a yearly study scholarship given to meritorious university age students, the Premi di Studio Franco Bertagnolli.

Associazione Nazionale Carabinieri Sezione di Ottawa

The birth of the Carabinieri Military Corps was officially sanctioned on 13 July 1814; the current Statute of the Associazione Nazionale

Carabinieri (ANC) was approved on 25 July 1956. Today, ANC consists of 1696 sections distributed worldwide with over 205,000 members. In Canada there are active sections in Toronto, Montreal, Ottawa, Calgary and Vancouver.

The Ottawa Chapter participates as honor guard at many community activities held during the year.

Associazione Nazionale Bersaglieri d'Ottawa

The Asssociazione is part of the larger Associazione Nazionale Bersaglieri fouonded in Bologna on 30 June 1924 following the merger of the Comizio Veterani Bersaglieri (18 June 1886) and the Società di Mutuo Soccorso ex-Bersaglieri (19 May 1887) that subsequently became the Federazione Nazionale Bersaglieri (4 November 1921). The Ottawa Section was founded in 1972 by Bersagliere Antonio Maggiore. There were 80 original members including sympathizers. In May 1980 the Ottawa Section convoked an extraordinary meeting to decide its uncertain future. The 13 Bersagliere present decided not to dissolve the Ottawa Section and continue forward despite dwindling membership numbers. Present at the meeting were Bersaglieri: Bonardi, Maurizio; Campagna, Enzo; Cassandra, Filiberto; Diodati, Amato; Iacobucci, Tonino; Leggeri, Andrea; Maggiore, Gino; Mazzarello, Luigi; Merenda, Vito; Poggione, Antonio; Rizzuti, Antonio; Silvestro, Giovanni; Villani, Ernesto. The meeting was presided by Padre Sebastiano Pagano, Section Chaplain. A new Executive Committee was elected by acclamation and included: Tonino Iacobucci, President; Maurizio Bonardi, VicePresident; Padre Sebastiano Pagano, Treasurer and temporary Secretary; Enzo Campagna, Andrea Leggeri, Gino Maggiore, Counselors.

Though the Section has further dwindled in numbers over the years, they are still present at all community events where an official Honor Guard is required. The Current President remains Tonino Iacobucci.

Associazione Pratola Peligna di Ottawa

The Associazione Pratola Peligna di Ottawa was founded by the late Mario Tofano in 1992. The founding executive committee included: Mario Tofano, President; Ferdinardo Gianantonio , Vice President; and councelors Filiberto D'onofrio; Franco Gualtieri; Ezio Dibacco; Lino Dibacco; Vittorio Di Cioccio; Fatina Panetta; Ferdinardo Panetta; Rina Ceccato; Loreta DiPelino; Leonardo Notarandrea; Golfea Notarandrea; Marco Notarandrea. The group's history boasts only three presidents: Mario Tofano, Ezio Dibacco and current active president Rocco Petrella.

The Association was founded in the spirit of bringing together the many families from Pratola Peligna that had settled into the Abruzzese community of Ottawa. The group remains very active in the celebration of their customs and traditions and hosts annual dances and community picnics. Chief among these celebrations is the *Festa dell'Uva*, a popular annual Fall festival and dinner dance.

The Association is also proudly committed to addressing the needs of the less fortunate both in Canada and in Italy and participate in and generously support local fund-raising activities for humanitarian relief.

The Associazione Pratola Peligna di Ottawa is a proud member of the Federation of Pratola Peligna Associations who together celebrate the yearly Pratolani Interstate Picnic alternately in the cities of Toronto, Hamilton, Brantford, London, Ottawa, and Hartford, Connecticut, U.S.A..

Associazione Pretorese

The first Pretoresi emmigrated to Ottawa in the early 1920s and initiated a chain of arrivals that make them one of the largest groups of Abruzzesi in the nation's capital. The Association was founded in October of 1971. The founders of the Association were Emidio Peloso, and Francesco DiTiero. The first Executive Committee was composed of Rocco Marcantonio, President; Emidio Peloso, Vice-President; Carlo D'Angelo, Secretary; Francesco DiTiero, Treasurer. Directors: Carlo Marcantonio, Vincenzo Micucci, Valerio DiTiero, Giovanni

Mattioli, Domenico D'Angelo, Tony Bassi, Lino Santurbano, Rosano Giamberardino, Camillo Bassi. The group was Federally incorporated on 19 June 1972.

The non-profit organization aims to foster a sense of community and culture within Canada while contributing to the enrichment of their community and their multicultural nation by advancing the traditions of the village of Pretoro. Towards these ends, the Association has supported notable charitable foundations including, amongst many others, The Children's Hospital of Eastern Ontario, The Canadian Cancer Society, The Children's Wish Foundation of Canada, Kidney Foundation Villa Marconi Long Term Care Facility. Ever mindful of their origins, the group has also raised funds for earthquake relief in Abruzzo and has supported repairs to the San Nicola Church of Pretoro.

Associazione Rapinese di Ottawa

One of the oldest fraternal clubs in the Ottawa Capital Region, The Associazione Rapinese di Ottawa was founded by Benito Colasante along with friends Vigilante Ferrante and Carmine Micucci. The stated purpose of the association is to unite the many local Abruzzesi of Rapinese descent in the spirit of fraternity and good will. Over the years the club has generously aided its members through difficult financial times but has also provided cultural, educational, recreative, and social opportunities to deepen and discover the traditions of the village of Rapino.

Associazione Roccamontepiano S.R. Ottawa

Founded in 1994 by Verino Dinardo and a group of fellow Roccamontepiani, the club is dedicated to preserving the traditions and culture of the mountain region of Abruzzo. Beyond the usual social events and annual picnics, the most important event on the club calendar is the *Festa di San Rocco*. The saint's Feast Day is celebrated yearly on the 16th of August. The saint's statue is of paramount importance to devotees and as a sign of devotion by club members, a faithful reproduction of the statue of San Rocco in his home parish in Roccamontepiano was commissioned and donated to St. Anthony's Church in 1998. The statue of Saint Rocco is unique because it traditionally depicts him pointing to an open sore on his left leg. It is faithfully carried in procession on his feast day by club members and normally sits in view in the main nave of St. Anthony. At its height, the club had blossomed to 160 members. The current President is Romeo Donatucci.

Associazione Trevisani di Ottawa

The Associazione Trevisani di Ottawa was founded on 3 September 1992 by Luciano Pradal, Gino Gallo' and Mario Francescin; supporting cast members included Steno Rossanese and Erminio "Moro" Zanette. It celebrated its 25 year anniversary in 2017. As part of the larger worldwide Associazione Trevisani nel Mondo, the local club's primary objective is to maintain the culture and traditions of Trevisani and Veneti in the world. The club is also committed, above all, to the well-being and education of children of former emigrants and their descendants. It therefore actively undertakes initiatives to find points of contact between its youth and tradition. The Association wishes to remain a reference point for all Trevesini and Veneti outside Italy.

The Association holds a well-attended annual summer picnic and a Fall celebration of *radicchio* that has become a community standard. The older members of the club meet regularly at scheduled afternoon socials. The club remains confident that the constant ingress of young members promises continued success for the future of the group.

Associazione Unione Sloveni Friiuli (VG)

The Associazione Unione Sloveni Friiuli (VG) is part of the larger and international Unione Emigrati Slovene del Friuli Venezia Giulia.

The Association is a voluntary, non-political, and non-profit group that pursues social and cultural activities and initiatives that promote, maintain, and strengthen Slovenian identity. Over the years the group has organized cultural sojourns and internships in Italy for its youth as well as cultural events that have made their unique traditions known to the local community. The association considers itself a focal point for arriving immigrants and their descendants and will continue to inform them about the rights and opportunities offered by the Friuli Venezia Giulia Region.

Centro Abruzzese Canadese Inc.

The idea for the Centro Abruzzese Canadese Inc. began in 1973 when a small group of passionate Abruzzesi, Francesco Di Tiero, Rinaldo Palanza, Antonio Cavalancia, and Antonio Peca, met at Giuseppe Corda's house to discuss the possibility of creating a social club that embraced all community members of Abruzzese origin regardless of village affiliation. The first public recruitment meeting was held soon afterward at St. Anthony's Church where more than 150 participants ratified the new club as the Centro Abruzzese Canadese Inc.. Founding members of the club are: Rocco Breda, Antonio Cavalancia, Giuseppe Corda, Fernando D'Innocenzo, Fernando Dirienzo, Francesco Di Tiero, Angelo D'Urbano, Mauro Filoso, Domenico Micucci, Rinaldo Palanza, and Antonio Peca. They became the association's first Executive Committee.

Over the years the group has dedicated itself to forging a cosmopolitan Abruzzese identity by fashioning a wonderful fusion of deeply-rooted traditions within a Canadian cultural experience. From regular fall and winter dinner-dances to yearly summer picnics, the association has forged a meaningful identity within the growing community. Its many socio-cultural events have included an annual and very popular Miss Abruzzo Pageant, as well as folklore and pageantry celebrations provided by the club's youth group I Fiori della Maiella. The association has remained a strong voice and a constant positive fixture in the Italian-Canadian community landscape and has promoted the best of Italian culture in the community at large. The group's ties to the Region of Abruzzo have remained strong despite the obvious distance. Abruzzese dignitaries, politicians, dance and theater troupes, choirs, and students have been invited to Canada to continue the cultural exchange that is at the heart of the Centro Abruzzese's ongoing mandate of community service.

Adding to its community profile and stability was the acquisition in the year 2000 of a permanent two-story clubhouse, Casa Abruzzo, located at 705 Gladstone Avenue. The location soon became a community meeting place making the Centro Abruzzese Canadese Inc. the only social club in Ottawa to maintain a functioning and profitable daily locale for youth and seniors alike. Casa Abruzzo provides a friendly, healthy, and caring environment, where all members are treated with honesty, courtesy and respect. It has become a home away from home for seniors to pass time amongst friends, a location where youth can gather to plan events and express an evolving abruzzese consciousness. The locale is situated in a former restaurant. Now fully renovated, it provides small banquet services as well as daily meals for an ever-increasing clientele.

But the Centro Abruzzese Canadese Inc. also remains conscious of its humanitarian mandate. In 2009, the Centro spearheaded the Earthquake Relief Fund for L'Aquila in Ottawa and was instrumental in helping to build a multifunctional community center in the earthquake zone. The Centro Polifunzionale "Insieme per Camarda" is a shining example of the efforts of Abruzzese associations, both local and worldwide, to support and aid the peoples of Abruzzo.

Past Presidents have included Joe Corda, Benito Colasante, Donato Di Nardo Adriano Rossi, Luigi Ricottilli, Delio D'Angelo, Franco Ricci, Antonio Mariani and Nello Scipioni.

Circolo Ricreativo Cleto Inc.

On 31 August 1973, the Circolo Ricreativo Cleto Inc. was officially recognized with a Letter of Patent by the Deputy Registrar General of Canada. The primary objective of the group was to promote an exchange of understanding between the peoples of Canada and the citizens of Cleto, Calabria. The club and its members have remained faithful to their stated purpose and have fostered a sense of community as ambassadors of the culture and traditions of the village of Cleto. Founding members include: Maurino Paradiso, Frank Nicastro, Giuseppe Bentivoglio, Franco Berardini, Rocco Nicastro, Frank Ienzi, Francesco Plastino, Corrado Nicastro, Frank De Carlo, Eugenio Chiarello.

Club Carpineto Romano di Ottawa

The club was born as a fraternal society of mutual and financial beneficial assistance to fellow *Carpinetani* in financial distress. Originally proposed by Mario Ricci, Domenico Cacciotti and Aldo and Ferdinando Campagna, the idea came to fruition when the club was officially catalogued in the Registry of Voluntary Associations and recognized by the Government of Ontario on 19 November 1969.

The founding Committee included: Aldo Campagna, President; Belisario Bernabei, Vice President; Romano Cacciotti, Secretary; Aldo Campagna, Treasurer. Counselors included: L. Pagani, T. Calvano, D. Fabiani, A. Burri, and G. Calvano.

A first inaugural dinner was held in March 1970 with the participation of the club's 34 members and numerous sympathizers. An ad hoc activities committee was soon struck and the first *Festa di Sant'Agostino*, patron saint of Carpineto Romano, was held in August of the same year. The highlight of the well-attended evening, beyond a sumptuous banquet and music, was a folklore group of 11 dancers dressed in traditional garb sponsored by the Italian Consulate. The club now moved to officialise its status by electing a new Directive that included: Aldo Campagna, President; Mario Ricci, Vice President; Isidoro Campagna, Secretary; Roberto Campagna, Treasurer. Counselors included: B. Bernabei, V. Campagna, L. Testa, G. Calvano, L. Castrucci, G. Pagani.

The club enjoyed great success and organized many eagerly anticipated social events that gathered the entire Italian-Canadian community. Of festive note is the *Ballo dell'Agnello*, a popular yearly event normally held two weeks before Easter where a live lamb was raffled to eager participante; the *Festa della Fragola*, and *Festa di Sant'Agostino* that animated the long winter months and brought great numbers of participants, *Carpenitani* and not, to relive moments of nostalgic joy.

Other activities soon followed: a respectable soccer team named *Semprevisa* became an important player on the Ottawa soccer scene, and an upstart bowling league that animated Sunday afternoons for seniors and children, and an annual summer picnic normally held at Vincent Massey Park. A truly active club full of initiatives and, let it be said, rough patches that served to inspire the club to reinvent itself often, the club now suffers, as many social clubs in the community, from benign neglect and memories of better, bygone days.

Sons of Carpineto Romano

The Club began with a Facebook Page: Carpineto Romano – Ottawa. This small action has connected over 1500 fellow Carpinetani from Italy, Australia and Canada. Their motto is Friendship, Food and Fun, but their heart is in the joy of giving back to the community and the tremendous opportunity to make the world a better place through fundraising. Since its inception in 2014, The Sons of Carpineto Congone Golf Day has raised over $17,000 and has supported the Youth Training Centre, Ottawa Children's Breakfast Program, Children's Neuro Blastphoma, and the Proud to be Me Campaign. A continuing fundraising event is the annual St. Valentine's Day Dance with all proceeds donated to The Canadian Breast Cancer Foundation, a disease that has affected members' grandmothers, mothers, wives, sisters and daughters. The extremely successful event has raised over $50,000.

The remarkable *new and latest club* on the scene, The Sons of Carpineto Romano has shown that fundraising can be tremendously satisfying for everyone involved. The members take pride in their immigrant inheritance, are proud of a shared Italian heritage, and are dedicated to supporting the Italian-Canadian community of Ottawa. Members of the current Executive include: Frank Cacciotti, Enzo Cefaloni, Ken Farquar, Giuseppe Castrucci.

Though short in history, this new generation of Canadian-born sons and daughters of Carpineto Romano are proving that the sacrifices of their elders were not for naught, and that their dreams of creating a better place for their children has produced extraordinary results.

Fogolar Furlan di Ottawa

In early 1969, an ad hoc committee of Friulian friends headed by Anselmo Bortolotti organized a banquet dedicated to Sante di Valentin in order to celebrate the success of an exhibition of his paintings organized by the Dante Alighieri Society at the University of Ottawa. The spontaneous enthusiasm of the many Friulians present gave the required spark to a more formal association dedicated to maintaining and promoting Friulian culture in their newly adopted land. Shortly afterwards, over 100 volunteers gathered at the Ambassador Hall on 9 March 1969 to lay the framework for a future social club. On 27 April 1969, the Fogolar Furlan in Ottawa was founded under the Presidency of Dino Vanier. They chose the name Fogolâr, a word that arouses in every Friulano the profound emotions of belonging to a regional family spread across five continents but bound by common socio-cultural ties.

The Fogolâr Furlan of Ottawa was formally incorporated and registered with the Ontario Corporations Act and its official seal was conferred on 23 April 1975. It is a member of the *Ente Friuli nel Mondo* and works closely with the Federation of Fogolârs of Canada and the Ente Friuli in the World. Yet, as a Canadian provincial corporation for non-profit purposes the local chapter maintains autonomy and local focus.

Always active in the community, the club is a cornucopia of recurring festivals that animate the local scene. These have included the *Fieste dal Bocâl*, the *Festa dei Cacciatori*, the extremely popular *Carnevale*, the *Festa di Natale*, as well as sponsored group excursions to Quebec, Ontario, and the U.S.A. It has organized local exhibits, and hosted choirs, dance groups, card tournaments, and personalities from Italy. An initiative that highlights the collaborative and philanthropic spirit of the group is the honorific title of Bon Furlan proposed by Enrico Ferrarin. This recognition is given to a member of Fogolâr Furlan for exceptional contribution to Fogolâr. The recipients of this recognition have included: Paolo Brun Del Re, Ezio Manarin, Piero Buttera, Toni and Nilde Morielaz, Olita Schultz, Benito Schifo, Catherine Fiorin, and Franco Riva.

With the passing of years and natural attrition of membership, the once super active group has redirected its energy to singular events such as the *Fieste de Patrie* from Friûl, the annual summer picnic, the autumn *Castagnata*, the Friendship Lunch with the Vicentini, and the Christmas Lunch. Most recently, the Fogolâr has agreed to participate in the ICAP project (Italian Canadian Archival Project) thereby continuing to collaborate with other local groups in coordinating activities of mutual interest. These include, for example: The Friendship Festival with the Club Vicentini, the Annual Children's Carnival, the Aviation Exhibition with the NCIC.

Past Presidents of the Fogolâr Furlan di Ottawa include: Dino Venier (1969-1972), Lino Brun del Re (1972-1974), Nino Croatto (1974-1976), Benito Schiffo (1976-1978), Renzo Vidoni (1978-1983), Nick Urban (1983-1987), Paolo Brun del Re (1987-1990), Enrico Ferrarin (1990-1994), Ivano Cargnello (1994-1998), Enrico Ferrarin (1998-2002), Gustavo Mion (2002-2003), Ivano Cargnello (2003-2005), Roberto Mazzolin (2005-2009), Enrico Ferrarin (2010-2014), (Roger Serafini (2014-2018), Ivano Cargnello (2018-2020).

Italo-Canadian Senior Citizens

The non-profit social was begun by Gino Tiezzi in 1976. Originally restricted to men only, the club opened its doors to women upon suggestion of Tiezzi's wife. The original founders include: Gino Tiezzi, President; Andrea Carrier, Parroco; Andrea Bortolotto,

Vice President; Domenico Russo, Secretary; Sam Macli, Treasurer. Counselors: Antonietta Casagrance, Antonio Donatucci, Vernardo Campagna, Salvatore Musca, Luigi Vecchio, Pietro Graziani, Amadeo Pagani, Francesco Smillovich. Mario Pontiroli served as Group Coordinator, while Amadeo Zuana became the club's Accounts Reviewer.

The group is fundamentally a recreational club that programs events for seniors. Monthly dinners, dances, Thursday lunch and bingo, as well as special occasion events for members (such as birthdays or anniversaries) keep the group active and engaged. Minimum age for membership is 50 years.

The Executive at this writing includes: Salvatore Maio, President; Nicola Maroncelli, VicePresident; Rita Antonelli, Secretary; Anna Frabotta, Treasurer; Counselors: Giulio Ricciuito, Amina Maroncelli, Rosa Provenzano, Santina Bellocci, Secondo Barozzi, Jim Corbett, Maria Di Pietto. The Group Coordinator is Santina Di Rienzo.

Juventus Soccer Club

The local Ottawa Juventus Soccer Club Bianco Nero was officially registered on 23 May 23 1991. The club is proudly affiliated with Juventus S.P.A. 1897 Torino, one of the oldest, greatest, and most successful soccer clubs in the world. The founding officers were Franco Ienzi, President; Franco Arlotta, Secretary; Renato Del Cul, Treasurer; with Antonio Battisti, Elio Lepri Berlutti, Raffaele Cellucci, Fidele Palumbo and Paolo Toscano as Directors. The principles underlying the social club are fair play, the friendly sharing of sporting experiences, and learning to appreciate the vicissitudes of both victory and defeat. The club has been active in promoting junior hockey in the Ottawa area. Presidents have included: Joe Cama, Cristina Del Castello, and Tony Panuccio. There are currently 48 members.

Milan Soccer Club of Ottawa

The spirit of the *rossoneri* is alive in the Milan Soccer Club of Ottawa. Officially affiliated with the Associazione Calcio Milan S.p.A, the local sports club was founded by a group of loyal fans in 1987. Presidents have included Tony di Domenico, Vito Merenda, Giuseppe Nicastro, and current President Eugenio Bubba. The club boasts 45 official members and a battery of fans throughout the community. It is very active in local events and helps organize a yearly soccer party that embraces all local soccer clubs in a spirit of mutual friendship and sportsmanship.

St. Anthony's Knights of Columbus Council 11726

The fraternal benefit society known as The Knights of Columbus was chartered by the Connecticut state legislature on 2 March 1882, thanks to the efforts of Father Michael J. McGivney, assistant pastor of St. Mary's Church in New Haven. The aim of the society was to encourage men to follow the Charity, Unity, Fraternity, and Patriotism. The knights are still true to their founding principles. Over the years the single council has grown to 15,900 councils worldwide with 1.9 million members throughout the United States, Canada, the Philippines, Mexico, Poland, the Dominican Republic, Puerto Rico, Panama, the Bahamas, the Virgin Islands, Cuba, Guatemala, Guam, Saipan, Lithuania, Ukraine, and South Korea. Originally formed to render financial aid to members and their families, the knights provide assistance to the sick, disabled, needy members and their families. Educational, charitable, religious, social welfare, war relief and public relief works are also part of the social, economic, and intellectual fellowship promoted the group.

In Ottawa, the St. Anthony's Knights of Columbus was established in March of 1996 by Sylvio Lemire and Giovanni Manca. The founding Executive included Marco Pagani, Founding Grand Knight; Giovanni Manca, Deputy Grand Knight; Bernard Battistin, Financial Secretary; Raffaele Pagani, Treasurer. The newly founded mission aligned itself with the initial vision of Father McGivney and sought to aid the community of St. Anthony's parishioners by organizing community events, fundraisers, and by contributing money to the parish and local charitable organizations. The local knights have donated over $100,000 and countless volunteer hours towards the aims of the group. Noteworthy events have included hosting Knights of Columbus Degree Ceremonies, numerous church fundraisers, basketball free-throw competitions for St. Anthony's School, and organizing the annual St. Anthony's Church Barbecue during Italian week. The local council continues its activities and maintains a membership of over 60 knights.

Patrica Social Club

The notion for an Ottawa based Patrica Social Club sprang in 1993 during the tenth anniversary celebrations of the Toronto Patrica association. Discussions among the Ottawa attendees eventually led to the birth of the Ottawa sister club. Founded by Bruno Giammaria in 1994, the original group numbered only 45. Its spirit of cooperation and fraternization, however, was immense. In its heyday, the club held annual dinners, regular group trips to Toronto, Niagara Falls, and the United States. Its most important festivities were normally held at Tudor Hall, (owner Franco Giammaria, a proud son of Patrica) include the *Festa della Famiglia, Festa della Fondazione,* and the *Festa di San Rocco.*

The original Exevcutive Committee elected 17 April 1994 was comprised of Bruno Giammaria, President; Franco Giammaria, Vice President; Ernesto Pantusa, Secretary; Patrizia Giammaria, Treasurer. Counselors: Gina Costanza, Isabella Pantusa, Norma Giammaria, Francesca Giammaria, Maria Pia Palma, Lisa Giammaria.

Società Sicula

On 2 January 1973, Padre Sebastiano Pagano, Antonio Cuffaro, Antonio Prinzo, Carmelo Gagliano, Paolo Diaguardi, Giuseppe Pappalardo, Dott. Ladelpha, Antonio Princiotta, Pat Piemonte, Domenico Lentini, Carmelo Giambillo, Giuseppe Lamonica, met to found the Società

Sicula, an association dedicated to the promotion of the culture, traditions, and wellbeing of Sicilians and friends of Sicily in Ottawa. The group is long-standing member member of the *Assessorato Regionale del Lavoro della Regione Siciliana* and is an Incorporated Patented Society Chartered by the Province of Ontario.

The club no longer charges dues to its membership in an effort to promote the notion of Italianicity amongst all members of the Italian-Canadian community. The club hopes to continue its pan-Italian strategy with the scope of promoting cultural events that include cinema viewings, public lectures, culinary evenings, as well as cultural excursopms to Italy. The club promotes the National Congress of Italian Canadians in fundraising efforts but also provides financial assistance to needy families fallen on hard times in the Italian-Canadian community. A very noble organization that is proud of its 200 members that include over 40 Medical Doctors, 30 practicing engineers, and a myriad of diverse professionals within their ranks. The club's cofounder, Tony Cuffaro, remains its most ardent supporter and indefatigable worker.

Club Vicentini di Ottawa

One of the oldest and most active associations in the community, the Club Vicentini was founded in the Fall of 1969 and celebrated its 50 year anniversary in 2019. The current President is Mario Cinel. He has been President for many years and has led the club with dignity, distinguished activity, and calm grace. The club is part of the larger *Associazione Vicentini nel Mondo* and dedicated to the promotion of every form of activity suitable to the preservation and strengthening of bonds and relationships with their common land of origin. Their mandate: to maintain and strengthen friendships. The local chapter was founded by Giancarlo Errante, President; Giorgio Zanetti, Vice-President; Giorgio Grappolini, Secretary; Mario Dal Grande, Treasurer; Tarcisio Caron, Umberto De Pretto, and Renzo Fracasso, Counsellors.

PROFESSIONAL GROUPS AND ENTITIES
The Canadian Italian Business and Professional Association (CIBPA)

One of the oldest professional associations in the community is the Italian Business and Professional Men's Association (currently CIBPA). Founded by three local businessmen, Nicholas Di Labio, Amelio Durie, and Benny Licari in 1961, the association wished to promote "strong community and family ties," take "pride in our [Italian] heritage," and contribute to the cultural, business, and social facets in Ottawa and Canada." From its outset, the association wished to create a social network that united business and professional persons of Italian heritage in order to foster the general welfare of the Italian community by promoting "higher social, business, cultural and professional standards." Towards these ends, the name of the association was changed to the Italian Canadian Business and Professional Association in the 1970's, reflecting a modern and less gendered business and professional profile. In June of 1989, CIBPA became a founding member of the National Federation of Canadian and Italian Business and Professional Associations Inc. This established a national network and voice for the many businessmen chapters that spread throughout Canada.

CIBPA has been active in local community events since its founding. For over 25 years, the Association organized the *Carnevale Italiano*, first held on 14 February 1965 under the chairmanship of Sal Pantalone. The popular event engaged the entire community and normally sold over 6,000 tickets. It was the premier winter event in the City of Ottawa before the advent of Winterlude. It has remained at the forefront of iconic community events and projects that include the *Carnevale Italiano* and the Central Canada Exhibition Parade. CIBPA is also a major supporter of The Villa Marconi Centre. In 2002, CIBPA Ottawa established a scholarship program that assists worthy students of Italian-Canadian heritage who reside in Ontario in their post-secondary studies. Since its inception, the program has awarded more than $50,000 to commendable Italian-Canadian students.

CoMiTes

The *Comites*, or *Comitato degli Italiani all'Estero*, (acronym for Committee of Italians Living Abroad) are democratically elected representative bodies of Italian communities residing outside of Italy. Members of *Comites* are elected on the basis of lists of candidates signed by Italians residing in each consular district. Established by proclamation by the Italian Parliament in 1985, the committee is active in circumscriptions where at least three thousand Italian nationals reside and are registered in the updated AIRE (*Anagrafe Italiani Residenti all'Estero*; Registry of Italians Living Abroad), a list referred to in Art. 5, paragraph 1, as promulgated in Law 459/2001.

The role of each individual *Comites* committee is to identify the socio-cultural needs of its constituency in order to act as an effective liaison for defining frameworks of cooperation with the Italian diplomatic and consular missions in the district in which it operates. Towards this end, each *Comites* committee seeks to develop and promote a myriad of initiatives that contribute to the general well-being of the community it represents. This may include, but is not limited to, promoting opportunities that ensure a sense of meaning, purpose, and belonging to the community, supporting activities that stimulate the collective strength and wellness of the community, initiating scholastic assistance for youth and their professional training, in sport and leisure activities. *Comites* is especially concerned in ensuring equal civic opportunities to members of the Italian community residing in its district.

But the *Comites* is also invested by consular authority to perform a host of activities that include the protection of the rights and civic interests of Italian citizens residing in the consular district, with particular regard to the defense of civil rights guaranteed to Italian workers by the laws in force in the individual countries. It collaborates with the consular authority for the purposes of compliance with employment contracts and the granting of benefits granted by countries where the Committee is based in favor of Italian citizens. It may report to the consular authority any violations of the rules of local, international and EU legislation that damage Italian citizens. In short, the powers and initiatives of *Comites* committees are many and are moved by a mandate that favors the cultural and recreational well being of the Italian community it serves.

The Ottawa *Comites* was officially enacted on 29 November 2001 by proclamation of then Ambassador Marco Colombo. The idea for an Ottawa caucus to join those already formed in Toronto, Montreal, Vancouver, and Edmonton, originated with the local CIBPA and its spokesman Augusto Capitani. Community elections were held in Spring 2001. The first elected *Comites* committee was formed by: Marco Pagani, President; Romano Molo, Vice President; Annamaria Borrello, Secretary; Fiore Pace, Treasurer; and Counselors: Sharon Buglione, Luigi Carozzi, Elio Coppola, Maddalena Ianniti, Antonino Mazza, Franco Ricci, Caterina Vogrig, Patrizia Vogrig. Coopted Members: Rosanna Antinarella, Danita Midena, Del Gesso Giampiero, and Office Assistant: Rina Mafrici.

Since its founding, the committee has sponsored and participated in local community activities, supported Italian language teaching, organized well-attended cultural events, and has been a positive driving force in promoting civic equity for the community's many cultural and regional associations. Of special note, among its many initiatives *Comites* Ottawa sponsors a yearly *Italian of the Year Award* that recognizes two individuals, a man and a woman, who have contributed significantly to the promotion and enhancement of Italian culture and identity in the Ottawa region in activities that may range from the cultural to the entrepreneurial, from the arts to sports.

At this writing, members of the *Comites* include: Francesco di Candia, President; Giuseppe Pasian, Vice President; Antonio Romeo, Executive Counselor; David Mollica, Secretary; Mariano Carrozza, Treasurer; and Counselors Olimpia Bevilacqua, Delio D'Angelo, Corrado Nicastro, Frank Palermo, Tony Prinzo.

The Italian Canadian Community Centre of the National Capital Region Inc.

The Italian Canadian Community Centre of the National Capital Region Inc. was incorporated in 1995. The first directors were President

Angelo Filoso, Vice President Gino Buffone, Secretary Pat Adamo, Treasurer Nello Bortolotti and Director Peter Scott. The organization has worked tirelessly in support of St. Anthony's Church since its first day of operation. Whether it be the renovation of walls, the reparation of exterior stairs, or restoration of statues, the Centre remains at the forefront of community initiatives to sustain and enrich St. Anthony's Church and its parishioners. But the Centre has also promoted fundraising efforts for numerous projects in the community. These include: the operation of a regular Bingo event since 1997 that has raised in excess of $175,000; the construction of a handicap ramp for St. Anthony's Church; $113,000 for the restoration of the stained-glass windows of St. Anthony's Church by Guido Nincheri; the reconstruction of Piazza Dante and the raising of over $500,000; the creation of the Historical Wall in Piazza Dante commemorating the Italian-Canadian soldiers who died in the WWII and members of the local community who were interned.

The Centre is also active in National Capital Region projects. It has co-sponsored events with Opera Lyra, with the Ottawa Senators Foundation, it has organized cultural exchanges between Italy and Canada for the Ottawa Firefighters, and has worked unremittingly in fundraising drives for The Villa Marconi Centre. No cause is too large, no event too small. The Centre works with all community groups in an effort to improve and consolidate community life.

The Italian Canadian Historical Centre

Situated as an entry portal to the Marconi Centre, The Italian Canadian Historical Centre's mandate is to contain and preserve primary source documents that pertain to Ottawa's Italian Canadian community. It also serves to recognize, protect, and perpetuate the important contributions that Italians have made across Canada. It thus serves as a memory institution for both local and national Italian-Canadian culture, supports scholarly research and community projects, as well as formal and informal learning and research activities.

The Centre was officially inaugurated on 29 January 2013 with initial funding from the Federal Government's Community Historical Recognition Program, the Ontario Provincial Government, as well as the City of Ottawa. It operates with the official patronage of the Embassy of Italy. During its short history, The Centre has become the official venue for many historical, cultural, and educational activities. Primary among these is the story of the Italian internment experience that has been captured in literary, filmic and archival objects. It also reviews and accepts donated personal or family memories and histories into its collection. These accounts help construct a shared community meaning from individually lived historical experiences.

The Centre is open to the public and used by many of the local Italian-Canadian associations and clubs (as well as other ethno-cultural communities) in the Capital region. In its short tenure, it has become a true focal point for the community, a willing guide to the community's past and optimistic leader towards its future.

The Italian Canadian Youth Formation Centre

Today's increasingly globalised economy and effortless communication suggests an ever-broadening interaction across cultures in a manner never before imagined. In such a world, the importance of learning a second language, along with the ability to function comfortably within a second culture becomes self-evident. Learning a second language helps one to communicate across cultures and to conduct business in lands one may never have previously considered viable markets or enriching destinations. Imagine the importance, then, of providing language and cultural training to the Italian-Canadian youth of one's own community.

This is the motivating spirit of the Italian Canadian Youth Formation Centre, an incorporated non-profit organization, founded in 1974, with the purpose of fostering Italian language and culture in Ottawa. Though not officially located on Preston Street, the Centre nevertheless is a lynch pin of the Ottawa Italian-Canadian community. Begun primarily as a Saturday morning school program focusing mainly on the teaching of Italian language and culture at the elementary level, the Centre has evolved to offer adult courses as well. For the Centre, Italian is the gateway to a world of knowledge, commerce, and culture; a lingua franca that gives each student access to their heritage, traditions, and culture in a way that other languages cannot.

The Centre seeks to maintain the highest levels of professionalism and operates its elementary and adult programs in co-operation with the *Conseil des Écoles Catholiques de Langue Française du Centre Est* (Council of French-language Catholic Schools in the Center-East Ward). It normally employs between 10 to 17 instructors, a Director of the educational program, one secretary and an adequate number of supply instructors. An 11-member Board of Directors advises the Director of the educational programs who, in turn, makes recommendations to the Board of Education regarding curriculum and staffing. The Board of Directors also makes decisions regarding the Centre's many other activities. These include: cultural and school exchanges with Italy, professional development workshops and symposia for teachers of Italian language and culture, as well as annual summer camps for children. A Parents' Committee is also elected annually to provide feedback to the Director of the educational program regarding school-related events. The Parents' Committee is also active in fundraising efforts and community support, and helps provide the supplemental funding needed for extra-curricular activities such as traditional dancing.

The Centre relies upon three main sources of funding to support its initiatives: The Ontario Government's Ministry of Education and Training, the government of Italy's Ministry of External Affairs and International Cooperation, and the Parents' Committee. Together, these sources provide funding for staff, site rental, textbooks and educational materials, and support for many special initiatives.

St. Anthony's Ladies Aid

In 1948, Father Jerome Ferraro, Pastor of St. Anthony's Church, approached a group of 10 women of the Parish and suggested they form a charitable group with the mandate of aiding the Church,

St. Anthony's School, and the community. Many of these women had spouses who belonged to the all male Sons of Italy and the St. Vincent de Paul Society yet were already active in helping regardless of the community event. Many, born and schooled in Ottawa, helped newly arriving immigrants settle into the community in the aftermath of WWII.

The newly formed charitable group was aptly named St. Anthony's Ladies Aid (Auxiliary). The first elected Madame President was Eleanor Menchini Guzzo. The group soon proved popular enough to hold a regular Sunday afternoon monthly meeting that was soon moved to the first Wednesday of each month. The meetings were held at 77 Norman Street in the home of Mary and Domenic Disipio up to 1995.

Though the meetings were primarily devoted to discussing ways to serve their parish, school, and community, an active social network was quickly formed that spawned long-lasting friendships. The members soon became a sisterhood that supported each other and their community during family events such as births, baptisms, marriages, deaths and burials. A key element of their aid was sustainment during personal strife.

In those early days, the group held Saturday bingo nights to help pay the mortgage on the new Church Hall. The all-volunteer group continues to hold fundraising events year-round with all proceeds donated to charitable causes in the community that include, to name only a few, The Dalhousie Food Cupboard, The Villa Marconi Center, St. Anthony's School, and of course, the Church. Their social events enriched the community with initiatives such as the much-anticipated annual pasta feast held during the St. Anthony's Day celebration, or the annual Communion Mass and Breakfast, normally held on the Sunday following Easter and generously catered by the Knights of Columbus. The Ladies Aid annually holds a popular bake sale and many of those recipes are found in their cookbook, *The Spirit of our Kitchen*.

A wonderful initiative called the "Friendly Visiting Program," sponsored by UIM (Union of Italians in the World) once saw members visit lonely and often isolated seniors in the Italian-Canadian community who have requested social companionship.

But as much as the ladies accomplished in their outreach and parochial duties, they also left time to enjoy each other's company in their many planned trips outside of Ottawa. Past excursions have taken them to Expo 67, St. Joseph's Oratory in Montreal, and Villa Colombo in Toronto. Shopping getaways to Syracuse, Watertown, Montreal and New York City were always popular and fruitful.

The group recently celebrated its 70th anniversary and remains socially active and relevant in the lives of many women. Membership has currently peaked at 50 and is comprised of women aged 30 to active 92. Many members represent multi-generations as mothers entice daughters who bring granddaughters, while sisters, aunts, and cousins all commit to the inspirational string of becoming lifelong friends. This true sisterhood still marks the cornerstone of Christian faith, hope and charity proudly sustains the rich traditions of their shared Italian ancestry.

Notable past presidents include Lena Cuccaro (25 years) and Jennie Prosperine, an indefatigable worker whose service to the community has been recognized with awards and honors. This type of unselfish service to the community continues in the most recent Past President, Trina Costantini-Powell who served for 12 years before becoming President of the Ottawa chapter of the National Congress of Italian Canadians.

Symptomatic of current times, however, we are saddened to learn that St. Anthony's Ladies Aid, similar to many worthwhile and energetic groups to grace the community, is also closing shop after 71 years. Although membership remains solid and the need for community aid is still present, a lack of interest in holding executive positions signals the end of this longstanding and benevolent community mainstay.

The Ottawa Philodramatics

The Filodrammatica Drama Company of Ottawa was born on a whim. In the late 1990s, Matildi Zinni, President of the Golden Age Group, would stage theatrical presentations at Christmas in order to entertain the residents of Villa Marconi. Members of the community were invited to act in these friendly productions that quickly gained the sympathy of participants and audience alike, lending the actors welcomed notoriety and local fame. The small drama troupe soon began to present authored theatrical pieces in community venues that included the Villa Marconi community center, St. Anthony's Church, as well as the Laurentian High School auditorium.

The actors and directors of the troupe are worth mentioning and included: Elio Coppola, Daniele Ruiu, Alfredo Mazzanti. The actors include Elio and Renata Coppola, Pasquale and Maddalena Iannitti, Antonio Mauriello, Fabio Romano, Lucio Appolloni, Franca Bellizzi, Barbara Rizzi, Orazio Rizzi, Marco Agostini, Ugo Silvaroli, Nilde Morielaz, Nick Urban, Elvira Boselli, Franca Mastroluisi , Mario Cospito, Davide Cospito, Maria Serena Cospito, Maria Antonietta Fiori Paolo Siraco, Ivano Cargnello among others. Set production normally came under the aegis of Antonietta De Giovanni.

Theatrical productions worth mentioning include: *Ditegli sempre di sì* by Edoardo De Filippo; *Maneggi per sposare una figlia* by Niccolò Bacigalupo; *Due dozzine di rose scarlatte* by Aldo De Benedetti; *Peppone e Don Camillo* by Giovannino Guareschi; *La sposa venessiana* by Mirella Ioly. The group's last performance, *La Patente* by Luigi Pirandello, directed by Manuel Caro Torres, was held in December 2017 at Villa Marconi under the aegis of Ottawa's Dante Alighieri and the Ottawa Comites.

The Ottawa UIM

The UIM, or Union of Italians in the World, is a non-profit organization whose aim is to assist members of the Italian-Canadian community. Although autonomous by statute, the UIM shares the scope and aims of ITAL-UIL and undertakes socio-cultural activities that benefit the needs of the local community. The UIM was founded in Rome in 1995 by the ITAL-UIL and remains under its patronage. The Ottawa branch was founded soon afterwards by Berardino Carrozzi who also became its first President. Succeeding presidents have included Luigi Ricottili, Elio Coppola, and Lucio Appolloni. The current president is Maddalena Iannitti; the Vice president is Michele Di Pentima.

The Ottawa UIM has organized information events on Italalian legal matters for the community and has sponsored many cultural and support projects, especially for the elderly. Among these, the "Friendly Visit," an initiative designed to support the elderly in need of company. These visits then gave rise to the publication of a book, *Pier 21*, that recounts stories of emigration. Today, the UIM continues to work as a voluntary entity in close contact with ITAL-UIL.

CONSTRUCTION
BUILDING A NATION AND AN IDENTITY

Ethnicity is a social paradigm that undergoes a continuous process of renegotiation, of re-visitation, of adaptation, of deliberate and, above all, laborious construction. There is no romanticized history of Italian success, prodigious and widespread across all fields of endeavor and in the farthest reaches of the planet, that does not highlight the reality of often backbreaking labor as the hallmark of Italian immigrancy.

It is the laborer who, in many cases, lost fingers on frozen worksites, lost personal dignity in dirty menial tasks, lost their lives in the bowels of the earth, survived the intolerable conditions of garment industry sweatshops, accepted their fateful exploitation on the factory assembly line, all the while enduring the accompanying derisive epithets and frightful prejudices with hard-headed pragmatism. Assimilation is a hard bargain. It is the laborer, it must be said, that provided the steely backbone for any political, social, cultural, or economic success the Italian diaspora may have carved for itself.

Work is the indelible mark of man and an enduring sign of his shared humanity. It is his badge of honor. It is the defining expression of a person operating within a community of persons; and this mark decides the community's intrinsic characteristics. By whatever name: work, toil, travail, industry, sweat, grind, struggle, or drudgery, labor constitutes the very nature of community.[57] Laborers merit special attention as their work produces tangible evidence of a community's passing.

Many of those arriving in Canada did not intend to remain. Searching only the opportunity to work and send money to their

---

57 "By the sweat of your face you shall eat bread, till you return to the ground, for out of it you were taken; for you are dust, and to dust you shall return." *The New Oxford Annotated Bible, Genesis* 3:19.

families back home, seasonal laborers departed for their villages yearly; and indeed, a not insignificant number returned to Italy permanently.

Why? Because staying exacted a toll.[58] The economic benefits of becoming a future middle-class Canadian included the mixed-blessing of displacement and personal adaptation. The arriving immigrants were an insular people deeply rooted in local village tradition and place. Their arrival into a relatively modern and alien world and inhospitable climate triggered a protective existential reaction that refused to completely surrender identifying markers from the past. Very few, if any, immigrants arrived with marketable skills. At a time when a strong back and stubborn necessity were the only sellable requisites, many simply exchanged the burdensome farm toil of sharecropping for the steady drudgery and sweat of construction. They toiled as the classic pick-and-shovel immigrant, digging ditches, cleaning sewers, melting steel and becoming, in the disparaging words of contemporary historians, part of the human dung that fertilized industrial growth.

Rewards were immediate and palpable. Homes were purchased, families grew, children were educated. Yet the psychic sense of displacement due to the unending routine of uninterrupted seasonal labor was long-term. It is a process that spanned and often continues to influence the successive generations that followed their fathers onto worksites. The loss of traditions and a psychic sense of displacement in these youth commix with the decided benefits of becoming a middle-class Italian-Canadian. There are always two sides to every bargain.

The two primary facets for immigrant Italians normally revolved around the central core of work and family. Their work on roads, tunnels, dams and railways, their tedious labor in factories and mines,

---

58   In "Assimilation is a Brutal and Necessary Bargain," political scientist Peter Skerry writes that assimilation "has typically meant that immigrants have adapted and changed in disparate domains, rejecting their immigrant past in some ways (forgetting their parents' mother tongue and speaking English, or learning to tolerate individuals with sharply different values) and holding on to other aspects of their heritage (ethnic cuisine, specific religious holidays, family traditions from the homeland)." In response to the question "Can America Remain a Nation of Immigrants in the 21st Century?" 20 October 2014. See the *Law and Liberty* blog at: https://www.lawliberty.org/.

their perilous toil on suspended scaffolding built the infrastructure of nations and granted them an economic anchor. Their dedication to family, children, traditions, and faith generated the social foothold centered on the home, church, and ethnic associations.

Joining, or better, forging a successful laboring class implicated the loss of a romanticized old neighborhood for the greener lawns of larger suburban houses and more prosperous future. Despite the long hours and usually backbreaking work, many of these laborers became businessmen, thereby creating conditions that ensured job opportunities for their fellows and subsequent immigrant arrivals. Slowly, a few became successful and pragmatic entrepreneurs.

There are many Italian and Italian-Canadian entrepreneurs in the Ottawa region that dedicated their talents to the construction trade. These are individuals that measured themselves by a different yardstick and navigated their way into the Canadian mainstream by a slightly different route. Driven by an unconscionable faith in progress, they became prominent industry players with local, regional, sometimes international impact.

Though I will concentrate on those whose name and reputation has moved beyond the confines of the Italian-Canadian community of Ottawa, this by no means disparages or neglects the many small, middle, and larger companies that built, be it said, Canada. This company of men admits that they aren't any better than others. They merely represent the brighter lights in a general fluorescence of Italians and Italian-Canadians in the Canadian building industry, a fluorescence that is confirmed and measured on a continuing daily basis.

The following lists are not complete. They suffer not from my own wanted neglect but by the sheer impossibility of assembling all the successful persons who eventually created thriving companies. Despite my online, and archival research, my many queries to community members and colleagues, my repeated efforts to contact the greatest number of companies possible, and my desire to include the greatest number of companies possible, I am able to mention only the most prominent and better known companies.[59]

---

59   The number of companies that did not reply to my queries or complete my questionnaire is unfortunate.

I hope in this small way, however, to give a flavor of the supreme professionalism, dignity, perseverance, intelligence, pride, and downright spunk that every Italian-Canadian laborer, whether past, present, or emerging future entrepreneur, commands.

Bellai Brothers Construction Ltd.

Bellai Brothers Construction Ltd. is an Italian-Canadian company engaged in every type of construction activity in the Ottawa-Gatineau area. The company was founded by Antonio Bellai, patriarch of a large extended family that remembers him as a hard worker and proletarian philosopher. "Do what you love and you will stay young," was his motto and credo in life.

Antonio's love for stone and masonry work began in San Martino di Lupari (Veneto) where he learned his trade working in local churches. At the age of 17 he felt the urge to broaden his artisanal skills and, like many youth, left Italy for Switzerland, eventually immigrating to Canada in 1950 because he had heard of the need for skilled laborers. He settled in Toronto, ultimately moving to Ottawa where he worked for Mel Durie Marble and Tile. Antonio's professional ambition and restless spirit soon had him searching for renewed challenges. And so in 1954 he founded Bellai Brothers with his newly arrived brother Rizzieri. In very short order, no job was too big or too complex. Their reputation for honesty, integrity, and hard work quickly placed them on the top of the list of Ottawa contractors and they were soon involved with major projects with the major regional players including Irving Greenberg and Minto Developments.

During the 60s and 70s the company was involved with many of Ottawa's capital projects, notable among these the Terrace La Chaudiere for Robert Campeau, The National Gallery of Canada, and the Museum of Civilization, the Library of Parliament, Canadian War Museum, National Archives, CBC Building, World Exchange Plaza, Constitution Square, Canadian Tire Place, and the Ottawa International airport. Indeed, it is almost impossible to travel the streets of the National Capital Region without espying a building, bridge, or monument that has not been constructed or rehabilitated by Bellai Brothers Construction.

Winners of numerous awards, a proud moment was the *Premiazione del Lavoro, del Progresso Economico dei Padovani che hanno onorato l'Italia nel Mondo*[60] given to the Bellai brothers Antonio and Rizzieri in 2004 by the Chamber of Commerce of the city of Padova. They are also founding members of the Canadian Construction Association, known as the CCA for short.

From its humble, but genuinely artisan stone and mason beginnings, the company has evolved over the years to specialize in structural concrete work for buildings, footings, and concrete walls. It now serves the Industrial, Institutional, Commercial, and Residential sectors. Their services include low-rise and high-rise formwork, concrete placing and finishing, mobile concrete pumping, mobile and tower cranes.

But despite their role and influence across the region, the company remains a quiet family business, true to the temperament, beliefs, and demeanor of the original founders: simple men who enjoyed simple pleasures. The company has remained a family business. Besides Romeo and Gianni (sons of Antonio), Mirella and Nadia (daughters of Rizzieri), and Sonia (daughter of Antonio), along with cousins Pietro and Gianni as co-presidents, agile management keeps the company running smoothly.

Bellai Brothers Construction now numbers 600 employees in all fields of construction including carpentry, masonry, crane operation; it remains heavily engaged in concrete superstructure in the regional Ottawa area.

Central Precast Inc. / The Precast Group

Luigi Mion was born in 1927 a small town near Udine. He immigrated to Canada in 1954 and worked as a laborer on the railway in British Columbia. Drawn to Ottawa by a distant cousin, he quickly found work with Durie Mosaic and Marble, one of the largest suppliers and

---

60   The Award for Work and Economic Progress of Paduans who have Honored Italy in the World.

installers of tile, granite, and marble in the area. In 1956, Luigi's keen insight, skills and personal strength soon channelled his bountiful energy towards a small garage on Preston Street where, armed with a bag of cement, a wheelbarrow and a telephone, he and a long-time friend began a small business that produced concrete patio slabs and steps. In 1958, the fledgling company, now named Central Precast, moved to St Laurent Boulevar where the company product line was expanded to include manholes, catch-basins, and concrete poles. By 1963, land expropriation, forced the company to move to its present location in Nepean. Shortly afterwards, Luigi's younger brother, Gustavo, joined the company as plant manager.

Times were good, business was booming. As the city of Ottawa grew, so did the company product line that now included precast precast panels and utility boxes. In 1976 Luigi bought his partner's shares. In the early 80's his two sons John and Rudy joined the business and he began diversifying the company to include sister companies Utility Structures and M-Con Products. The range of construction materials was again expanded to offer precast cement patio stones, highway barriers, underground structures for sanitary and storm sewers, concrete pipe, architectural panels, interlocking paving stones, concrete poles, Bell and Hydro utility vault structures. Luigi would eventually step back and pass the business to sons John and Rudy and daughters Marcella and Anna in the mid-1990s, but not before establishing a legacy that still resounds in the community.

No man, it has been said, can become rich without himself enriching others. This adage, pronounced by Scottish-American magnate, industrialist, and philanthropist Andrew Carnegie, aptly describes the humanitarian bountifulness of Luigi Mion. Always willing, enthusiastic, persevering, and seemingly tireless, Luigi gave of himself and of his time to countless charities and projects. He served on the Board of Directors for the Ottawa Construction Association, The Ottawa Hospital Foundation, The Kidney Foundation, and of course Villa Marconi where he served as Chair of the Fundraising Committee, but also as President of the Board of Directors for Villa Marconi for many years.

The company, but especially Luigi, has been honored by a multitude of distinguished honors including The Canada Award for Business Excellence for Entrepreneurship, he has been appointed a Knight of the Order of Merit by Rideau Hall, and has received community awards from the former City of Nepean, The City of Ottawa and by the Kidney Foundation's Annual Fundraiser for his philanthropic contributions to the community, from Villa Marconi, and a special award of recognition from his hometown in Italy. Luigi was awarded the Gold Medal for Business Achievement of Success Internationally by the city of Udine, and also granted the title of *Cavaliere* in the Order of Merit of the Italian Republic by the Italian Parliment for his lifetime dedication to public service, social, philanthropic, and humanitarian activities.

The company today is very distant from the company John and Rudy assumed from their father. In 2001, the brothers opened the largest paver plant in North America in Metcalfe Ontario (eventually sold to Oldcastle/CRH). In 2005 a second M Con location was opened in Cambridge to serve the southern Ontario market. The company continued to expand Central Precast and sister companies Utility Structures and M-Con Products to meet the ever-growing region of Ottawa and eastern Ontario market. The two operated the companies together up to 2018, when John took sole ownership of Central Precast and M Con. His three sons, Marco, Stefano, and Carlo, the third generation of Mion, have all joined the company.

Together with their cousins Claudio, Carlo, and nephew, John has begun the next chapter for the amalgamated companies, now called the Precast Group. John has restructured the companies to allow growth and responsibilities for the next generation, allowing them the same opportunities that his father provided him and his brother. Ottawa has reached 1,000,000 in population and as such the demands for their many construction products has never been greater. Though there is inevitable inertia in any trade, as long as roads need repair, highways require expansion, and buildings keep reaching skyward, The Precast Group is determined to remain at pace with demand. The family remains proud of their heritage and faithful to the lessons of hard work and sacrifice bequeathed them by the legacy of their father.

De Marinis Group of Companies

When Vincenzo De Marinis (Jimmy to his friends), arrived in Ottawa in November 1950, he was part of the immigration chain that had brought a good number of Abruzzesi from their hometown of Pretoro to the Canadian capital. His wife, Rosa Salvatore, arrived in Ottawa in May 1952 from Rapino, a neighboring town.

A Master mason, Jimmy quickly found work and his skills were soon part of the crew building the new extension to the Prescott Hotel in 1951. His persistence, drive, and above all, skills as a Master mason, soon drove him to begin his own company in 1958: De Marinis Construction Ltd..

1960s Ottawa was on the cusp of transformation into a capital city. With major parts of its commercial heritage purchased by the federal authority preserved for national purposes, the newly constituted National Capital Commission became the principal steward of significant public places. The De Marinis Construction company was especially prepared and poised to become a creative partner committed to providing quality masonry services on new and existing structures in the growing capital.

By 1962, the company won a major project: the Edgeworth Apartments on Carling Avenue. To handle the work, Jimmy hired a larger workforce to meet the occasion and began another company: D.M.A. Masonry Ltd.. Many more projects followed and include the Billings Bridge office tower, the Public Service Alliance Building, as well as many buildings on the Carleton University campus. As the workforce grew to over 250, the two companies also restored the O'Keefe Brewery in Lebreton Flats, Canada Packers (Maple Leaf Foods) in Hull, the Pure Spring Building, refurbished St. St. Anthony's Church, and built the church hall and daycare center. Large-scale projects were also tackled and encompass many 1967 Centennial projects such as the Bell and Merivale arenas, the Nepean Sportsplex, the Walter Baker Sports Complex, the Ottawa Public Library, the Nepean Police Station, the Heart Institute at the Civic Hospital, and the Teron Albert Street Hotel (presently the Sheraton Ottawa Hotel).

While success is ephemeral in all areas of life, it can indeed be defined in the actions that bring joy, a sense of accomplishment, and community service. For Jimmy De Marinis, the philosophy of life was simple: "in life, we must not become angry with all of the rocks that we trip upon as we follow our chosen path but, rather, we need to move forward." Sons Mario and Tony have continued the proud tradition of their father. In 1979 they founded their own business, De Marinis (DMA) Inc., a multi-award-winning company specializing in masonry, stonework and the restoration of historic masonry structures.

The contemporary trend of saving existing historical structures has worked in the company's favor. Their contracts are normally high profile and dot the most important corners of the Ottawa region. The highly specialized niche company remains involved in the ongoing restoration work on Parliament Hill but has also completed work on the Victoria Memorial Museum, the Cartier Square Armoury (for which it received the Ottawa Architectural Conservation Award), the National Library and National Archives exterior restoration, and the Chambers project on Elgin Street. A challenging project was the restoration of the Earnscliffe Residence, former home of Sir John A. MacDonald and now the residence of the British High Commissioner. Says Tony De Marinis: "Along with stone repointing and restoration of the exterior, we had to rebuild eight masonry chimneys on top of the roof, which was difficult because of the various slopes of the roof."

But the company is not limited to historic restoration and is both masterful and proficient in masonry work on new commercial, institutional, government, and residential buildings. In addition to the stone selection, anchorage & support details, drawings, and stonework on the Canadian Museum of Contemporary Photography, their most recent projects include the addition at the Lord Elgin Hotel and the Granite Ridge Long Term Care Residence in Stittsville.

The company has been continuously recognized for its state-of the-art work and is gracious recipient of many numerous and prestigious awards that include 2000 Ottawa Architectural Conservation Award of Excellence – Special Category for the Plaza Bridge/ Confederation Square Restoration project, the Masonry Project Design Award Competition for St. Peter Catholic High School in Cumberland, and have received the Gold Seal Certification for their work as Project

Managers in Restoration of Historic Masonry and Stonework, to name a limited few.

Mario and brother Tony are the only two Gold Seal certified project managers in the field of historic masonry structure restoration. And indeed, it is difficult to speak of one brother without mentioning the accomplishments of the other as their symbiotic relationship extends beyond family and onto the professional field. Mario was the 2000 winner of the Canadian Masonry Contactors Association's Outstanding Achievement Award. He has served on the CMCA's Board of Directors and was the association's President between 1997 and 2000. Tony has served on the Board of Directors of the Ottawa Construction Association from 1995-2002 and was the Board's Chairman in 2000. He was on the Board of Directors of the Ontario Masonry Contractors Association from 1995 to 2017 and was President from 1999 to 2001.

The brothers invest heavy time and mentoring effort in the Ontario Masonry Training Centre (OMTC), an institution that trains future masons and for which Tony has served as Chairman since 2000. He has also provided leadership as Chair of the Provincial Advisory Committee for Brick and Allied Crafts. The brothers are also an active ambassadors for the industry. For Tony, "there are always fads and different kinds of designs and finishes, and a lot of times people just come back to masonry. It is tested and has long-lasting quality."

Father Jimmy would be proud of both not solely for the efforts and accomplishments of his sons who have become and remain prime movers in the construction industry but because they are also distinguished promoters of one of the oldest and noblest of professions, masonry, and lead by intelligent example and hard work.

Durie Mosaic and Marble / Instile Design Build

Brad Durie is proud of his Italian heritage. A certified Marble and Tile Mechanic, as well as a certified Heritage Stone Restoration Mason, he inherited a love or marble and stone from his grandfather. The dictates of genetics might guarantee children the same eye color as the father or the same gait. But not much can ensure that a child will share the same interests and passions, let alone inheriting the same career as the old man, or indeed the great grandfather.

Amelio (Mel) Durie (the original family name was Duri), great grandfather, Ignatius (Ignatcio), and his three sisters arrived at Ellis Island, New York from Udine in 1927. Rather than remaining in the United States, familial ties pulled them towards Toronto where they settled with their aunt. Amelio attended school for two years but soon began work in the tile trade, eventually managing a branch office of DeSpirit Tile and Marble in Kirkland Lake.

In 1945 he opened a field office in Ottawa for the same company which he eventually purchased in 1948. He changed the name to Durie Mosaic and Marble; the final e was added to Duri to anglicise the company profile. Even in those early days, the company engaged over 100 employees. Mel filled his labor ranks with newly arriving immigrants, mostly Italian. Indeed, the company became both a haven and a training ground for arriving masons. Many of Ottawa's successful individuals and future trade companies cut their teeth with Durie Tile & Marble.

From the beginning the company was a family-run business that included Brad's father and three uncles. It was Durie Mosaic and Marble that supplied and installed most of the tile, granite, and marble to the interiors and exteriors of buildings in the greater Ottawa area between 1948 and the late 1980s. If there was a building that needed stone or marble, Amelio and his crew were the trusted masons and allied craftsmen to complete the job.

The late Amelio Durie supplied and installed most of the tile, granite and marble to a many of the interiors and exteriors of buildings in the greater Ottawa area between 1943 and the late 1980s. "Nonno Amelio," remembers Brad, "was a pioneer in exterior precast, slab granite, terrazzo, tile, marble floors and walls. It can be said, without exaggeration, that any school, mall, hospital, hotel lobby, or large building that boasts terrazzo flooring was probably done under his supervision." Among the many projects the company completed are recognizable Ottawa landmarks and include the Island Park Towers, The Westin Hotel, the National Arts Center, National Defence Headquarters, the CHEO and General hospitals, the Ottawa/Macdonald–Cartier

International Airport. One of Amelio's final jobs before retirement was the construction of the Centennial Flame on Parliament Hill, first lit on New Year's Day in 1967 to mark the 100th anniversary of Canadian Confederation. A fitting memorial to a lifetime of dedicated masonry excellence.

Brad is the fourth generation Durie to join the family business and was involved with installations at a young age. The rest came by osmosis. He remembers hanging-out with his father, Richard, at the workshop. At the age of 15 he worked full-time summers sorting bags of terrazzo, cleaning the shop and loading the trucks in the mornings for the workers. It wasn't long before Brad was on the installation sites helping with installations. Upon successful completion of the necessary schooling and hands on apprenticeship, he became a certified Marble and Tile Mechanic, as well as a certified Heritage Stone Restoration Mason.

His skills have permitted him to work on many notable Ottawa projects and have included, to name only a few, all the exterior walls of the World Exchange Plaza, the Nortel Building, Christ Church Cathedral, the Peace Keeping Monument, all exterior and interior stone and masonry work of the United States Embassy. He was also heavily involved with the rebuilding of the Ottawa Locks, the Rideau Falls, as well as the occasional rebuilding and routine maintenance of the Parliament Hill Buildings.

In 2000, Brad decided to begin his own company and, like his father and grandfather, has never looked back. Four generations of marble and stone purveyors have led to Instile Design Build, one of the most successful companies in the Ottawa Region. The company offers broadened services beyond masonry and, regardless of the size of the job, the company boasts a distinguished list of accomplishments and many satisfied customers. The work, although taxing, is also rewarding. Whether working with architects, builders, or homeowners, he maintains a generational commitment to total client satisfaction that is backed by creativity, innovation, and family reputation, and enduring integrity. Admittedly more artisan than businessman, Brad still remembers the lessons of his great grandfather and grandfather, men who coordinated some of the largest projects in Ottawa at a time when man-power was wanting and skills even fewer.

The Durie family, true pioneers who built the city and whose legacy continues.

Giamberardino Contracting

Giamberardino Contracting is a full-service construction management company and general contractor that specializes in building and maintaining Industrial, Commercial & Institutional Construction. The company was begun by Nick Giamberardino in 1955. Brothers Roberto and Domenico soon joined the company at which point Nick Giamberardino and Brothers was formed. The three brothers remained the driving force behind the company's success and growth for over 40 years.

The company has survived not only the odds brought by competitors in the marketplace but the odds of second-generation passage.[61] Uncle Nick would eventually pass the business torch to his son Carmine, (he actually sold him the company. As Carmine recalls: Uncle Nick always said: "Nothing for Nothing" and has seen the company continue to prosper ever since.

Motivated by all the sad tales of one generation building it, and the next generation squandering it, Carmine, always one to march to the beat of his own drum, didn't want the company to flounder into the status quo. Carmine grew-up in the business; remembers working on site in his teen years, becoming a foreman and then a project manager. He worked his way up the ladder to prove himself and became the owner and trusted President after more than 30 years of practical, hands-on experience. He has ably demonstrated his expertise in all aspects of construction and fine carpentry; the company is deeply rooted in a heritage of craftsmanship.

The company's dedication to detail and commitment to client confidentiality are the reasons why they are called upon to build

---

61 A study of 1,600 family-run businesses conducted by consultancy *PriceWaterhouseCoopers* found that only 36 percent of the businesses surveyed survived passage into the second generation.

and maintain capital investment portfolios that serve both industry leaders in high technology as well as classified government enterprises. Building managers and government development officers know that Giamberardino's team can be trusted to design sustainable action plans that build and maintain capital and business investments with the utmost security. Giamberardino not only manufactures but also maintains professional, fashionable, and truly sophisticated work spaces in the Ottawa area. They are the leader in made-to-measure general contracting because of dedication to detail and total commitment to craftsmanship. The company is proud of its family of career employees that remain loyal and committed to the firm despite the industry tendency towards transient workers. Their list of accomplishments are numerous. Three that stand-out, however, include the personal residence of a past Prime Minister, the Senate Chambers in East Block on Parliament Hill, and the Canada Post Head Quarters. The Company plans to be around for at least another generation . . . or two.

Mar Gard Builders

Entrepreneur Tony Mariani is a local boy with international experience. He is an ambitious man that acts with steely purpose and cold resolve but allows himself room to enjoy and appreciate the beauty and subtleties of his Italian-Canadian roots. This heartfelt earnestness has allowed his natural resourcefulness to experiment and grow in often unexpected ways. More an executer and facilitator than a builder, Tony humbly describes himself as someone "who gets shit done." And indeed his company, Mar Gard Builders Limited, is a leading protagonist in projects that span the civil, mechanical and electrical disciplines throughout Ontario and the Caribbean.

Mar Gard Builders Limited was established in 1986 on little more than a shoestring and a prayer. "I was very scared but at the same time confident I could get the confidence of construction buyers to trust me and allow me to build their projects buildings," Tony recalls. "I was 32 years old, working at Fuller Construction and running a very successful division. I had a wife with two small children. It was July of 1986 and I just did it. I took a leap of faith."

Early in the company's history, an enormous 53,000 sq. ft. project was asking for bids. Tony submitted a proposal, but knew he needed to be bonded. "I was not very financially sound, had been in business only 2 short years, but the bonding agent knew I could get the job done; so he gave me the bond and we were successful in securing the job. It turned the page for us." This initial success bred confidence and, as with so many ambitious individuals, parental world view was a motivating factor. "I was extremely proud the day I took my father to the job site to see the work I had done. My father thought I was the real estate agent for the site. He was so proud when he understood that I was actually the builder."

Shortly thereafter, Tony was chosen as the Construction Expert for Intelcan, a Canadian company building the Havana International Airport in Cuba. This proved to be the experience of a lifetime as he spent 10 years traveling to Cuba to integrate and adapt Canadian construction methods and technology to Cuban government regulations and requirements.

The company continues to do selective design work on projects in the Caribbean and has an extensive list of satisfied customers and the honour of many outstanding building awards including the Butler Building Systems Wise Owl Award for innovation and creativity in Commercial Construction and the Architectural Building Awards. He also sits on the Behlen Building Systems Advisor Council. Known internationally for its quality, experience, and customer commitment, Mar Gard controls all phases of construction, thereby significantly reducing project risk for investors. It has a long history of working with pre-engineered buildings and have expanded their capabilities to include fit-outs, large warehouse complexes, and specialty structural wood ICI buildings. The company's largest timber structure to date is the Kemptville Dental Clinic building in Kemptville, Ontario. Other projects include a Kids' Kingdom facility, a Clean Water Works building, a unique Argyle Cosmetic Surgery building, and the Barrhaven Honda dealership.

The greatest satisfaction, however, is with repeat clients. "All my clients say, 'If you want something done, ask Tony.' That is what I am most of; the respect and confidence of my clients who then become my friends." The company plans to expand its reach into the lucrative, but hard-bid public sector, adding more employees as needed. Whatever the future, Mar Gard Builders will continue to improve and consolidate its presence in the community and abroad as engineering consultants, and revel in the prospect of being responsible for every physical detail of a project from beginning to end.

Nicolini Construction and Engineering Limited Ltd

Nicolini Construction and Engineering Limited Ltd. has been providing construction services for clients across Ottawa and the Ottawa-Valley Region since 1976 and has a long a proud tradition of successful performance in the construction industry. Its founder, Gino Nicolini, a well-known figure in the community, is intimately familiar with local construction conditions, trends, and the specific requirements of his clients. Not surprisingly, the company has delivered a large number of important projects to Federal, Provincial, and local Municipal Government.

NCEL has constructed numerous educational facilities and has completed renovations and additions to existing school buildings on behalf of many of the Ottawa area school boards. They have also constructed buildings, residential high rises and fire stations for the City of Ottawa, as well as industrial projects for various municipalities outside the Ottawa area that include Water Treatment Plants, Waste Water Treatment Plants, and pumping stations.

The company has successfully kept abreast of construction trends and has continued to grow in the multi-faceted and ever-changing construction industry. The ability to respond to a client's business needs, the professional discipline needed to see a project through to its successful and satisfactory completion, and the dedication to get the job done are the hallmark of the company. For Gino Nicolini, "By evolving our experience into better methodologies and improved delivery methods, we allow our clients to benefit from the successes of similar organizations while still obtaining a solution customized to their unique needs." Gino is proud of his company's ability to employ and retain the services of the most qualified professional staff and reliable subcontractors. He is a promoter of the soft skills not taught at college or university such as the ability to effectively communicate, negotiate and judiciously delegate each important task. These are aptitudes are learned on the construction site, and it is Nicolini's contention that qualified resources must be available to the client in a timely manner, that financial control of the client contract is carefully maintained, and that quality control be assured and vigorously monitored at every stage of construction.

Currently retired after practicing his profession for 41 years, Gino recalls the many challenges but above all the experienced solutions that the grand variety of diverse and interesting projects that cap a satisfying career. Of notable significance among these is the People Mover project at the Toronto Zoo. A fully automated Electric powered guiderail system that transported visitors through the Rouge valley site of the Metropolitan Toronto Zoo completed in 1975.

Worthy of mention is the TTC Spadina Subway Rail Vehicle Storage Facility locate immediately north of the Yorkdale Shopping Centre, known as the Wilson Yard. This was followed by another impressive Highway Project, the extension leg of the Don Valley Parkway from Hwy 401 to Steeles Avenue. The extension consisted of 5 miles of highway and 4 bridge structures.

NCEL also contributed to the growth of the City of Ottawa in relevant and timely projects. Most notable is the YOW Control Tower at the Ottawa International Airport constructed in 1989 for Transport Canada. Housing projects for City Living in Ottawa as well as the neighbouring towns of Arnprior, Pakenham, Cornwall, Pembroke, and Greely, to name only a few, populated the rural landscape. NCEL constructed the Blair Road OC Transpo Station in 1997 as well as the Greensboro Station at South Keys. The most noteworthy project for the City of Ottawa was the AAA Baseball stadium known as Lynx Stadium. It was built in a record 10 months.

In the education sector, the company constructed several schools including Saint Marks in Manotick, Mother Teresa in Orleans,

Rockland High School; numerous community centres: Manor Park and Greenboro; and long-term care facilities, especially the Peter D. Clark in Nepean, and of course, the company helped in the construction of the Villa Marconi Community Centre. The company was also responsible for building Firestations throughout the Ottawa area and a wide array of Federal Projects that include the Parliament Hill Aboriginal Conference Room, the Rideau Hall extension and refurbishment, the South African Embassy Addition and Rehab of the Residence.

The lengthy list of accomplishments and high-profile projects is impressive and long. Though retired since 2004, Gino remains active and has served on several Boards both locally and provincially. These include the Ontario Clean Water Agency, the Villa Marconi Long Term Care Board of Directors, and the City of Ottawa Committee of Adjustment.

Rome Floor Cleaners Ltd.

Rags to riches story chronicle the history of anyone who attains far greater success than original circumstances would have indicated as possible. Normally, these individuals defeat circumstances and overcome obstacles to achieve goals. Self-made men attain their success either through education, hard unending work, or sheer willpower.

Joe Cama is proud that he is a self-made man. The founder of Rome Floor Cleaners Ltd., a thriving family business he began in 1969, has recently celebrated its 50th anniversary and demonstrates no signs of stopping. He never imagined that the upstart janitorial business he once ran from his garage on …… Street would one day become one of Ottawa's leading flooring companies. Honesty and respect are the trademark emblems of the company but Joe insists that the major reason for his success is trust. "The person who runs the company makes the name of the company something to trust."

Born in Calabria but reared on the outskirts of Rome, the name seemed a natural extension of his life and ideas of corporate growth. And grow the company did. From humble beginnings as a janitorial service Rome Flooring now offers industrial, commercial and residential janitorial services, floor installation, sanding and refinishing. It has become a major supplier for quality prefinished hardwood flooring as well as laminates and cork flooring products, tile, and stone. All the while building a solid reputation for quality service and customer care.

The fulcrum of the company's success lies in the character of Joe himself. Limited only by his drive and ambition, Joe became a recognizable personality in the community. Whether advancing the business through impeccable customer care, building and coaching soccer teams, leading charitable campaigns, tending to executive board meetings, Joe set a course for greatness and proceeded to work without rest until goals became a reality. He seemed to be everywhere. And everywhere he went honest success followed.

Now semiretired, Joe has placed the next phase of Rome Flooring's growth in the capable hands of his three sons. The thriving company is ably managed by sons Vincent (Site Supervisor), Michael (Vice President), and Mark (Project Manager). "Our size may have changed," state the brothers, "but the company remains focussed on personal care, attention to detail, quality product, and the small finishing touches that guarantee customer satisfaction regardless of job volume."

Located at 4-58 Antares Dr. the company boasts 25 employees, a fleet of 10 vehicles and is the largest Vintage Flooring Dealer in Ottawa. Its product line includes quality materials from industry leaders Torlys, BMB, Loba, and Lauzon.

No longer catering solely to the home improvement projects, the brothers have a resume of prestigious projects across the region. These include the entire Parliament Hill Center Block, the Envie Student Residences, and exclusive condominiums by Ashcroft Homes. They are also the floorers of choice for Urbandale Homes, Cardel Homes, Doyle Homes and Bulat Homes.

The future is indeed exciting for Rome Floor Cleaners Ltd. A family firm that proudly boasts traditional family, and business, values.

THE VILLA MARCONI CENTRE
ELDER CARE, AN ENDURING LEGACY

It began with a group of citizens concerned for the needs and well-being of the community's aging seniors. This concerned group formed the original Board of Directors and applied to the Ontario Ministry of Health for a Nursing Home License; approval was received in 1990. Over the next five years consolidating community support, fund raising efforts and securing a suitable property were the focus of this group. In 1995 the old Convent of the Holy Cross was purchased, plans were drawn and renovations begun. Exceptional volunteers from the community donated their time and expertise to make this part of the vision a reality. In May 1999 Villa Marconi began operation of a 60-bed Long Term Care Facility. One year later, in May 2000, the Province of Ontario awarded an additional 65 beds to Villa Marconi and construction began on a new wing that opened in September 2001. That same year, Villa Marconi opened The New Marconi Centre which provides barrier free access to the community center and events hall.

Historical Timeline

At a preliminary meeting held 17 May 1989 the Ontario Ministry of Health informed ethnic communities of the possibility of long-term care beds destined for the ethnic communities of Ontario. Present at this meeting were Elisa Bonardi, Nello Bortolotti, and Lucio Appolloni. On 19 June 1989 the trio called a community meeting inviting the local chapter of the National Congress of Italian Canadians and the many associations of Ottawa to discuss the possibility of preparing an application for this government initiative. More specifically, the meeting discussed the possibility of building of a long-term care facility for the Italian community of Ottawa-Carleton.

A number of meetings followed this initial contact with the community. These meetings were held at the Circolo degli Anziani and, as interest grew, so did the number of volunteers willing to lend support to the project. They included: Lucio Appolloni, Betty Bergin, Elisa Bonardi, Nello Bortolotti, Lorenzo De Franco, Nina Della Zazzera, Andy Molino, Mario Nicoli, Luigi Petro', Philip Piazza, Marino Pontiroli, and Olita Schultz. The volunteers worked throughout that summer in anticipation of the government's pending decision.

The government proposal became reality on 25 October 1989 when the Ontario Ministry of Heath announced the availability of 600 beds to be distributed for Nursing Homes throughout Ontario. These beds were destined exclusively for ethnic communities and would be mandated primarily to non-profit organizations. The deadline for submission to the Ministry of Health was 15 February 1990.

Now began a fevered and frenzied period of activity as the committee worked feverishly and along many parallel lines to meet the deadline. Tasks included the completion of a complicated and demanding grant application, finding a suitable location to situate the Nursing Home, developing a plausible architectural plan and rendition of the site, all the while maintaining a positive interface with the community, informing it of progress while striving to consolidate the community into a cohesive and supportive component of the dream.

Towards this end, many information meetings were held in the community, surveys were circulated, and fundraising events were planned. The first such event was held 17 December 1989 in the basement of St. Anthony's Church: a plate of pasta with sausage or meatball went for $8.00.

From these humble, honest, and heartfelt initiatives, the *project*, as it came to be known among enthusiasts, began to take form. Yet many in the community mistakenly believed that the future site would become a Senior Citizens Residence. This caused an initial public reticence and a brooding disinterest among many skeptics.

But the community eventually fully understood the scope of the enterprise and slowly accepted the notion of a community-supported Long-Term Care Nursing Home for its elderly.

And so, after nine propitious months of work from the initial informal information session with the Ministry of Health, the Committee *Casa di Cura Villa Marconi*, as the Nursing Home had come to be known, submitted its application for the 60 long-term care beds that were to be allotted to the Regional Municipality of Ottawa-Carleton. The document consisted of 111 pages of densely written responses to ministerial questions and 60 additional pages of supplementary required material. It was the product of hectic, prolonged, hotly discussed yet measured and intelligent effort on the part of the entire committee. Now it was only a question patience and time.

With the passage of time, the Villa Marconi project became less a question of individuals or individual glorification or petty rivalries and more one of community necessity, community cooperation, and moral public imperative. As a noble initiative it provided a rare opportunity to demonstrate social cooperation, heartfelt volunteerism, and Italian Canadian pride. As enthusiasm within the community grew, so did earnest generosity. The fundraising events that were held during this time are too many to mention, yet the effects of contributions from local Italian businesses, professionals, individuals and families helped sustain the drive for Villa Marconi.

On 7 August 1990, local Ottawa newspapers announced Health Minister Elinor Caplan's decision to grant the licensing of 600 new nursing home beds to the diverse cultural communities of Ontario. Sixty of those beds had been designated to the Italian community of Ottawa-Carleton. The application had been a success and the community was ecstatic. Expectations were high. It was hoped that the 60-bed nursing home would be built within three years. And indeed, parcels of land in Nepean and elsewhere were already under consideration. The only stumbling block remained financial. The community needed to match the grant monies allotted by the Ministry of Health. The committee was given until 15 May 1991 to develop a viable financial and appropriate building plan for the future nursing home.

On 28 October 1990, an Executive Board was struck. Its members included: Lucio Appolloni, Betty Bergin, Maria Bonacci, Nello Bortolotti, Dino Chiumera, Maria Chubb, Tony Ferrante, Lorenzo De Franco, Kathleen Gottfried, Ariella Hostteter, Saro Panuccio, Philip Piazza, Olita Schultz, and Dr. Max Della Zazzera. Its first order of business was to faithfully adhere to ministry prerogatives. On 29 March 1991, the Board invited interested parties to submit "Expressions of Interest" to provide land and/or develop a nursing home as required by Ontario law. The announcement was posted in both English/French and Italian local media. Several articles followed informing the public of the Villa Marconi Nursing Home Project. By expanding the search to the entire Ottawa community, the committee hoped to find an architect who wished to design the nursing home and a land developer that would construct the project and subsequently return the unit back to the community with a contracted lease.

It was reasoned that if adequate land could be found and purchased, the nursing home could evolve into a multi-use facility, thereby becoming a focal point for the Italian community. A Villa Marconi Nursing Home could become the focal point of a long-dreamed community center that would become the premier facility for special events and simple occasions for the Italian community. Architects were thus asked to plan for eventual expansion of an initial nursing home and provide for meeting space for social clubs, sporting and youth events, day care, banquet and catering services. The building itself would be surrounded by benches, trees, balustrades, and walking paths. In essence, it was hoped that Villa Marconi would embrace both young and old, the able and the infirm, in a harmony of community solidarity.

The Building Committee, as it was called, now began meeting on a weekly basis. By October 1991 it had developed specific land and location requirements according to regulations stipulated by the Ministry of Health. The proposed 2 to 4 needed acres were to be located in the greater Ottawa area, suitable for a nursing/retirement home complex or potentially rezonable to meet Ministry requirements. Offers would be accepted from private individuals but public lands would also be considered. The deadline for offers was 15 November 1991.

Estimated costs for the purchase of land and construction was between $6 and $7 million. The region was scoured for potential sites. The preferred site, however, remained southwest Ottawa, especially the area known as Carleton Heights where many Italians had settled in the 1970s and 1980s. All the while community support was encouraged through fund-raising events that included gala evenings and bingo nights, informal picnics, pasta dinners and charity soccer matches. Money was raised through raffles, donations, letter campaigns, and door to door solicitation. Local papers were constant in their promotion of Villa Marconi; volunteers offered both time and advice on initiatives to advance the cause. These start-up funds were necessary for inevitable administration costs, demographic studies, design estimates, and publicity. The entire Italian community was abuzz with anticipation, anxious to have this propitious dream become an auspicious reality. Momentum became mired, however, as the search for an appropriate site proved more difficult than anticipated. A city location was not viable given land costs; more distant country sites seemed too far and unacceptable to the community.

As the months turned to years that inevitably passed, the community was kept regularly informed through local media about the slow, but steady, progress. The Board of Directors was kept busy fielding phone inquiries and writing public responses to often critical letters that appeared in the local *L'Ora di Ottawa*. At times it seemed that all the initial enthusiasm and sincere anticipation had turned to despair; that what had seemed an impossible undertaking was in fact revealing the fissures and cracks of the Italian-Canadian community. Consolidating public support now became the major concern of the Directors as they attempted to maintain the project's momentum while abating the community's increasing fears. Golf tournaments continued to raise necessary funds by attracting major sponsors, casino nights attracted unexpected revenues, small donations from generous individuals helped boost community morale.

In the meantime, attention was also given to the future clients of Villa Marconi, the aged and the aging members of the community. In an effort to educate the public, the newspaper rubric titled *L'Angolo della Terza Età* was created. In the rubric, informed local professionals answered questions on healthcare issues, available social services, diet, and overall general care for the elderly. Villa Marconi was still a distant reality, yet the tutelage and concern for the declining members of the community had already begun.

And then it happened. On Wednesday, 28 December 1994, a brief article in *The Ottawa Citizen* announced that: "A non-profit group wants to convert the Holy Cross Convent on Baseline Road into a nursing home for Ottawa residents of Italian descent." The belated Christmas present could not have come at a better time. *L'Ora di Ottawa* proudly proclaimed the news shortly afterwards on 2 January 1995. "*Habemus Terram et Aedificium*" (*We Have Land and a Building*) exclaimed the celebratory headline. After months and years of active and intensive searching Villa Marconi had found a home. And what a home indeed! Not only had the Directors found a centrally located and magnificent parcel of prime land (8 acres on Baseline Road directly across from the Experimental Farm) but had a beautiful, and, as it was deemed, a dignified structure that would soon become the home of the community's elderly.

Activity now reached a fever pitch. An information campaign designed both to inform the public of purchase details and to marshal support in the community for the ongoing negotiation process began in earnest. The purchase offer for the property was $3,450,000.00. The Board of Directors of Villa Marconi, upon consultation with both the Building and Fundraising committees, needed to decide, before the end of February, whether the purchase was feasible. Determining factors not only included the adaptability of the convent to a Nursing Home facility given the standards required by Ministry of Health, but whether the Italian Canadian community could realistically raise the needed amount in the appropriate time frame. The first objective was a material one; architects, engineers, electricians, and contractors needed to assess the structure for its projected use. The second objective was more difficult and toilsome;

it was deduced, through surveys, that the community could indeed raise the required amounts, but it would unfortunately require five years, well beyond the established deadlines.

The information campaign proved beneficial. Having received optimistic reports regarding the adaptability of the existent Holy Cross Convent to a future Nursing Home, the Board of Directors now felt comfortable enough to launch the Villa Marconi Down Payment Fund on 13 March 1995. The objective: $250,000.00 before 31 March 1995. The funds were needed to close the deal; another $1,000,000.00 was due 1 September 1995. All told, the community was to raise $2,5000,000.00 to purchase the 47-year-old convent.

Money for the down payment was raised without difficulty and exceeded the established goal. Indeed, on that fatidic Friday 31 March 1995, Lucio Appolloni proudly officiated the unveiling of a public sign on The Holy Cross Convent grounds denoting the Future Home of Villa Marconi. Six years of tenacious faith and resolve were now his personal crown and the community's glory. Yet, he was fully aware that the historical event marked the successful conclusion of only the initial phase of fundraising and the beginning of a long-term, and potentially difficult, capital campaign to amass the remaining funds.

For the moment, however, the Italian-Canadian community was allowed to revel in its accomplishment. Enthusiasm was euphoric; emotions were at fever pitch. Villa Marconi, that fantastic dream that had awakened the latent spirit of the Italian-Canadian community of Ottawa-Carleton, was one step closer to realization. When completed the project would provide a long-term care and health center for seniors, non-profit housing, and a long-desired community center. As a bonus, the beautiful and elegant religious chapel, a hallmark of the building, would be saved, further consolidating the full spirit of Italian tradition that would animate the future center. Villa Marconi, it was felt, would become a symbol of community solidarity and hope, of renewed faith and pride, of unified purpose and moral commitment.

The second phase of fund raising would prove more difficult. Originally anticipated to run 13 months, that is to June 1996, the amount to be collected was a considerable hurdle: $2,500,000.00. Given the seemingly overwhelming sum, the Board of Directors was careful to maintain transparency in all its endeavors. Hoping to assure the community that capable businessmen were at the helm, on 24 April 1995 it was announced that Luigi Mion, founder of Central Precast and a supporter of numerous other charities and organizations, had accepted the Chairmanship of the Capital Campaign Fund. In his acceptance interview he called Villa Marconi "the heart of our community... a fulcrum for its future." The official fundraising campaign was slated to begin 8 May 1995. Meanwhile, the Villa Marconi thermometer became a steady feature of the local paper informing the community, with its slowly rising mercury, of the temperature (or progress) of the fundraising campaign. The community was enthused about Villa Marconi and it was immediately apparent that while the fundraising campaign progressed, activities could begin in the newly purchased convent. Indeed, the community was eager to view the site and helped transform its use to more community-oriented activities.

Although Villa Marconi was, so to speak, a community affair, its progress did not escape the notice of local Italian dignitaries. The then Italian Ambassador to Canada, His Excellency Andrea Negrotto Cambiaso, eager to demonstrate his support for the community's drive for a nursing home, decided to invite a childhood friend to Ottawa to visit the future site of Villa Marconi. Community excitement was palpable as it was announced in the local papers that Princess Elettra Marconi Giovanelli, daughter of Guglielmo Marconi, would be present in Ottawa to attend the Italian Week/ *La Settimana Italiana* exhibit commemorating the centenary of Marconi's discovery of the wireless telegraph (the exhibit was on display at the National Museum of Science and Technology from 1-18 June 1995). The Princess would also tour the Villa Marconi site and dedicate a commemorative plaque marking her visit on 13 June 1995. Her visit greatly increased the profile of the nursing home project in the Ottawa community at large as local mayors, city councilors, then Regional Chair Peter Clark, and Supreme Court Justice Frank Iacobucci attended the unveiling of the commemorative plaque. All pledged their support to the success of Villa Marconi thereby sanctioning its importance as part of the Italian-Canadian community's burgeoning profile on the Ottawa scene.

The emotion and impetus of this extraordinary event carried the fundraising drive throughout the summer months. As hoped and expected, a *Festa del tetto* party was held on 17 September 1995 marking the official inauguration and grand opening of the long-term health care facility known as Villa Marconi. The $1,000,000.00 needed for the initial down payment for the capital project had been raised in only six months. The entire Italian-Canadian community and its many associations as well as enthusiastic Ottawa residents, attended the open-house party. Happy revelers paraded around the neighborhood, played in card and bocce tournaments, feasted, sang in chorus, and danced to musical entertainment into the night. As the festivities wrapped up, renovations to adapt the convent to a nursing home were set to begin.

As the months of difficult and seemingly endless fundraising continued, days of hard work and charitable labor transformed the old convent into a construction site. Under the supervision of Architect Vincenzo Colizza, workers demolished, renovated, and converted the once reclusive rooms and spaces into open communal areas and appropriate, well-lit nursing rooms.

In the meanwhile, an office for the Board of Directors was set-up in the facility, and space was cleared for a *Centro di ritrovo e attività per anziani* (Meeting and Activities Center for the Elderly) under the direction of Dr. Rosa Paliotti. Both events were tangible evidence that Villa Marconi was well on its way to becoming a permanent fixture serving the Italian-Canadian community. As 1995 came to a close, a flurry of activities that included conferences, dinners, and concerts animated the first few months of occupancy as the community eagerly adopted Villa Marconi as its new home. The serenity of the holiday season was reflected in the traditional *presepe* (Nativity scent) that graced the lawn before the building, symbol of both the culmination of a vision and the birth of newfound community spirit.

The new year (1996) began with calls for monetary contributions and volunteers to help top-off the fund-raising campaign at its project target of $2,500,000.00. By mid-April $1,500,000.00 had been generously donated. The goal was nearer, but much work remained. In the meanwhile, another cornerstone to the completion of Villa Marconi was laid with the grand opening of the *Salone Comunitario* (Community Hall) in February 1996. Completed under the direction of Engineer Gino L. Nicolini, the work was concluded in relatively short order by volunteers who graciously donated their time and skills. The hall, replete with a proscenium theatre stage, roman columns and bar service, provided the community with its own banquet hall; a space for meetings, conferences, dinners, and concerts. These events cemented community solidarity by celebrating Italian culture and tradition, all the while helping to forge another positive Italian-Canadian footprint on the Canadian landscape.

By mid-February 1997, the name Villa Marconi had become synonymous with community activism. Renovated convent space regularly housed local association meetings and dinner dances, the newly formed clubs *L'età d'Oro* and the *Jelly Bean Club* stimulated both the young and the aged, while aerobic classes invigorated participants towards better health. All that remained was the final push towards topping-off the Fund Raising Campaign with the $1,000,000.00 needed to receive final Government of Ontario approval and distribution of funds.

In April 1997, Director Lucio Appolloni was finally able to thank *San Michele* (St. Michael, a jocular reference to Ontario Premier Mike Harris) for a single-matching grant of $2,400,00.00 towards Villa Marconi. After seven years of intense and often suffered fund raising, everyone involved was allowed a sigh of relief. The construction on the long-term care facility could now begin in earnest. During the summer of 1997, tenders were requested from local architects for the modification of the existing convent structure and construction of a 60-bed facility. In November of 1997, the proposal for Villa Marconi - Long Term Care Centre by Architect Vincent P. Colizza, were made public.

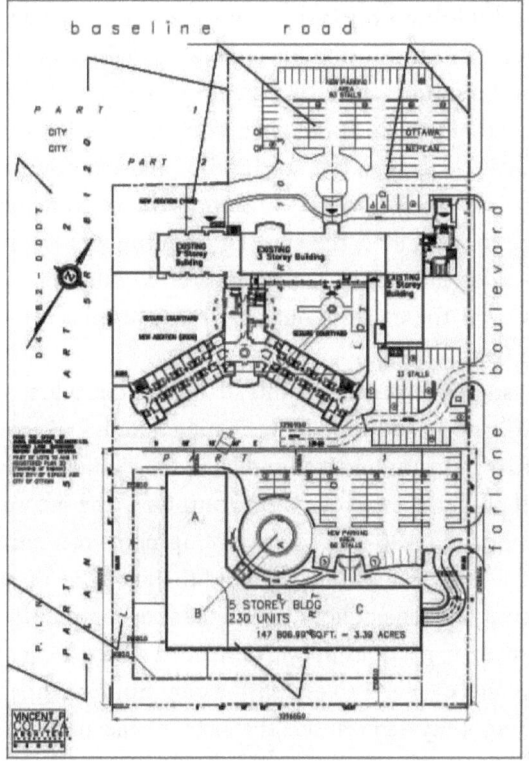

Request for Proposal
Vincent P. Colizza Architect Incorporated

Villa Marconi Master Plan - Long Term Care
Centre, Community Centre, Supportive Housing

The eight-acre parcel is situated in Nepean, Ontario bordering the City of Ottawa. The existing building housed 200 Sisters of the Holy Cross within a two and three storey building. The Italian Community purchased the facility with the intent to develop a Long Term Care Centre, a Community Centre and Supportive Housing for Seniors. The campus provided for a continuum of care based on a wellness model. The solution to achieve these objectives was both intriguing and challenging in that the existing building had to be adapted and reused, and the location of the existing building presented limitations to the development of the site. The study for the reuse of the existing building explored various income producing options, including supportive housing for seniors, medical arts, a pharmacy, a community resource centre and a cultural centre. The community proceeded with a renovation of an existing meeting area to establish a banquet hall cloak area, bar, washrooms and community kitchen. The response to the mixed uses did not produce sufficient revenue to retire the mortgage on the existing building and the funds were limited to cover the cost of renovation for community uses. It was determined that the existing building must be reused in part for a Long Term Care Centre.

The master plan focused on this strategy and produced a series of options involving an addition to the existing building to accommodate the long term care centre and community uses including a new entrance, daycare and program areas for cultural purposes. The site was analyzed to accommodate a 180-bed LTC development, recreation centre, supportive housing for seniors, freehold market driven town homes, medium density retirement housing and outdoor community recreation areas. A partnering relationship was developed with the City of Nepean (Recreation and Culture) to establish a community centre for Fisher Heights Community Association. The income generated by a long-term lease financed a retrofit and an addition to accommodate an elevator and lobby. The development of the master plan reflected the parking and servicing requirements of the community centre and the Long Term Care Centre. The Regional Municipality of Ottawa Carleton expressed interest in a RMOC Day Care Centre within the campus. A study was prepared to locate and accommodate the requirements of a Day Care Centre for 100 children. The re-use of the existing building on the community side accommodated various day programs for seniors, meeting, conference, and banquet functions. The master plan exercise continues as private and public interest is realized. The remnant lands yield approximately 100 apartments for seniors, in various formats utilizing services provided by the Long Term Care Centre for food services, housekeeping and health services including monitoring.[62]

---

62   Printed with permission, Vincent P. Colizza Architect Incorporated.

The wheels of the project now began to turn quickly. By month's end, demolition of the central external staircase had begun. The convent was well on its way to receiving a rejuvenating facelift as windows, doors, partitions and hallways would be modified to better suit the building's new function. The work was accomplished by community volunteers who lent both their time and often the materials required. Architect Colizza recalls that "The entire journey was full of experiences with people and volunteers who were completely dedicated to the cause of building Villa Marconi and offered support whenever and wherever it was needed. It was a pleasure to work hand in hand with them as we transformed the interior of the original Convent for the Sisters of the Holy Cross into the wonderful center it was to become."

The new year began with a renewed call for workers, for volunteers, and support for the many *ad hoc* programs for the elderly that were already active in the partially demolished interior of the once convent. No time was lost in establishing the site as a community focal point. No momentum was lost as social events often coincided with work schedules and the sounds of construction accompanied conversation.

In the meanwhile, approval was pending from the Ministry of Health for the construction plans that would transform the convent into a health care facility. The long-anticipated approval finally arrived in early August 1998. By 24 August, work began on the construction of the new wing that would house the 60 long-term care beds. It was estimated that one full year would be required to complete the wing and all the ancillary work in the convent proper. Estimated costs exceeded $5,000,000.00.

As work progressed, the community was kept informed with a constant gallery of photographs and updates that followed the growth of Villa Marconi as if it were a community child. A Ground Breaking party was belatedly held 5 September, testament to the work already accomplished and affirmation that there was no turning back! The day-long open-air event attracted young and old, politicians and diplomats, workers and dignitaries. The day's activities included a ceremonial turning of the soil, tangible symbol of the project's growth and community pride. The closing fireworks were a touching tribute to the work accomplished and to the bright future of Villa Marconi.[63]

The propitious and long anticipated *taglio del nastro* or ribbon cutting ceremony finally arrived in early summer of 1999. On 16 June 1999 with much fanfare, official observance, tears of happiness and heartfelt joy, the community reveled in the miracle that was Villa Marconi. During the festivities, the first residents of the care facility were admitted. These included Vincenzo Pellegrini, Concetta Imbesi, and Loretta Chiarelli. Others were soon to follow. Indeed, by May of the following year, all 60 beds had been filled and a waiting list of 160 persons attested to the need for a larger facility. A request was made to the Ministry of Health for 64 more beds and in May 2000 the request was granted. All the success, the open doors, the occupied beds, the musical concerts, and the theatrical exhibitions did not salvage, however, the gaping debt that the Board of Directors needed to repay. More beds had meant more construction, more expenses, more calls to the community for financial assistance. Yet, once again the community responded generously.

The birth of the New Millennium saw the inauguration of a new Fundraising Campaign whose goal was to amass $1,500,000.00. These monies were needed to complete the new autonomous entrance to Villa Marconi, a new wing that would house the recently granted extra bed space, and a public elevator. As work continued throughout the summer, Villa Marconi began to assume its current architectural profile. By 2004, however, the euphoria that had been rampant throughout

---

63 Many such events began to animate the life of Villa Marconi and touched the lives of persons once associated with the Convent. One such story is retold by Architect Vincent P. Colizza: "One day a few sisters visited the newly renovated site and looked for their former bedrooms which they had occupied in the former Convent and viewed the transformation which the community had undertaken to create a new home. The sisters were absolutely amazed as the former stairs to the second floor were removed and the underbelly was upgraded to a new accessible entrance complete with a view to a courtyard and a bistro and reception space forming the hub. They toured the new community center and adaptive reuse of the former classrooms and stage to a banquet hall. The tour generated strong emotions amongst the Sisters and all present who expressed a sense of pride for the accomplishment of the community."

the community was soon tempered by a financial crisis that threatened the facility's very existence. Though the mounting problems could not be laid at the feet of any one individual, a collective culture of blind hope and unfortunate personal politics had fostered an untenable financial nightmare. It had been assumed that the community would always support the nursing home, would continue its monetary generosity and, in short, would remain faithful to the dream. In reality, the community lacked the collective will to further the project and had grown tired of the constant monetary appeals. Villa Marconi's financial standing had become truly fragile. Since opening its doors, the facility had never operated at a break-even point where revenues met expenses. Monthly shortfalls were the unfortunate norm rather than exception. Furthermore, the severely regulated long-term care operations governed by the Ministry of Health strangled revenues. As a result, debts, interest costs, and promissory notes, coupled with reduced income resulted in a sizeable financial commitment that could not realistically be met. Any organization, let alone a not-for-profit community organization like Villa Marconi, would struggle simple to survive on a daily basis.

The Board of Directors elected in 2004 thus inherited a non-expressed mandate to resolve the mountain of debt that had been accumulated through inauspicious, yet well intended, practices. To its merit, the Directors tackled the considerable problems with a sense of clarity, forthrightness, and professional resolve. Of prime concern was the inability of the facility administrators, MetCap, to adequately satisfy Ontario standards. It was decided to engage the services of Diversicare, a healthcare provider of post-acute care. The move was positive and resulted in Villa Marconi quickly becoming one of the best long-term care facilities in the Province. But the financial situation would prove to be a harder nut to crack. By this time in history, community support had all but vanished; meetings and public gatherings could not garner the needed funds to maintain solvency; weariness and lethargy had set-in. Like all public projects, Villa Marconi had reached its moment of truth. If it were to continue to move forward, it would need a serious revamping of business policies. After unsuccessfully exploring numerous avenues and viable options to find a long-term solution to its continuing financial challenges, the Board began entertaining possible alternative uses for the 4 acres of vacant land adjacent to the building. In August 2004, the Board began actively evaluating strategies for the land's profitable use. The preferred solution was to develop the land in a joint venture with a third-party developer. The land would thus remain within the operating structure of Villa Marconi. Appeals were made to the community at large but few feasible plans materialized. Furthermore, it was estimated that the lead-time for any such construction was a painstaking 12-18 months. Also, significant financial resources and time would be required, commodities the Board did not have.

In 2005, after a series of meetings held at St. Anthony's Soccer Club, a Community Commission selected an "unbiased few from the community" it was noted, to audit the Villa Marconi books and determine if the proposed selling of Villa Marconi property was truly the only real option. The ad hoc committee eventually reported that it had become painfully apparent that for the body to survive, it would need to sever a limb. In the same year, two events occurred that would change the future profile and fate of Villa Marconi. First, a member of the ad hoc committee that had recommended the selling of the property, Marco Pagani, future President of Villa Marconi, was asked to join the Board of Directors as a community member. Second, in late January 2005, an unsolicited offer to purchase the parcel of land was tendered to the Board. The offer carried a limited acceptance period. In a last-ditch effort to maintain the parcel within the scope of Villa Marconi, the community was immediately informed and encouraged to further offers and ideas for developing the land.

After a series of community meetings held in order to effectively appraise and seriously evaluate all possible alternatives and, after much deliberation, the Board publicly advertised the sale of the vacant land and requested offer of purchase from interested parties. The unpopular sale of the land nevertheless resolved many of the institutions lingering problems. In one fell swoop, the transaction extinguished problematic secondary financing, saved the organization approximately $100,000 in annual interest costs, provided Villa Marconi with needed cash flow, and gained additional time to continue organizational improvements.

Ultimately, the sale permitted the Board to work towards an eventual break-even fiscal point. Although this initial period of Villa Marconi's history was both difficult and often desperate, the unwavering diligence and steadfast loyalty of the Board to the success of the long-term care facility guaranteed its very survival.

The 2006 Board saw the election of Marco Pagani as President of Villa Marconi. The newly elected President brought considerable professional skills to the job. After a notable 20-year career at Nortel Networks, he had served as Chair of the Board of Directors at a number of high-tech companies. His leadership skills would now help steer Villa Marconi to a position of market leadership. Towards this end, he immediately instituted a fiscal recovery plan that included a) mortgage renegotiation; b) budget restructuring; c) fund raising initiatives (one ongoing and successful initiative was the Raising the Roof Annual Corporate Event that continues to raise up to $120,000 yearly). He also enlisted the help of Maria Ricci who quickly became a fixture amidst the increasing financial activity. The creation of a Capital Reserve Fund for capital expenses, mortgage disbursements, and sundry sources of revenue also assured that Villa Marconi would continue to operate on the positive side of the budget ledger.

Marco Pagani's priorities were evident from the beginning of his mandate. Along with his successful three-pronged plan to restore both short and long-term financial stability, he advanced two collateral initiatives that revamped and rejuvenated Villa Marconi's image in the community. The Residents First Program drew upon the values that best express the spirit of the long-term facility. The goal of the program was to create an extension of the Italian-Canadian household by ensuring that love, respect, good food and impeccable cleanliness became the hallmark of a patient's stay. Steps were taken to guard the proper training of staff personnel and incentives were set in place to guarantee the proper fulfillment of Board requirements. The Residents First program became such a raving success that it was acknowledged by the Provincial Ministry of Health and elements are being considered for standardization as the operating model for long-term care facilities for the Province of Ontario.

The time was ready for Villa Marconi to regain a sorely merited and renewed credibility within the Italian community. Towards this end, community events were drawn to the Villa Marconi Center in an effort to render the socio-cultural side of the complex a viable point of reference for community activities. The revitalized center witnessed an influx of events that testify to the growing potential and professional competence that Villa Marconi Center has come to represent not only within the Italian-Canadian community but within the community at large. With a stable financial footing secured, a modicum amount of community support regained, and long-term care stability firmly established, the future of the Villa Marconi Center complex had acquired new luster.

The Villa Marconi Center is effectually composed of two distinct entities; Villa Marconi long-term care and the adjacent community center. The Center has prospered under the able directorship of Executive Director Domenic Ricci. The Center is a beehive of constant activity. Whatever is raised by the events held in the Marconi Center go directly towards the long-term care facility. The Center has built good community rapport and has become the long-awaited community center that the community had long craved. Furthermore, the Center is home to a retirement group called *L'età d'oro* (The Golden Years) which, under the direction of Teresa Barbera, has become a 300-member strong social network group for the elderly that is perhaps the largest recreational group in the Ottawa community.

The Center has no immediate plans for expansion but is determined to allow community needs dictate any possible future growth. These plans might include retirement residences on the property that would enhance the social life of the Villa Marconi community. But whatever the future holds, the Villa Marconi Center is a legacy gift to future generations who will hopefully remain committed to advancing long-term resident care and community services thanks to a glowing culture of philanthropy and a caring community.

VILLA MARCONI BOARD MEMBERS 1989 TO 2019

Working Committee August 1989 - October 1990
First meeting held Wednesday, 30 August 1989

Lucio Appolloni	Elisa Bonardi	Mario Nicoli
Marino Ponteroli	Agustino Monteduro	Olita Schultz
Enrico Del Castello	Nina Della Zazzera	Philip Piazza
Luigi Petro	Nello Bortolotti	Luigi Mion
Betty Bergin	Gianna Aitken	Lorenzo De Franco
Andy Molino	Nancy Shank	Clara Pannarella
Max Della Zazzera	Elizabeth Greenberg	Luigi Mion
Saro Panuccio	George Flumian	Kathleen Gottfried

FIRST BOARD MEMBERS
Elected Sunday 28 October 1990
Elected for 2-year term (1990-92)
Elected for 3-year term (1990-93)

EXECUTIVE
President - Lucio Appolloni
1st Vice-President - Lorenzo De Franco
2nd Vice-President - Ariella Hostteter
Treasurer - Dino Chiumera
Secretary - Olita Schultz

DIRECTORS: Maria Chubb, Betty Bergin, Tony Ferrante, Maria Bonacci, Kathleen Gottfried Nello Bortolotti, Saro Panuccio, Max Della Zazzera, Philip Piazza.

BOARD MEMBERS 1991

EXECUTIVE
President - Lucio Appolloni
1st Vice-President – Lorenzo De Franco
2nd Vice-President – Ariella Hostteter
Treasurer - Dino Chiumera
Secretary - Olita Schultz

DIRECTORS: Betty Bergin, Maria Bonacci, Nello Bortolotti, Maria Chubb, Tony Ferrante, George Flumian, Kathleen Gottfried, Andy Molino, Saro Panuccio, Walter Squazzin, Max Della Zazzera, Nina D'Onofrio – *Ex Officio*.

BOARD MEMBERS 1992

EXECUTIVE
President - Lucio Appolloni
1st Vice-President - Nello Bortolotti
2nd Vice-President - Lorrenzo De Franco
Treasurer - Tony Ferrante
Secretary - Olita Schultz

DIRECTORS: Marco Basile, Elisa Bonardi, Bernard Bouchard, Maria Chubb, Tony D'Angelo, Enrico Del Castello, Dr. Max Della Zazzera, Rosamaria Durand, George Flumian, Saro Panuccio Nina D'Onofrio – *Ex Officio*, Walter Squazzin – Honorary Member.

BOARD MEMBERS 1993

EXECUTIVE
President - Lucio Appolloni
1st Vice-President - Marco Basile
2nd Vice-President - Nello Bortolotti
Treasurer - Tony Ferrante
Secretary - Olita Schultz

DIRECTORS: Maria Chubb, Lorenzo De Franco, Joel Diena, Rosamarie Durand, George Flumian, SaroPanuccio, Walter Squazzin, Angelo Spadola, Helen Tape, James Zamprelli, *Ex Officio Members*: Nina D'Onofrio, Josephine Palumbo.

BOARD MEMBERS 1994 / 1995

EXECUTIVE
President - Lucio Appolloni
1st Vice-President - Marco Basile
2nd Vice-President - Nello Bortrolotti
Treasurer - Tony Ferrante
Secretary - Franco Marinelli
DIRECTORS: Anna Bevilacqua, Joel Diena, Rosamaria Durand, Raffaele Basile, George Flumian, Giuseppe Nicastro, Saro Panuccio, Angelo Spadola, Helen Tape, Luigi Mion, James Zamprelli, *Ex Officio Members*: Nina D'Onofrio, Josephine Palumbo.

BOARD MEMBERS 1995 / 1996

EXECUTIVE
President - Lucio Appolloni
1st Vice-President – Luigi Mion
2nd Vice-President – Marco Basile
Treasurer – Tony Ferrante
Secretary – Franco Marinelli / Anna Bevilacqua

DIRECTORS: Nello Bortolotti, Gino Buffone, Augusto Capitani (replacing Franco Marinelli), Joel Diena, Angelo Filoso (replacing Angelo Spadola), George Flumian, Romano Molo, Saro Panuccio, James Zamprelli, *Ex Officio Members*: Nina D'Onofrio, Josephine Palumbo, *Honourary Members*: Tony Cuffaro, Domenic Ricci.

BOARD MEMBERS 1996 / 1997

EXECUTIVE
President – Lucio Appolloni
1st Vice-President – Luigi Mion
2nd Vice-President – Marco Basile
Treasurer – Domenico Ricci
Secretary – Anna Bevilacqua

DIRECTORS: Nello Bortolotti, Gino Buffone, Augusto Capitani, Giuseppe Castrucci, Joel Diena, George Flumian, Dalia Malandra, Saro Panuccio, James Zamprelli, *Ex Officio Members*: Nina D'Onofrio, Josephine Palumbo.

BOARD MEMBERS 1997 / 1998

EXECUTIVE
President – Luigi Mion
1st Vice-President – George Flumian
2nd Vice-President – Mario Giannetti
Treasurer – Tony Ferrante
Secretary – Angelo Filoso
Past President – Lucio Appolloni

DIRECTORS: Frank Allevato, Anna Bevilacqua, Gino Buffone, Giuseppe Castrucci, Delio D'Angelo, Mario D'Angelo, Joel Diena, Dalia Malandra, Rosa Paliotti, Saro Panuccio, Frank Tonon, James Zamprelli.

BOARD MEMBERS 1998 / 1999

EXECUTIVE
President – Luigi Mion
1st Vice-President – George Flumian
2nd Vice-President – Mario Giannetti
Treasurer – Bob Landry
Secretary – Angelo Filoso
Past President – Lucio Appolloni

DIRECTORS: Frank Allevato, Anna Bevilacqua, Gino Buffone, Delio D'Angelo, Mario D'Angelo, Joel Diena, Luciano Gervasi, Cesidio Mariani, Rosa Paliotti, John Saracino, Tony Variano, James Zamprelli.

BOARD MEMBERS 1999 / 2000

EXECUTIVE
President – Luigi Mion
1st Vice-President – Mario Giannetti
2nd Vice-President – Angelo Filoso
Treasurer – John Saracino
Secretary – Ross Talarico
Past President – Lucio Appolloni

DIRECTORS: Frank Allevato, Anna Bevilacqua, Gino Buffone, Delio D'Angelo, Mario D'Angelo, Joel Diena, Maryantonett Flumian, Luciano Gervasi, Cesidio Mariani, Tony Variano, James Zamprelli, Executive Director: Domenic Ricci.

BOARD MEMBERS 2000 / 2001

EXECUTIVE
President – Luigi Mion
1st Vice-President – Mario Giannetti
2nd Vice-President – Angelo Filoso
Treasurer – George Flumian
Secretary – Ross Talarico
Past President – Lucio Appolloni

DIRECTORS: Frank Allevato, Gino Buffone, Paola Cargnello, Berardino Carrozzi, Walter Cibischino, Maryantonett Flumian, Luciano Gervasi, Marcello Pecora, John Saracino, Tony Variano.

BOARD MEMBERS 2001 / 2002

EXECUTIVE
President – Maryantonett Flumian
1st Vice-President – Mario Giannetti
2nd Vice-President – Mary Pitt
Treasurer – Marcello Pecora
Secretary – Ross Talarico
Past President – Luigi Mion

DIRECTORS: Luigi Bastianelli, Paola Cargnello, Berardino Carrozzi, Walter Cibischino, Angelo Filoso, George Flumian, Luciano Gervasi, Lino Panetta, Richard Raymond, John Saracino, Tony Variano.

BOARD MEMBERS 2002 / 2003

EXECUTIVE
President – Mario Giannetti
1st Vice-President – Ross Talarico
2nd Vice-President – Gino Buffone
Treasurer – Marcello Pecora
Secretary – Angelo Filoso
Past President – Luigi Mion

DIRECTORS: Luigi Bastianelli, Rocco Caminiti, Joel Diena, Genoeffe Filoso, Angelo Fiore, Gino Marrello, Gino Nicolini, Peter Scott, Honorary Director: Lucio Appolloni.

BOARD MEMBERS 2003 / 2004

EXECUTIVE
President – Ross Talarico
1st Vice-President – Gino Nicolini
2nd Vice-President – Gino Buffone
Treasurer – Marcello Pecora
Secretary – Angelo Filoso
Past President – Mario Giannetti

DIRECTORS: Rick Campagna, Walter Cibischino, Angelo Fiore, Pina Giorgio, Michael LeClair Gino Marrello, Vince Mastrogiacomo, Luigi Mion, Peter Scott, Honorary Director: Lucio Appolloni.

BOARD MEMBERS 2004 / 2005

EXECUTIVE
President – Walter Cibischino
1st Vice-President – Rick Campagna
2nd Vice-President – Robert De Toni
Treasurer – Marcello Pecora
Secretary – Gino Nicolini
Past President – Ross Talarico

DIRECTORS: Gino Buffone, Angelo Filoso, Pina Giorgio, Michael LeClair, Tony Marcantonio, Vince Mastrogiacomo, Luigi Mion, Marco Pagani Honorary Director: Lucio Appolloni.

BOARD MEMBERS 2005 / 2006

EXECUTIVE
President – Walter Cibischino
1st Vice-President – Robert De Toni
2nd Vice-President – Rick Campagna
Treasurer – Marcello Pecora
Secretary – Tony Marcantonio
Past President – Mario Giannetti

DIRECTORS: Angelo Barone, Stefano Biscotti, Angelo Filoso, Luigi Mion, Kevin O'Neill, Marco Pagani, Honorary Director: Lucio Appolloni.

BOARD MEMBERS 2006 / 2007

EXECUTIVE
President – Marco Pagani
1st Vice-President – Robert De Toni
2nd Vice-President – Stefano Biscotti
Treasurer – Dino Chiumera
Secretary – Lee Pavan-Farnworth
Past President – Walter Cibischino

DIRECTORS: Angelo Barone, Eolo Bevilacqua, Rick Campagna, Tony Campanale, Christopher Chong, Rosetta Giammaria, Mario Giannetti, Luigi Mion, Kevin O'Neill.

BOARD MEMBERS 2007 / 2008

EXECUTIVE
President – Marco Pagani
Vice-President – Robert De Toni
Treasurer – Dino Chiumera
Secretary – Lee Pavan-Farnworth
Past President – Walter Cibischino

DIRECTORS: Marcello Bentivoglio, Eolo (Ian) Bevilacqua, Mona Campanale, Christopher Chong, Rosetta Giammaria, Mario Giannetti, Vince Mastrogiacomo, John Mion.

BOARD MEMBERS 2008 / 2009

EXECUTIVE
President – Marco Pagani
Vice-President – Eolo (Ian) Bevilacqua
Treasurer – Madhavan Madhu
Secretary – Lee Pavan-Farnworth
Past President – Walter Cibischino

DIRECTORS: Marcello Bentivoglio, Mona Campagna, Christopher Chong, Frank Falsetto, Rosetta Giammaria, Mario Giannetti, Vince Mastrogiacomo, John Mion.

BOARD MEMBERS 2008 / 2009

EXECUTIVE
President - Mario Cuconato
Vice-President - Vince Mastrogiacomo
Treasurer - Silvana Gandolfini
Secretary - Daniella Sicoli-Zupo
Past President – Marco Pagani

DIRECTORS: John Abbenda, Frank Falsetto, Mario Giannetti, Luc Imbeau, Carmela Marrazza-St. John, John Mion, Gino Nicolini, Mary Pitt

BOARD MEMBERS 2009 / 2010

EXECUTIVE
President - Mario Cuconato
Vice-President - Vince Mastrogiacomo
Treasurer - Silvana Gandolfini
Secretary - Daniella Sicoli-Zupo

DIRECTORS: John Abbenda, Frank Falsetto, Mario Giannetti, Luc Imbeau, Carmela Marrazza-St. John, John Mion, Gino Nicolini, Mary Pitt, Marco Pagani

BOARD MEMBERS 2010 / 2011

EXECUTIVE
President - Mario Cuconato
Vice-President - Vince Mastrogiacomo
Treasurer - Silvana Gandolfini
Secretary - Daniella Sicoli-Zupo
Past President – Marco Pagani

DIRECTORS: John Abbenda, Frank Falsetto, Mario Giannetti, Luc Imbeau, Carmela Marrazza-St. John, John Mion, Gino Nicolini, Mary Pitt

BOARD MEMBERS 2011 / 2012

EXECUTIVE
President - Mario Cuconato
Vice-President - Vince Mastrogiacomo
Treasurer - Silvana Gandolfini
Secretary - Daniella Sicoli-Zupo
Past President – Marco Pagani

DIRECTORS: John Abbenda, Frank Falsetto, Mario Giannetti, Luc Imbeau, Gino (Eugene) Milito, John Mion, Gino Nicolini, Mary Pitt

BOARD MEMBERS 2012 / 2013

EXECUTIVE
President - Mario Cuconato
Vice-President - Vince Mastrogiacomo
Treasurer - Silvana Gandolfini
Secretary - Daniella Sicoli-Zupo
Past President – Marco Pagani

DIRECTORS: John Abbenda, Luigi Caparelli, Anna Chiappa, Frank Falsetto, Mario Giannetti, Gino (Eugene) Milito, John Mion, Mary Pitt, Oriana Trombetti

BOARD MEMBERS 2013 / 2014

EXECUTIVE
President - Mario Cuconato
Vice-President - Vince Mastrogiacomo
Treasurer - Silvia Gandolfini
Secretary - Daniella Sicoli-Zupo
Past President – Marco Pagani

DIRECTORS: John Abbenda, Luigi Caparelli, Anna Chiappa, Frank Falsetto, Gino (Eugene) Milito, John Mion, Mary Pitt, Oriana Trombetti

BOARD MEMBERS 2013 / 2014

EXECUTIVE
President - Mario Cuconato
Vice-President - John Abbenda
Treasurer - Silvana Gandolfini
Secretary Daniella Sicoli-Zupo
Past President – Mario Giannetti

DIRECTORS: Luigi Caparelli, Anna Chiappa, Frank Falsetto, Claudio Gerebizza, Gino (Eugene) Milito, Mary Pitt, Oriana Trombetti

BOARD MEMBERS 2014 / 2015

EXECUTIVE
President - Mario Cuconato
Vice-President - John Abbenda
Treasurer - Silvana Gandolfini
Secretary - Daniella Sicoli-Zupo
Past President – Mario Giannetti

DIRECTORS: Riccardo Campagna, Luigi Caparelli, Anna Chiappa, Claudio Gerebizza, Gino (Eugene) Milito, Mary Pitt, Oriana Trombetti

BOARD MEMBERS 2015 / 2016

EXECUTIVE
President - Riccardo Campagna
Vice-President - John Abbenda
Treasurer - Silvana Gandolfini
Secretary Claudio Gerebizza
Past President – Mario Cuconato

DIRECTORS: Luigi Caparelli, Anna Chiappa, Frank Falsetto, Mario Giannetti, Vince Mastrogiacomo, Franco Manarin, Gino (Eugene) Milito, Oriana Trombetti

BOARD MEMBERS 2016 / 2017

EXECUTIVE
President - Riccardo Campagna
Vice-President - Vince Mastrogiacomo
Treasurer - Silvana Gandolfini
Secretary - Claudio Gerebizza
Past President – Mario Cuconato

DIRECTORS: Luigi Caparelli, Anna Chiappa, Frank Falsetto, Mario Giannetti, Franco Manarin, Paolo Siraco, Gino (Eugene) Milito, Oriana Trombetti

BOARD MEMBERS 2017 / 2018

EXECUTIVE
President - Riccardo Campagna
Vice-President - Vince Mastrogiacomo
Treasurer - Silvana Gandolfini
Secretary - Claudio Gerebizza
Past President – Mario Cuconato

DIRECTORS: Luigi Caparelli, Anna Chiappa, Frank Falsetto, Mario Giannetti, Franco Manarin, Paolo Siraco, Oriana Trombetti

BOARD MEMBERS 2018 / 2019

EXECUTIVE
President - Riccardo Campagna
Vice-President - Vince Mastrogiacomo
Treasurer (Appointed) Silvana Gandolfini
Secretary - Claudio Gerebizza
Past President – Mario Cuconato

DIRECTORS: Luigi Bastianelli, Frank Falsetto, Mario Giannetti, Fabio Madonna, Franco Manarin, Giuseppe Montuoro, Paolo Siraco

BOARD MEMBERS 2019 / 2020

EXECUTIVE
President - Riccardo Campagna
Vice-President - Vince Mastrogiacomo
Treasurer (Appointed) Silvana Gandolfini
Secretary - Paolo Siraco
Past President - Mario Giannetti

DIRECTORS: Luigi Bastianelli, Annalisa Bonardi, Mario Cuconato, Frank Falsetto, Sarah Macaluso, Fabio Madonna, Giuseppe Montuoro, Pasquale Santini

IMPORTANT DATES IN THE HISTORY OF VILLA MARCONI

June 1989: Committee formed to request 60 bed Nursing Home Licence.

25 October 1989: Ontario Ministry of Health requests submissions from ethnic groups for culturally sensitive Nursing Homes.

15 February 1990: Committee formally submits request for 60 beds

1 August 1990: Licence to build and operate a 60 bed Nursing Home granted.

1990/91: Villa Marconi Long Term Care Centre legally formalized

26 October 1991: First gala Fund-Raising Event with guest speaker Justice Frank Iacobucci of the Supreme court of Canada.

1991- 94: Various attempts to locate a suitable and affordable parcel of land; various fund-raising events including the first John Denofrio Golf Tournament; various architectural designs of Villa Marconi Nursing Home presented and studied.

November 1994: Sisters of the Holy Cross contacted for the purchase of the Holy Cross Convent and adjacent land.

1 March 1995: Beginning of Down-Payment Campaign to raise $250,000.

31 March 1995: Down-Payment Goal surpassed at $299,380.

3 April 1995: Beginning of Fund-Raising Campaign to reach $ 2.5 million.

13 June 1995: Visit of Princess Elettra Marconi Giovannelli, daughter of scientist Guglielmo Marconi.

1 September 1995: Possession of land and building at 1026 Baseline Road.

PRESTON STREET TODAY
UPDATING IDENTITY

Ethnicity, the art of maintaining one's essential and seemingly primordial traditions, language, and customs on foreign soil, is not a static project. Werner Sollers has remarked that the criterion of inclusion and exclusion that produces alien identities, is a constantly evolving socio-economic parabola of perceived winners and losers. Ethnicity, in other words, is really a social construction that undergoes a continuous process of renegotiation.[64] Unquestionably, life in the early days of Italian migration was a struggle; the adjustment to urban Canadian society was demanding and difficult; economic circumstances, as well as the weather, were always harsh and uncompromising; language differences and endemic illiteracy presented barriers that seemed insurmountable. Yet, the pioneer immigrants arrived with a sense of purpose and hope for the future that enabled them to endure initial hardships because, as this study has demonstrated, endure they did.

Preston Street developed its Italian identity and Italian-Canadian culture well before the 1950s when the more recent postwar immigration from Italy began. More importantly, in direct counterpoint to what some have contended, the area has definitely maintained and consolidated its identity in a process of settlement and redevelopment that gives the area its resilient energy, strength, and pseudo-authentic character. Preston Street/*Corso Italia* today is not only renewing its visual landscape but also reshaping its sociocultural and business identity to hopefully better reflect and serve an evolving Italian-Canadian community that has moved away from its humble origins and is struggling to maintain its original ethnic flavor. As the elders leave their place to younger, more

---

64 William Sollers, *Beyond Ethnicity: Consent and Descent in American Culture* (Oxford: Oxford UP, 1986).

demanding, and normally more Canadian than Italian offspring, to newer business store fronts and contemporary meeting places, the area is well poised to move beyond its perceived confines of fading ethnic enclave and become one of the trendiest areas of the burgeoning city. Question is, will it remain a *Little Italy*? Because of its proximity both to the downtown business section and the newly resurrected interest in the waterfront area of Lebreton Flats, Preston Street seems positioned to strengthen its identity as the Italian business islet of Ottawa, but only if it plays its cards right.

If Canada promised the arriving immigrant the opportunity for progress and change, Preston Street now permits the incoming business entrepreneur the opportunity to create a colorful and vibrant ethnic mosaic in a neighborhood that has been economically revitalized, socially gentrified, and continues to thrive, grow and visually prosper.

Endings and New Beginnings

Over the course of the 20th century, Preston Street lost much of its residential character in favor of commercial use. Years of stunted growth, normal community decay, unwarranted neglect, and a spotty snail's pace pattern of growth, however, only made way for the current encroachment of developers on vacant lots and sprawling parking areas. Multiple medium and higher rise apartment buildings and the ever-trendy glass office suite may have modernized *the look* of the street, but has done little to revive *the feel*. Rather than community-friendly smaller buildings and sites following a well-defined pattern of renewal, renovation, and rebuilding, the street has succumbed to variegated locales that have done little to reflect a perceived and desperately wanted pseudo-Italian vision for the area.

Instead, the aesthetic impact on the streetscape is decidedly underwhelming and undramatic. New businesses that have moved into the area opted to redevelop existing homes and storefronts usually without a second thought to contextualized design or form. The result is an uneven streetscape of recycled restaurants and assorted caffe's, neon hairdressers, and remnants of variety groceries that create a hodgepodge of odd-looking storefronts that do little to reflect the context and character of the local community. As overall commercial activity increased, so too did transient traffic volume and the frustrating congestion of cars, buses, predator bikes, and pedestrians. On-street parking issues have negatively impacted the intended mixed-use profile of the neighborhood and has further reduced needed pedestrian flow. The resultant confusion has sucked up what little neighborhood vitality remained. But dramatic change seems to loom on the horizon. Preston Street was about to receive a facelift thanks to the tireless initiatives of a revitalized Preston Street Business Improvement Association (BIA).

Preston Street BIA

The BIA's self-described mandate states that it will "improve, promote and undertake projects that will result in a stronger and more competitive commercial main street or business district." Founded in 1986 by a few enterprising businessmen from the immediate area, the group has succeeded in transforming a mostly bleak streetscape into a relatively vibrant stretch of specialty stores, boutiques, public artwork, and distinctive eateries. Consequently, the heighborhood area has experienced an increase in population and is attracting people migrating back to the city, reversing the decades-long trend of settling in the suburbs. The trend in city living is driven primarily by two groups: young professionals, who enjoy skyhigh living that rises above street level boutique shops, and aging Baby Boomers, who are retiring and moving back to the gentrified area of Preston Street/ *Corso Italia*. The increased urban density is directly attributable to the significant time and efforts of the BIA to consolidate the area as a desirable neighborhood. Impressively proactive in pursuing initiatives to encourage neighborhood revitalization (piggybacking, for instance, on the considerable City of Ottawa investment in infrastructure and transportation), the BIA continues towards its goal of developing a rejuvenated streetscape for the long-neglected street. As a result, Preston Street/*Corso Italia* is being pulled into the new millennium.

The Preston Streetscape Project: Executive Summary, was presented to The City of Ottawa by Commonwealth Historic Resource Management Limited in May 2005. The Summary was studied by The Planning and Environment Committee and Council and submitted by the Deputy City Manager for Planning and Growth on 25 October 2005. The Planning Committee approved the Preston Streetscape Project and made the following recommendations:

1. That the Preston Street Streetscape Plan be approved as outlined in Documents 2 and 3.
2. That the funding of the streetscape improvements outlined in the Streetscape Plan be shared between the City and the Preston Business Improvement Association on a 1/3, 2/3 basis respectively.
3. That the City enter into a Maintenance Agreement with the Preston Business Improvement Association concerning the funding of hydro for the decorative street lighting and the ongoing maintenance of streetscape improvements.
4. That the Planning and Environment Committee recommend Council approve the preparation and posting of the Municipal Class Environmental Assessment, Notice of Completion.
5. That the detailed design and construction of the streetscaping improvements be coordinated with the planned infrastructure renewal initiatives.
6. That the cost for the streetscape improvements outlined in Document 4, the related public arts funding and maintenance costs, be identified in the 2006 Long Range Financial Plan and in future capital budget submissions as an incremental cost to the Preston Street planned infrastructure renewal.

In short, after years of conceptual designs, traffic analysis, public screenings, revisions in response to public comments, updates, and alternative schemes (including the Preston-Champagne Plan of Development prepared in 1994 that provided an overall framework for future development of the street as well as the 1999 Project Patio), the City of Ottawa decided that there was a definite need to initiate a block-by-block study to identify the neighborhood's unique character and defining features.

Marketing analysis revealed the importance of selling the area with a recognizable brand. The branding concept for Preston Street became *Viva Italia*. The overall and far-reaching conceptual plan envisioned Preston Street as a natural gateway to a redeveloped Lebreton Flats, but also as a potential national attraction for Italian-Canadian culture. The ambitious rehabilitation plan was further studied, revised, subjected to routine public scrutiny, and amended to accommodate the technical requirements of the roadway and the desire of the local community to preserve both the unique ethnic character of the area while creating a pleasant environment for both residents and future visitors. The street had already been identified as a vital transportation artery and as a principal link within the city as early as 1950 in the Greber Plan. In this latest official plan, however, Preston Street was set to evolve from its moniker as important, though ethnic, side-street to full-fledged modern city Mainstreet; a veritable *Corso Italia* of upscale housing, niche boutiques, enticing restaurants, and welcoming outdoor caffe's.

Nevertheless, and unfortunately, the rebranded package named Preston Street/*Corso Italia* and the surrounding environs, remain devoid of any truly memorable landscape settings or inspiring memory landmarks that anchor the area to its fabled past. Though the same can be said of many other urban streets in the city of Ottawa, the flavor of the area as a legitimate Italian/Italian-Canadian public enclave suffers when comparing present-day Preston Street/*Corso Italia* to more traditional *Little Italy's* across North America that have maintained their equally deep roots and immigrant history.

When speaking of possible historical or meaningful landmarks on present-day Preston Street/*Corso Italia*, one must consider activity and function as elements that render a place an important commemorative political site, a venerable religious shrine, or a simple social reminder of a past event. A landmark is a vital nodal point of reference if any sense of community wishes to survive. They are necessarily external to the observer; they serve to characterize the general existential nature and relative symbolic gravity of an area that lie beyond the personal memories of any one person. Size, emblematic importance, and history are determining factors that establish shared community landmarks. Personal memories are powerful reinforcements in creating landmarks. But they remain personal, relative to an individual and, while noteworthy, do not impact the community at large. Once a lasting meaning is attached to a site that holds relevance and historical value to the entire community, its value as a landmark rises in time regardless of the physical transformations or sociopolitical conversions throughout the years.

The culture of Preston Street/*Corso Italia* was and remains an oral one. It is characterized by face-to-face communication and personal relationships that endow unknowing privilege (and sometimes power) to those members with a tale to tell or something to sell. Yet, these realms of oral memoryscape that privilege the personal are always problematic. Their symbols are often contrastive, their meanings too often distorted. When examining a present reality as it relates to the past, historians often refer to the collective memory of the group, the *mentalità*, in other words, of a given community. Culture is the result of the effort of society members to describe and determine (or raise) the individual according to the acknowledged and shared successes, accomplishments, losses, pains, and joys of the group. People who hold memories are not merely individuals but are a mirror of the values of a social group. History, in a general sense, is made when individuals, groups, events, and memories coalesce to invent rituals and traditions that keep the memory of a shared past, regardless of its perceived importance, alive. Thus history, like memory, draws from the shared stories, impressions, and images that form narratives of the past that condition individuals in the present. These narratives may be written, drawn, related orally, or simply, as could happen on Preston Street/*Corso Italia*, lived as local culture.

In other words, a seemingly meaningless and inconsequential meeting of old friends on Preston Street/*Corso Italia* can become an occasion to recount, to retain, to relive, in memory, the group's past while simultaneously weaving the anthropological fabric that guarantees the community's evolving future. When examined from this vantage, Preston Street/*Corso Italia* today is lacking such culture-creating happenings. Indeed, the street may slowly be coming alive. However, the unexpected local vibes being created will condition and change its ethnic heart.

The most recent metamorphoses on the street are due to a variety of factors. Not least of these are the herculean efforts of the BIA to beautify and revamp the street as it awaits what is anticipated as profound and radical change on Lebreton Flats. Lori Mellor, Executive Director of the BIA, reveals the efforts of maintaining a village feel to the area while following city protocols. "The big challenge for us was to get the beautification project. We'd had very little success. As I started to get to know my business owners, I found out 18 of our businesses were getting flooded every time we had rain. That's because we had a one hundred-year-old combined sewer system. I sent a letter off to our ward councilor and I received no response whatsoever. So I sent a newsletter to our neighborhood residents and I received 113 letters back. Suddenly we began to get some action from City Hall. What happens when you get a new sewer is that once the city puts the street back, you get your beautification project. That spurred the development of a secondary plan for the area that would define the zoning, height, and density. It's really one of those 'be careful what you wish for' scenarios. The BIA and the residents' association agreed that all the height [tall buildings] would be around the perimeter and we'd protect the village-like nature of the area. We were anticipating heights of 20 story buildings along Carling, Rochester and Champagne; but we've now got 45 and 55 story towers. This creates all whole new series of concerns: How are we going to manage increasing traffic? What about shadowing from tall buildings? Are we going to turn Preston into a cold wind tunnel? Those are our current and future concerns."

The street's prime location is as much its fortune as it is problematic. As more and more tourists choose to visit the area because of proximity to the city's two most picturesque cycling paths (the Ottawa River and the Rideau Canal Pathways), Dows Lake and Commissioner's Park, the Lebreton Flats redevelopment, and the downtown core, (all tied together by the new Trillium light rail transit line), the current interim strategies of streetscape change can only mitigate growth in order to survive and prosper for the next phases of development that foresee greater population and business intensification.

For the moment, the street has been revived from its doldrums days of the 70s and 80s and thrives with the social buzz of eagerly anticipated events, well-attended pubs, normally packed micro-breweries, award winning-eateries, and upscale boutique businesses. According to the Preston Street Business Improvement Area Census Project 2018[65], the following table represents the demographic distribution of businesses in the Preston Street area by category in 2018:

>Food & Drink 60 22%
>Entertainment 4 1%
>Shopping 19 7%
>Health, Beauty & Fitness 42 15%
>Financial Services 10 4%
>Professional Services 82 29%

The census identifies a total of 278 businesses and non-residential locations of which 271 are located in BIA-levied commercial properties. A few of them are iconic landmarks that give the street a marketable ethnic flavor. These include The Prescott, Giovanni's Restaurant, Preston Hardware, Pasticceria Italiana, Sala San Marco, Luciano Foods, etc., to name only a few. The newer businesses are quickly establishing themselves as future Preston Street/*Corso Italia* landmarks.

These newer businesses are using technology to provide greater versatility and marketability of the street shops in the naturally evolving social media world. In the mind of tech users, a business can improve the impact of its services and products with the help of technological tools to anywhere and to any location on any device to any potential customer. The following table lists the percentages of business with Publicly Available Contact Information and those that use social media 2018:

>Business with website 213; 77%
>Business with email 192; 69%
>Business with phone number 234; 84%

---

65 This Final Report was prepared by Michel Frojmovic, 15 September 2018. All references are to this document.

USE OF SOCIAL MEDIA:
Google Maps 202; 82%
Google Places 205; 83%
Facebook 165; 67%
Twitter 118; 48%
Instagram 86; 35%
Other 67; 27%

Since life in the villages of Italy was grounded on the social and economic foundations of the piazza with its myriad shops and stalls, Preston Street/*Corso Italia's* real and virtual piazzas, link owners and clientele in a new form of social interaction. The streetscape, in this sense, achieves a diverse public image that affects the changing infrastructure, efficiency, the culture, and relationships that are born and nurtured through Preston Street business. All these current locales, then, can be considered future memory landmarks because they are the new lifeblood of the street. Without them, Preston Street would be in ruins. Most importantly, these small business owners are self-employed and often employ others, producing private-sector jobs and livelihood for the neighborhood economy.

PRESTON STREET BUSINESSCAPE
Preston Hardware

A familiar business with a rejuvenated look is Preston Hardware. Located on the same original location on Preston Street since 1945, Preston Hardware was started by William Germain and brother-in-law Angelo Locatelli. It was the first self-serve store in Ottawa. The goal of the two entrepreneurs was to provide the local community with the highest quality of products and service. In 1973, the business was purchased by the current owners, Mario and Sam Giannetti and brother-in-law Mario Frangione, who have since both modernized and aggrandized the business becoming Canada's largest independent hardware retailer.

Mario Giannetti is rightfully proud of his trade, his career, the store, and his life-long calling. Arriving in Ottawa in the late 50s, he worked the aisles of Preston Hardware part-time during the school year, full-time in summer. His education and degree eventually landed him a job with the Federal Government. But after much deliberation both with his family and Mr. Locatelli, Mario assumed the role of store manager and has never looked back. Under the tutelage and steady hand of the Giannetti family, Preston Hardware became the go-to place not only for the Italian community but for the city at large. At a time when small hardware shops, often found in city centres, were disappearing in the shadow of the big suburban chain stores that came to dominate the market, the Giannetti brothers not only consolidated their position but were able to position themselves as major players. Their goal had always been to move beyond the normal mom and pop corner hardware store. They did so by competing honestly, and by providing the best customer service possible.

As the market and customer demands changed over the years, Preston Hardware changed along with it. Not only was product diversified and upgraded, but small in-store showrooms were designed, thereby creating stand-alone specialized business sectors in the store. In 1975, the store was enlarged; the second floor converted into a separate bathroom and fixtures showroom. In 1983, the hardware segment was moved to a larger adjacent building while the older hardware portion of the store was transformed into one of the city's finest bathroom emporiums.

This specialized showroom concept was extended to include a premium quality paint sector, a finishing hardware and home improvement sector, a wine and wine supply shop, and a tool and equipment zone. This long-term strategy has proved to be a winning formula. By providing the highest quality product in a user-friendly and luxurious atmosphere staffed with informed and highly capable professional salesclerks, Preston Hardware has further defined and differentiated its banner in an extremely competitive marketplace.

But Preston Hardware is also a beloved icon in the community. The Giannetti family is always at the forefront in support of community fundraising events and are major contributors to local hospitals and national fundraising campaigns. Service is the key. Be it within the store or within the community, the Preston Hardware family, from the original three clerks in the early days to the 120-person operation today, has worked tirelessly to serve the community.

As Mario Giannetti contemplates the future, he notes that Generation 2, as he has baptized them, will continue to move the business forward, continue to evolve and become even bigger players in large construction projects. But he is also proud that they have continued the personal and friendly approach, combined with individual practical advice, which only a small retailer can offer. Knowing their strengths and their ability to react quickly to market pressures have guaranteed Preston Hardware a lasting place on the Preston Street landscape, a place where personal respect and community involvement is the norm, and where honest business is the message.

Franks Auto Centre Ltd

A significant part of the Preston Street business landscape, Franks Auto Centre provided professional car care and service, as well as a 'hang-out' for local patrons and neighborhood friends, for more than 40 years.

Established in July of 1973 by Giovanni Centofanti and Delio D'Angelo, the two long-time friends had always wished to open a full-service auto repair since their apprenticeship as mechanics in Italy. Originally located on Pamilla Street, the business moved to 95 Norman Street two years later. Third partner Francesco De Angelis remained with the business until 1984. Known for their integrity, honesty, and professionalism, patrons of Franks Auto Centre could expect warm relationships and personal care. No job was too small, no general overhaul too large for the intrepid duo who seemed to resolve major problems with consummate knowledge, exceptional skill, and practical expertise.

The centre represented major automotive brands including Blaupunt and Agip and specialized in all makes of cars, eventually creating a niche market for expensive European models. In 1986 Giovanni and Delio became major Canadian players with Lada, the Russian automaker sold new in Canada up until 1998. They opened a successful Lada dealership and showroom on nearby Preston Street. At the time the Lada Signet was the cheapest car available in Canada.

Their slogan: "At $4,998 no other car in Canada comes with so much and sells for so little." In the mid 80's Lada started importing the Niva compact 4x4 that is still sold today in Europe and Russia. Their dealership built quite a reputation, but they excelled in service. They became the only authorized Lada dealership to rebuild transmissions from Lada Canada. But Franks Auto Centre's total service commitment also extended to Genuine Service Maintenance for high-end new and vintage Ferrari, Porsche, and Maserati models. Their clientele knew their cars would remain in perfect working order and at superb levels of performance and quality over time.

A side hobby of the two mechanics was the *Settimana Italiana* car parade. A fledgling feature of the festival, in 1978 Franks Auto Centre became the sole sponsor and organizer of the annual event up to 2012. In 2013 Giovanni, Delio and friends founded ICCO, the Italian Car Club of Ottawa. The yearly car parade has since been conducted under the aegis of ICCO and the unlimited support of Joe Cotroneo, a Preston Street businessman and car collector. From its humble beginnings of 20 cars, more than 140 cars parade on Preston Street arriving from as far as Quebec and northeastern United States.

Always busy and chock-full of innovative ideas, the civic-minded automotive centre hosted local parties, benefit dinners, and improvised feasts for its many clients and community friends. Yet, after 40 years of mechanical and community service, the doors of the popular institution closed its doors in December 2012. Both Giovanni and Delio miss the daily interaction with people who filled the shop and became friends, the daily routine of demanding work, but above all they fret the excitement and challenge of solving the most disparate of mechanical problems. The two may indeed regret no longer having their brand on Preston Street but both can revel in the confidence of having created a revered Preston Street memory.

Saro's BP Station and Milano Autobody and Paint

Saro Panuccio, founder and owner of Saro's BP Station and Milano Autobody and Paint, is remembered on the street as a visible and vital fixture of the Preston Streetscape. Unselfish and philanthropic by nature, Saro believed that a vibrant, healthy business and social community offers opportunities for everyone. He therefore devoted much of his spare time in community activities that fostered goodwill and inspired happiness.

Sponsored by sister Lucerta (married to Vincenzo Zito), Saro immigrated to Canada in the winter of 1951. Never known as someone who wanted for things to do, Saro immediately set to work inserting himself within the community fabric he had chosen as his home. Surprisingly resourceful, he began helping newly arriving immigrants find gainful employment and eventually acquire Canadian citizenship. Ever the soccer fan, he assisted Fathers Jerome Ferraro and Domenico Fiore found St. Anthony's Soccer Club (Saro was Presient of the club for 6 years, 1952-1958). Even in those early days, Saro realized the importance of a political voice for the community and actively supported the local Liberal Party. While not volunteering his time in these pursuits, he found time to work as a mechanic at a local garage.

A diesel mechanic, rare in those days, by trade, Saro quickly progressed from garage work to Smith Transport, indisputably Canada's largest and most recognizable trucking firm, where he became a trusted, skilled, and respected diesel mechanic. Many's the time, he would recall, when he was awakened in the middle of the night to repair transport trucks stuck somewhere on the TransCanada highway. Many nights were spent away from Ottawa as his skills were required on-site on many occasions.

But Saro's ambitions ran beyond merely working as a mechanic for others. In 1964, he acquired the service station on the corner of 241 Preston Street run by Rino Mazzocato and rebaptized it Saro's BP Station (this building first appeared in the Ottawa city directory in 1959). Milano Auto Body and Paint soon followed in 1974. Both establishments quickly became centers of social activity on Preston Street as clients and friends would drop-by for coffee and the inevitable lively debate about that week's soccer match.

More than a working office, the walls of Saro's office attested to the heartfelt love for the black and white of his soccer team, Juventus, but also displayed the many community service awards awarded to

Saro and his company. These included the Queen Elizabeth II Golden Jubilee Medal and the Caring Canadian Award. His dedication and lasting contributions to both the Italian and Canadian communities were acknowledged by his native Italy with the prestigious *Cavaliere al Merito* medal.

Sons Tony, an engine mechanic, and Giuseppe, a painter by trade, continued their father's legacy and maintained their father's trademark honesty and devotion to excellence and customer satisfaction up to 2016 when both officially retired from the trade. The Panuccio family continues to own their father's property but the body shop continues under new management as does the gas station, now known as the Preston Street Garage or Gabriel's Auto (the gas pumps were removed before the end of the 1990s).

Saro's BP Station and Milano Autobody and Paint recall a simpler time when the Preston Street neighborhood gave the community the advantages of shopping, working, and congregating at the same place people lived. Though not official bars or caffe's, these establishments represented credit-worthy community hang-outs, where anyone with a little spare time could find a place to chat and a friendly ear. Saro's philanthropic spirit of selfless community service and dedicated labor is and remains the heart of place-making; keys to appreciating people as lasting social fixtures.

Sala San Marco

Forever modern, forever new, Sala San Marco is constantly updating its professional profile. Named for the patron saint of Venice, birthplace of Maria Bonacin, Tony Zacconi's maternal grandmother (his grandfather, Luigi Vigliotti moved the family to Oslo, Norway after marriage), Sala San Marco has been an important Preston Street anchor since 1987. Tony proudly recalls how his parents opened a restaurant called Caffe Italia in 1982 immediately across the street from Sala San Marco, in a building the family had purchased in the 1970s. The banquet hall opened in 1987.

Sala San Marco was the brainchild of Tony's father, Joe Zacconi, and his uncle Luigi Aprile who purchased the land in 1985 in order to build a future banquet hall. At the time, the City of Ottawa, but especially the Italian community, lacked a large venue for special events and an event center to celebrate gala occasions. The notion was well-thought and farsighted. Over the years, these well-appointed and multi-functional event centers have become increasingly popular venues because they help transform small family gatherings, or large receptions and banquets, as well as community events and special occasions into memorable moments of celebration.

The Sala was an immediate success. Its well-appointed rooms helped make important and special moments even more memorable. The first memories current owner and manager Tony maintains is helping to assemble chairs and table set-up at the age of eleven. The first weddings were held in the Fall of 1987, and Tony remembers them all. Over the years, the community has become accustomed to celebrating Easter Sunday and Mother's Day with sumptuous brunches. New Year's Eve celebrations are also a yearly appointment as generations of revelers continue the tradition at Sala. These events are routinely sold-out, attesting to the continuing quality and festive promise that the Zacconi family provides the community.

But Sala San Marco is also a proud organizer and sponsor of many charitable events that return the love and support it has received from the community. Millions of dollars have been donated to local charities while event space, deeply discounted prices, and flexibility care have solidified the Zacconi family's position as one of the most generous families in the Ottawa community. Mother Zacconi is still deeply involved in Sala activities. Over 500 women attended the International Women's Day event she organized where all proceeds were donated to Nelson House. The family's generosity extends all the way back to Italy as local fundraisers for overseas projects in the family's native Calabria are regularly supported.

Son, and current owner, Tony is very comfortable in his role, very proud to serve his heritage community with dignity and love, respect and honor. After stints in government work, as restaurant owner, and in other sundry activities, Zacconi receives the greatest satisfaction from his banquet business. "I am proud that for decades people have trusted Sala for the most important events in their lives and that the community continues to support us. What I have learned is that there are no 'do-overs' in this business. We have to nail-it the first time, every time. And we normally do. We have a fantastic and professional staff that guarantees event success." Tony is particularly gratified by Sala San Marco's reputation in the community; a community he loves and that he serves with passion, pride, and professionality. "We are big on innovation and being on-trend but are proud to maintain deep family business values because we are part of this community. We are happy to build long-lasting relationships with our clients who are more like friends rather than clients. In this sense we are very accessible."

As a true ambassador of Italian culinary traditions and purveyors of excellence, Sala San Marco boasts a loyal following not only in the Italian-Canadian community but in the Ottawa community at large. The locale boasts four fabulous banquet halls that when connected can accommodate 800 guests but can certainly be scaled down to fit smaller gatherings of 20. Tony believes that Sala's strength and success lie in the honest efforts of his staff to unite the community in a spirit of convivial enjoyment, while their location, interior amenities and comforts, quality of service and cost guarantee satisfaction and ongoing loyalty. "I am happy to continue our reputation of excellence and luxury, but above all of professional value. I love my work. I could not imagine doing anything else."

Pasticceria Gelateria Italiana

A favorite stop on the street is the Pasticceria Gelateria Italiana, co-owned by award-winning Pastry and Chocolate Chef, Joe Calabro. An established all-season icon, the shop offers professionally inspired and meticulously prepared desserts for the most discriminating tastes. Joe brings all his unique skills to bear in the production of award-winning pastries and sumptuous gelati. As a member of the Canadian Federation of Chefs, a member of the European World Master Chefs Society and member of Les Toques Blanches International, he provides the street with a bone fide world-class establishment that caters creative and inspired traditional sweets.

Photo-Lux, *now* Photoluxstudio

The official website of photoluxstudio informs its patrons that "It's more than just a photo, it's about the experience." A motto that aptly sums the long years of service and seminal importance of this community landmark. Ubaldo Cava, founder of Photo-Lux, located at 197 Preston St., remembers the name of his very first camera: *The Comet*, made by Bencini, a camera manufacturer of Milan. The camera held 127mm film. "My mother gave me the camera. I started earning a few cents that I quickly used to buy cigarettes."

He began his career early, becoming a "traveling photographer" for the three nearby villages of his hometown Serra Pedace, located on the slopes of the Sila-Cosentina in Calabria. The work was slow, but constant; mostly photographs of children sent to relatives who had emigrated to America. Others required photographs of themselves to send to future marriage partners by proxy, a common occurrence that presented a vehicle of escape from village poverty. After a series of jobs as a photojournalist for local newspapers, Ubaldo had the good fortune of meeting Biagio Granata, a notable photographer of the period, and learned much under his apprenticeship. He remained a part of his studio, *Photo d'Arte Granata*, until 1961, the year he married and emigrated to Canada in 1962.

The Ottawa Italian community provided few opportunities for the eager photographer. While roaming through several nondescript jobs, he continued, nevertheless, to photograph weddings and became the community's official passport photographer. Eventually, and after continuing odd photography assignments, the first Photo-Lux studio was opened in 1967, a workroom built next to his father-in-law's carpentry shop, located at 354 ½ Preston Street.

Ubaldo is proud of his service to the community both as visual archivist of its many events as well as witness to the many families who booked the services of Photo-Lux for their most important family celebrations. The studio had acquired a reputation for punctuality, precision, and artistic photography. Its wedding photography was normally back-dropped by the beautiful views and exotic flowers of Ottawa's Experimental Farm (one of the first photographers to use the venue), while its in church photography of the sacraments became legendary.

As the years passed and the reputation of the studio increased, it became necessary to hire two new photographers, Tony Alloggia and Luciano Del Rio, and move to a larger space, the current location on Preston Street. The new location offered the possibility of studio photography with creative lighting and backdrops. The seasonal nature of the work now became yearlong and business increased exponentially.

This success was noted by sons Antonio and Francesco who, after an internship with their father and a university Masters Degrees in Photography, joined the firm and eventually became internationally recognized photographers in their own right. Today, photoluxstudio defines itself as "a multi-generational studio located in the heart of little Italy." Indeed, this dynamic studio remains one of the most respected and experienced in the industry.

Photographs are an invaluable record of the community, preserving and documenting normally unrecorded information about humanity and nature, visual realities, the details and essential processes of human interaction. They are a key towards understand the self-created image of the community and convey this meaning through both their content and through their use. In this sense, Photo-Lux, now photoluxstudio, remains an invaluable partner of the verbal history of the Italian-Canadian community.

Pub Italia

The most original, evident, and lasting icon of Preston Street business remains, however, the local caffé. Each can boast a loyal, if not specific, clientele. They continue to serve as a meeting place, initially catering solely to men, to discuss sports, politics, for passing time or playing cards; a large percentage of the social contact among men in the community takes place in the traditional confines of the local caffé.

These brick and mortar real caffe's remain salient, even today, for two reasons: the ethnic nature of the business and/or the relative and rising popularity of the street when compared to those in the downtown core. Both the number and quality of the businesses would improve if the fast and heavy traffic were redirected elsewhere, hopefully encouraging more walk-in trade. But the traffic remains, and cars bring with them consumers who look towards the newer establishments, as well as the older, revitalized locals, as the new beat on Preston Street.

Such is the case of Pub Italia. Festooned with antique photos and strewn with religious icons, the pub may appear to the casual observer as a campy locale with anything but local ties. Yet this iconic watering hole and eatery is firmly planted in the humus of the area. Its owner, Joe Cotroneo, is a homegrown neighborhood original proud both of his roots and his idiosyncratic locale. His crowd is mixed and upscale, sophisticated yet traditional; an appreciative clientele that animates Preston Street with positive vibes.

The popular eatery, Pub Italia, is a visually quirky establishment that caters to a mixed and upscale clientele; it is a destination place for the community beyond Preston Street. Resembling more a Medieval abbey than a local drinking establishment, Pub Italia is the unique creation of owner Joe Cotroneo. "I always said that I was in the wrong line of work, the former journeyman electrician confesses, so one day I simply hung up my tools and decided to mull life's mystery." A visit to Boston and the purchase of T-shirt at a Boston ethnic festival would alter the future pub owner's destiny. "The shirt featured an Italian and an Irish flag crisscrossed on its front with the words: 50% Italian, 50% Irish, 100% Perfect!" The similarity of the flag's colors, plus the fact that his wife was also Irish, consolidated a burgeoning dream. "I've always been involved, in one way or another, with the Preston Street area," he continues. "I grew-up on this street. I was naturally interested in preserving its space as part of the Italian community of Ottawa. The idea of creating an Italian pub intrigued me because no one had ever heard of an Italian pub. This gave me a chance to create something unique. The addition of my wife's Irish half simply made the dream even grander."

Anyone that has been to the British Isles knows that pubs are the traditional heart of the community in villages and towns all over the British Isles. But the pub's origins are surprisingly Italian. Long before the Isles caught the eye of the Caesars, Roman tabernae served food and wine to the locals and were known for their bawdy manners. Travelers used roadside tabernae as a stopping place along the extensive Roman road network. Over time, invaders came and went; but the one thing all had in common was a fondness for the hearty food and robust drink served by the tabernae. By the time the Romans had conquered and left the British Isles, the Saxons had adopted the custom of turning cottages into what came to be known as ale houses. An early association between the Catholic Church and ale serving establishments occurs in the Tenth Century. As the faithful were encouraged to visit the growing number of cathedrals rising in Europe, taverns became statutory stopping posts for travel-weary, throat-parched, and morally inspired pilgrims. This, along with burgeoning commerce, spurred an already flourishing public house trade to augment profitability by also providing room and board for fatigued travelers. These pubs, also referred to as inns, were often located near monasteries that had heretofore provided shelter for pilgrims but were now dreadfully overcrowded. A further connection with the Church came with the guild workers who were hired by the local prelates to build their cathedrals. These workers were housed in Church-owned inns, usually run by monks. The enriched spirituality of the place served ale (and religion) on tap. Many of these legendary medieval pubs remain to this day and have names linked to Christianity (Cross Keys, The Lion and Lamb, The Mitre, The Three Crowns, for example).

Two thousand years later, enter Joe Cotroneo. Mixing both the historical Irish thirst for ale and the Italian passion for wine and food, Pub Italia was born. The combination is both historical and interesting, if not amusingly logical. Pub Italia is indeed a good place to quaff beers and savor wines. There is a romantic, medieval, and willfully Christian atmosphere to the interior. Customers sit in high-backed stalls that remind patrons of monastic intimacy and create intriguing little eating areas. Like a Master Guildsman, Joe is meticulous in the selection and placement of decor. Stations of the Cross adorn the walls, a reminder of life's travail, stained glass figures beckon chaste thoughts, rough-hewn and heavy wooden beams visually link the interior to its rustic origins.

The equally original Abbey extension next door provides a further link to a remote past and also features a pleasant courtyard setting to enjoy a round or two beneath the image of a singing choir boy. Formerly a bakery the Abbey is separated from the Main building by a 12-foot driveway. The building was completely renovated to maximize the monastic atmosphere of the pub. The driveway became an internal courtyard. A loggia-style passage links the two buildings. It is adorned with murals and frescoes by Karole Maroise depicting the Garden of Eden. This sylvan passage leads to two doors of heavenly respite (washrooms) appropriately labeled Adam and Eve.

But Joe is also conscious of the pub's inheritance, situated as it is in the heart of the Italian community and significant for its historical importance as the repository of the community's memories. Prominently displayed in the pub are murals of his grandparents. Painted by Maroise the first depicts his mother's parents, Grazia and Giuseppe Palermo, in stoic 19th Century pose. They stand before the small village of Santa Lucia in southern Calabria. The second is of his paternal grandfather, Pasquale Cotroneo. He sits, appropriately enough, in a tiny bar in Santa Lucia wearing hunting boots, jacket, and fedora. Both murals signal Joe's indisputable love for his own ancestral roots and his fervent desire to share that love with his customers. This passion extends to the scrupulous selection of the establishment's liquid offerings. The menu lists over 200 beers and 36 draft taps from a truly international brew list.

Pub Italia is at the heart of the steadily improving streetscape that is re-seeding the new-look of Preston Street with traces of the old Village quality that once defined the area. Most of the original customers may be gone, but Pub Italia is an essential hub of the street's future providing an animated and exceptionally crafted social gathering place offering high quality food, a full-service bar, and an upscale casual environment. All this while maintaining a felicitous cross between Italian style, Irish informality . . . and Christian morality.

The Food Scene: Not by Bread Alone

Whether selling it, preparing it, or eating it, food remains the primary transmitter of culture. Food preferences and choices are important elements of the cultural heritage they represent. From a cultural perspective, ethnic foods serve as a familiar sociocultural link with the past and provide a comfortable buffer to an unfamiliar and threatening reality. Not only do ethnic foods help maintain ethnic identity but they provide opportunities for the larger community to experience the newly arrived culinary traditions of the smaller ethnic group. The interaction creates a zone of acceptance that can mature into lasting sociocultural relationships. An ethnic population thus inspires a more multicultural palate. Foods add a new flavour dimension that challenges the conceptions of both the purveyors of foreign product and its consumers.

In the Italian-Canadian community of Ottawa, local grocery stores and corner variety stores have provided more than simple product diversity to customers. Their importance and influence can be traced to the enterprising ambulant fruit peddlers that populated the cityscape at the beginning of the 20th Century. These hardworking local merchants have nurtured the evolving acceptance of cultural diversity and human acceptance in the surrounding English and French community. Their evolving trade was the bedrock of the growing Italian community. More than just bricks and mortar, these intrepid individuals were creating legacy, good family name, community reputation, and cultural honor. The grocery store was a vital property. It was meant to be preserved and passed-on to succeeding generations. More than simple merchants, then, they became and remain modern ambassadors of humanism that provide valued cultural social spaces for ethnic identity formation and recognition. Their work extends into and beyond the community through their generous donations of time and money to charitable events, community feasts, and religious festivals.

The role these retailers played in formulating ethnic identities and their acceptance through food security is crucial. Ottawa has been blessed with a good number of food retailers over the years. Some, like Attinello Foods, Pasqua Grocery Store, Guzzo-Adamo, Arnone

Foods, S. Abbenda Grocery, Petruzzi, De Falco, Zaccone, and J. Saso and Son are no longer part of the community.[66]

A few others have created a lasting niche for themselves because they have created trends. They are community influencers and have played a vital role in shaping both its ethnic direction and acceptance within Ottawa. They have gained respect because of their qualifications and experience, and for their unending generosity to community events.

Nicastro Foods

Though not located in the Preston Street area, the name Nicastro is iconic in the community and evokes memories of the sun-drenched streets of the quaint mountain town of Cleto, Calabria. Five generations of family have worked the grocery aisles since Pasquale Nicastro opened a butchery in the small village that overlooks the Mediterranean in 1928. Brother Leopoldo extended the shop, enlarging it to include groceries and other sundry items. Their sons and daughters all remember growing-up

---

66 Each of these grocery stores had a long and varied history but shared the same family work ethic. Known in the community for their honesty, unrelenting labor, and selfless generosity, they were neighborhood anchors for newly arriving families, one-stop shopping for housewives, convenient hang-outs for youth. Unfortunate victims to suburban box-stores and grocery marts, they are remembered for the many family memories they helped create and the nascent dreams they sustained in the growing Italian community. The following is a listing of the better-known Italian grocers. My apologies to those whose merited reputation did not cross my desk.

Attinello Italian Foods, owned by Salvatore Attinello located on Bank Street near Sunnyside; eventually moved to Preston Street; Pasqua Grocery Store, owned by Joe Pasqua, located at 40 Lett Street on the Lebreton Flats, moved to Bell Street; Arnone Foods, owned by Jimmy Arnone and located on Preston Street; S. Abbenda Grocery, located at 564 Gladstone, eventually sold to the Nicastro brothers; Petruzzi Grocery, owned by Rosina Petruzzi and located at Somerset and Booth Streets; DeFalcos Wine Making and Grocery, owned by Domenic DeFalco located on Preston Street; J. Saso and Son, one of the oldest stores, Joe Saso and wife Margerite open their wholesale fruit business in an old carriage repair shop in 1923 in the Byward Market. Son Charlie sold the locale to the Nicastro brothers in 1994.

amidst the stocked shelves, remember the customers who became their extended family, remember the passion of their parents for their trade.

But the family was large, times in postwar Italy were often difficult. Lidia and her brother Alessandro emigrated to Canada in 1956. They sought their fortune in Ottawa where Bartolo Marinaro, a tailor by trade, began the chain immigration that was to call so many fellow compatriots from Cleto. They were soon followed by Leopoldo in 1959 who left the grocery to younger brother Franco until he too emigrated to Ottawa in 1962. Both worked construction briefly, but their hearts remained in retail. Back in Cleto, the store was inherited by Rocco and Giuseppe who were helped by mother Irma and sister Nella. Already deeply involved in the family business since youth, the brothers' passion for retail and customer service only deepened their commitment to creating a full-service grocery.

In 1966 Franco Nicastro, tired of construction labor, opened the first Nicastro-run grocery. He called it Frank's Meat and Grocery. Located on Somerset and Cambridge, his business partners were brothers-in-law Pietro Falsetti and Fortunato Furano. The store was successful and attracted his other brothers to Canadian shores.

Rocco was the next Nicastro to arrive in Ottawa in 1968. He found immediate work at brother Frank's Meat and Grocery where he learned, he likes to specify, "the Canadian way" of doing business. Four years later, Rocco, Giuseppe, Salvatore, Alessandro, Ugo, and Franco proudly opened the first store emblazoned with the name Nicastro Brothers Food on Gladstone Avenue. The year was 1972.

The brothers had a knack for pleasing their customers and no one could dispute the quality of their merchandise. The store proved an enormous success and the Nicastro brand was finally born in Canada. Franco eventually sold the original Meat and Grocery market in 1977 and went to work full-time with his brothers in the recently opened 1580 Merivale Road location. Business was brisk, and the brothers revelled in their merited success.

The brothers divided their energies between the two locations, Gladstone and Merivale, and ensured that their second store became an immediate success. The burgeoning Italian clientele coupled with their increasing influence in the English and French community at large necessitated a move to larger locale. In 1990, the Nicastro Merivale grocery moved up the street (1558) and into a mall already owned by the brothers. The new location quickly became their flagship store. They remained there till November 2017 when the business was sold. Details of the agreement provide for the Nicastro Brand to remain an integral part of the premises.

The success of the Merivale store eventually caused the brothers to consolidate and close the Gladstone store in 1993. The year 1994, however, sees the younger generation of Nicastro youth begin to branch-out and achieve success. The trendy Pesto's Italian Delicatessen is a Nicastro spin-off that opened in Kanata and serves the needs of Ottawa's most western suburb.

In 1995 another Nicastro generation, Pasquale (Pat) opened La Bottega, a unique boutique grocery in the heart of Ottawa's Byward Market. Cousin Rocco Jr. soon joined Pat as a partner after finishing his high school education. The store occupies the old J. Saso and Son Grocery store space, one of the first Italian groceries in Ottawa that had occupied the location since 1923. The purposefully retro-grocery has maintained the old-time, small-town feel with over-stacked aisles, but has added a deli counter with over-stuffed fresh gourmet sandwiches, a crowded Italian-style caffé, and a full-service restaurant. The grocery has won many awards and recognition throughout Canada for its gourmet products, artisan foods, rustic pasta and sauces, and premium service. It has become a destination stop for out-of-town tourists.

The family name is strong and is well placed in the business community of Ottawa. There is hardly a party, event, or festival that is not catered, sponsored or supported by a Nicastro store. And now, with the fifth generation firmly entrenched and taking the reins with novel ideas and upscale products, all are happy and proud of their legacy, eager to continue the hard work and cultural traditions that began back on the sunny streets of Cleto.

Luciano Foods

A longtime fixture in the community for over 40 years, this grocery store, conveniently located at the corner of Preston and Somerset Ave., sees long lines of food gourmets that flock from both sides of the Ottawa River. Owner Luciano Gervasi is head of a family business that boasts reasonable prices and unique quality foods and excellent customer care.

RESTAURANTS
Angelo's La Roma

When Angelo's La Roma opened in 1962, there wasn't another Italian restaurant like it. In fact, there wasn't any other Italian restaurant in the area, the closest one located on the other side of Parliament Hill. Located on the corner of Bronson and Somerset Streets in a former Bank of Nova Scotia location, Angelo Costanza bought the building and set about to renovate. He and wife Tersilla Cedossi wished to open an authentic Italian restaurant in Ottawa, a daunting proposition even in today's heady foodie atmosphere. Imagine launching the enterprise in the middle of a working-class neighborhood back in the early 60s! But open he did, and the place was packed from that day forward. He had the right concept, in the right location, at the right time. Over the years the couple added or changed many items of the original menu but never changed the formula: simple but tasty food, quality ingredients, and most importantly: a place where everybody knew your name. the upstart neighborhood restaurant the soon became an Ottawa mainstay.

The couple was not new to the world of customer satisfaction and had skirted the food business. In Italy, Angelo and wife ran a convenience store that feigned as the town dispensary for non-prescription medicine, but also carried groceries and other sundry items that included liquor. From here, a simple matter of will allowed Tersilla's expertise as a cook to prepare sauces and meals in what must have been the first take-out restaurant in the small town of Albengo in the northern Italian region of Liguria. The family brought these skills and talents to Ottawa and introduced catering to the community at large.

The locale itself was stylish and sophisticated, elegant but not stodgy. The Costanza's were devoted to maintaining original flavors but updated and refined the traditional recipes of their villages for modern palates. They introduced square pizza before it became the staple of generations and regularly treated local Immaculata High School students to free pizza. They are proud to have introduced fried zucchini to their appetizer menu as well as spumoni ice cream (hand packed and made on premises) to their clientele. That clientele included parliamentarians, businessmen, sports teams, and professionals in the capital region. Pierre Elliott Trudeau, as well as subsequent Prime Ministers of Canada, used La Roma as a favorite haunt.

La Roma also sponsored local sports and was an active participant in many community events. The Costanza family's generous and heartfelt contribution of time, money, and food to nascent enterprises such as Italian Week, the Dante Alighieri, and Carnevale made them indispensable partners in these beginning initiatives that helped create and secure a sense of community for the Italian-Canadians of Ottawa.

Trattoria Caffè Italia

Another cornerstone of Preston Street is the Trattoria Caffè Italia. Originally known as Caffè Italia, it first opened on the corner of Balsam and Preston Streets in 1950. The locale was a popular male hangout for billiards and card playing.

After taking ownership in the late 1970s, Joe Zacconi continued to operate the locale as mainly a caffè and a place for Italians in the neighbourhood to play cards and just hang-out. In 1982 Joe and Gina Zacconi added a small dining lounge and renamed the establishment Trattoria Caffè Italia. There weren't too many authentic Italian restaurants around at the time. The food was hearty and the atmosphere was homey. Owners Joe and Gina were always there ready greet their guests at the door and share a laugh.

The restaurant was an immediate success and remains an anchor on the Preston Street foodscape. Current owners Dominic and Pasquale Carrozza moved Trattoria to their current location at the corner of Gladstone and Preston and have both renovated and increased dining space by adding a second-floor banquet hall.

Giovanni Ristorante

Exceptional detail, a professional staff, and superb cuisine are the hallmark of Giovanni's Ristorante. Founded by Lisa Cocco Pollastrini and late husband Giuseppe Pollastrini, their dream was to bring to their passion for Italian food to Ottawa. And indeed, since 1983 a loyal clientele has enjoyed only the freshest and finest of ingredients, handpicked and selected by stellar Chef Tomasz Gurzynski. Serving exquisite food and Italian charm the restaurant is a cornerstone of the Preston Street foodscape and a destination stop on the Ottawa culinary scene.

Ciccio Ristorante

The Eramo family opened the doors to Ciccio Ristorante in 1974. Their idea was simple: provide homestyle, but elegant, food service to the Ottawa community. Over the years the innovative décor, authentic Italian flavors, and excellent service have made their mark on Preston Street, making Ciccio one of the more popular restaurants on the street. Owner Leone Eramo, whose family originates in Carpineto Romano, Italy, is proud to have served the community and appreciative the tradition continues.

OFF-STREET COMMUNITY BUSINESS
Giovanni's Snack Bar

Italian caffe's have a long reputation for being home to superb espresso, heated discussions, and sports talk. Today's caffes have evolved from the *tavernae vinariae* of classical Rome; a place Romans would stop and enjoy a glass of wine and pass the time with other citizens.

Giovanni's Snack Bar is just such a social place; a friendly oasis amidst the often grey and depressed landscape of the local neighborhood. And it is different to anything that one might expect. Situated on the corner of Booth and Willow Streets, long-time proprietors Antonio Mirella (affectionately known as Bruno to his friends) and wife Rosanna Perini (official barista) managed one of the few caffe's in Ottawa at a time when the concept was a novelty.

Opened in 1969 by original owner (and brother-in-law) Giovanni Petrillo, the couple turned the corner establishment into an icon of the Italian community long before sipping coffee in Italian-style coffee establishments became a trendy North American pastime.

More than a caffé, however, Giovanni's Snack Bar was the home-away-from-home for community aficionados of soccer, politics, and local news all blended amidst cups of heady espresso. The standing-room only locale tripled as a newsstand, providing the weekly fix of newspapers and magazines imported directly from Italy (Italian embassy staff were regular customers), as a grocery store for those last-minute Sunday morning purchases, and as a deli. Sandwiches from Giovanni's were legendary, again beating franchised sandwich shops for quality and size.

But the real draw for most were the soccer games. Bruno boasted one of the few shortwave radios in the city and customers crowded the small locale to cheer their team. Television eventually replaced radio; but the bonds that tied passionate fans sanctioned their social connections and blossomed friendships formed through fandom. It must be said that Giovanni's Snack Bar, beyond having been an absolute gem of a family business, played a significant and positive role in the life of the community; it provided a vital daily focal signature in the lives of its many customers.

The corner location has recently changed ownership. Though it remains a traditional male hangout serving some of the best coffee in the area, the new owners have dramatically restored the interior and expanded its sandwich offerings to include pizza and alcohol.

Di Rienzo Grocery and Deli

Considered one of the best sandwich shops in Ottawa, Di Rienzo Grocery and Deli has been a fixture on the corner of Beech and Champaign streets since 1973. For over 40 years owner Paolo Di Rienzo and family have been spreading the joy of Italian food beyond the local community.

It is known as the place that created street food before it was popular. "It all began," recalls Paolo, "one day when city workers were replacing street sewers in front of the store. We made them sandwiches for lunch. Didn't charge them anything. We were just happy they were fixing the sewers." The workers must have liked them, and spread the word. Since that generous gesture, between 200-400 custom sandwiches have been sold daily to city crews, policemen, firemen, government office staff, and routine regular customers who drop by not only for the over-stuffed sandwiches but for the healthy and hearty food.

Older brother Gennaro works as cook and provides daily hot servings of homemade pastas and soups. Nephews Antonio, Laura, and Lima work the counter while wife Carolee Dunn oversees the books. A real family business that traces its Canadian roots to 1967 when the elder Di Rienzo sisters and brothers emigrated to Ottawa, soon followed by Paolo and his father.

The family is proud of having served over 10,000,000 sandwiches to date. But they have somehow found time to gain the reputation as one of the most generous philanthropists in the community. They regularly give-back to the community in both monetary donations, work, and food. Hardly an Italian-Canadian community event occurs without a Di Rienzo Grocery endorsement. They are also official sponsors of the Daffodil Campaign, the TELUS Ottawa Ride for Dad, and many other charitable organizations.

Musca Wine Pressing and Supplies

Wine has played a central role in human culture for more than 8,000 years. The practice of making wine is as old as the most ancient civilization. In its basic form, wine making is a natural process that requires little human intervention.

The Italian-Canadian community loves its wine-making. The yearly quixotic ritual softened the pain of immigration; became the primary object of an immigrant collective fantasy as vital as planting tomatoes; gave the sense of feeling at home; a welcomed and soothing balm both in its production (the companionship of relatives and friends) and in its consumption (with the same companions). A link to tradition and the homeland, for better or worse one's home made wine is one's signature, a liquid legacy hopefully passed-on to the next generation. The same is true of food traditions. From curing meats to canning tomatoes, first generation immigrants grew, harvested, processed, and preserved their food in much the same manner they would have in Italy. These traditions are recalled with fondness and with heartfelt longings for simpler times. They are never discounted nor dismissed.

One of the first purveyors of fresh produce, grapes, wine-making equipment, and canning material was the Musca Fruit Store. Begun by Giorgio Musca and wife Lucia (Pina), they ran the family variety store originally located on Rochester Street near Balsam. The store was open 365 days a year, usually from 7:00 am into late evening. The only official holiday, if it could be called such, was Christmas morning; the store opened at 11:00 am. Traditional Christmas dinner was eaten with the family in the back of the store. The family, similar to many family-run businesses at the time, lived upstairs. Business dominated domestic life.

Giorgio Musca was born in Sannicola, Lecce; wife Lucia Toscano was from nearby Chiesanuova. After the birth of their first child, Maria, the family immigrated to Canada. Silvano, their son, was born in Canada in 1954. Giorgio began his Canadian odyssey as a fruit vendor. He sold fruit door to door for the Gamble Robinson Produce Company. The job gave him a feel for the neighborhood and its arriving Italian residents. He would soon open his own store and cater to those same customers.

The Musca Fruit Store opened in 1954. From the very beginning the business was more of a variety store and sold almost everything. From shoes and sox, to pots and pans, fabric and thread, to glasses and plates. Groceries were the main staple, but the store offered much, much more. An intelligent and ambitious man, Giorgio was the first Italian grocer to import fresh grapes by the crate from California. 300 cases were imported the first year; all unloaded by hand, all sold-out. All helped soften the sting of immigration for his many customers. Through the years, the yearly purchase of grapes for home wine production helped soften the sting of immigration for his many customers that moved beyond the Italian community and included Portuguese, Polish, Hungarian, Croatians, Spanish, and, once winemaking became a trendy pastime, English and French Canadians.

The grocery side of the Musca Fruit Store eventually succumbed to the tide of large grocery chains. The ever-resourceful Musca family, however, changed with the trend. The bulk of their business has evolved into a one stop homemade wine supply store that sells wine testing equipment, wine bottling accessories, wine filters, sanitizers, and related sundry items. From Wine Alternatives, like Fresh Juices, Concentrates, Freshly Crushed and de-stemmed Grapes from Italy, wines made onsite for the client, as well as wine making kits, Musca has all the wine making supplies to make that special personal vintage for the discriminating customer.

The business is now run by Silvano Musca and wife Carmela. Serving in-store wine making services as well as home making wine supplies and equipment, the goal of Musca is to offer nothing but the best quality of grapes, fresh juices, and concentrates from all over the world. As a direct importer of award-winning fresh juices that are carefully blended and balanced by an in-house Oenologist, Musca has satisfied the community's evolving needs for over 60 years.

Mamma Teresa Ristorante

The city of Parma, in the Emilia Romagna region of Italy, is noted for sumptuous food, a legendary king of cheeses, a world-class prosciutto, and fine wine. When Giuliano Boselli and his mother Teresa established a restaurant that bore her name, they opened the doors to those traditions of legendary dishes that would honor the original flavors of their native land. It could be said that Mamma Teresa Restaurant introduced the National Capital Region to Italian food; to the food that made the peninsula famous. It provided an upscale venue that recalled the finest of dining experiences. But above all, it presented a refined Italian dining experience at a time when the Italian-Canadian community was still struggling for an identity.

Since 1970, the family has welcomed its guests to a friendly and warm ambiance. Their hospitality is legendary; their reputation, according to many, uncompromisingly unmatched. Beyond the city borders, the restaurant became a definite tourist destination. Located on the corner of Somerset and O'Connor Streets, the walls tell a tale of family gatherings, business dealings, political compromises, and intimate dinners for couples in love. Mamma Teresa not only brought Italian food into mainstream Ottawa, it helped create the culture of upscale dining that pervades the market today. It was a catalyst that provided a unique professional environment for the enjoyment of classic Italian food.

ART ON PRESTON STREET
Mural

The massive mural that visitors encounter beneath the Highway 417 viaduct is the brainchild of Joe Cotroneo, owner of one of the more popular, if not most unique, establishments on Preston Street/*Corso Italia*, Pub Italia. Joe is a long-time community resident, innovative businessman, and primetime area promotor. The idea of a neighborhood improvement project that celebrated the lives of Italian immigrants in paint is an extension of Joe's conception of the street as a pedestrian center of Italian-Canadian heritage.

Public murals are part of the successful and ongoing process of reversing decades of stagnation on Preston Street. Painted by artist Karole Marois, the mural's colorful and multifaceted images depict the symbolic heritage and social history of the Italian community in Ottawa. Its colors have brightened a once dark and gloomy underpass by creating an easily recognizable and visually appealing community gestalt that highlights the history of the people who lived and worked in the area.

The overall view of the west side of the street is divided into an upper and lower canvas. The lower space takes the viewer along a time-line of an earlier Preston Streetscape. It begins at Preston Street's southernmost extension, Carling Avenue and the Little Italy Millennial Arch, centers upon a CN train (the train tracks ran along the location of Highway 417 today), moves northward towards an arriving streetcar (reminiscent of days when they rambled along Preston Street), the Plant Bath on the Sommerset Street corner of (a heritage property built in 1924 to improve the hygiene and well-being of the community's citizens), and ends at the Booth lumber yards. The streetscape is corniced by Dow's Lake to the South and the Ottawa River to the North.

The upper canvas features individual panels that honor local associations, families, events, and businesses with colorful cameos. They include: the Associazione Emiliana di Ottawa, the Preston Street Bicycle Race, Frank Licari and Sons Stucco and Plaster, the Pasquale Zito and Sons Grocery Store, the Giovanni di Roma Hair Salon, Slan Printing, the Società Sicula di Ottawa, the Eramo Family, Musca Wine Pressing and Supplies Ltd., Saro Panuccio and his BP Station, the Joe Ierullo and Sons Barber Shop, the Order of Italo Canadians, the Centro Abruzzese Canadese Inc., Luciano Foods, Peloso Family Fuels, the Pretoresi Association of Ottawa, and finally the Ottawa St. Anthony Soccer Club. Though the paint-scape is thematically uneven, it nevertheless charmingly represents a visual patchwork of the community's bedrock businesses and societal soul.

The eastside view is again divided into an upper and lower canvas. The lower section symbolically depicts the immigrant's voyage to Canada. Indeed, whereas the western side of the street reveals a background scenario of trees and buildings, the eastern side displays the body of an ocean liner with the usual panels painted upon the ship's hull. The arriving immigrants, laden with their cardboard suitcases, appear as dark silhouettes against the same ship. They arrive at a mythical Pier

21 in Halifax, eventually making their way to the emboldened title Little Italy. The upper half continues the same themes as previously and include: St. Anthony's Church, the Servite Sisters of the Addolorato, the Feast of San Rocco de la Croix, the Angelo Fiore Memorial, Trattoria Caffé Italia, La Roma Restaurant, Preston Hardware, Il Lavoratore: Family Photos of the Crotoneo Family, Venice Steel Works, The Prescott Hotel, La Bottega, Pasticceria Gelateria Italiana, Domenico Licari and Family, Fleischer Photography, St. Anthony's Ladies Aid[67], the Guzzo-Adamo Grocery, the Ottawa Rapinese Soccer Team and the Associazione Rapinese di Ottawa.

The mural has rallied the community and re-established a lost sense of place and Italian-Canadian pride and accomplishment. As a composite of community pride, this public celebration of past immigrant arrivals, present individual successes, and future family aspirations has generated a new civic dialogue that encourages a more active participation in the visual renewal of the streetscape not only by local inhabitants but by the community at large. By affirming community presence without denying individual space; the mural visually shares the unique history of the Italian-Canadian community and its solidarity with outsiders who visit the area. The mural is thus one more component that visually distinguishes Little Italy from other city neighborhoods. Sponsored by the Preston Street Business Improvement Association (BIA), it also represents the first time that the provincial Ministry of Transportation has permitted a private project on a public structure.

Because Preston Street is first and foremost a place for people - something the mural promotes and emphasises - this outdoor art gallery is only one of the projects that animate the new heart of the old community, giving it a new and sustainable self-identity. The fact that it located beneath a 6-lane highway viaduct makes it striking and visible. But it is not the sole representation of the new visual culture sprouting on Preston Street.[68]

---

67 Funeral director Lorne Kelly sponsored the Ladies Aid mural as he had acted as their banner carrier for many years in the St. Anthony's Day procession.

68 For a more detailed description of each individual mural including

Postcards from the Piazzas

A suite of 15 granite, bronze, and stainless steel sculptures now line the rejuvenated streetscape of Preston Street. Commissioned by the City Of Ottawa, the project continues the outdoor gallery approach adopted by the Preston Street BIA. Immediately visible to pedestrians and drivers alike, the human-sized sculptures line both sides of the street in a processional colonnade of eclectic themes and subjects.

The sculptures are the brainstorm of c j fleury, described as "a multi-media artist and cultural researcher who is deeply interested in the role of art in contemporary society."[69] Viewing the Preston Streetscape as a living, organic entity, fleury set out to animate the street with signposts of Italian-Canadian culture that wish to connect "the old country" to *Little Italy*.[70]

The sculptures are human-sized, inviting people to stop and dialogue, touch and interact with the many motifs, patterns, literary excerpts and the statuary atop the pedestals. Imemories of the cultural history of Preston Street come alive as one discovers the multifaceted realities of the Italian-Canadian community. There's a simple large brimmed hat atop one column, a reminder of the many lone men who braved the immigrant voyage to forge a new destiny for both themselves and their future families. The tools of their trades are emblazoned on the column plinth, while an epocal letter informs Maria that "I found work . . . I will send for you soon. Love, Your Berardino."

---

pictures, see John Sankey, *Outdoor Murals of Ottawa Canada: Corso Italia Heritage Mural*, www.johnsankey.ca/mural4.html.

69   Her practice includes drawing, shield-making, performance, writing, video, large-scale sculpture and pilot projects for social-justice and social-entrepreneurship education. She has completed commissions for seventeen permanent public works in Ontario and Quebec including: Ottawa - *Postcards from the Piazzas* (15 bronze and granite sculptures on Preston St); The "Women's Monument against Violence" (Elgin Street); The Dorothy O'Connell Anti-Poverty Activists' Monument (City Hall); Gatineau - "The Condition of Rosetta Stones" (C.E.G.E.P. Heritage College). See: http://www.masconline.ca/en/artists/directory/cj-fleury.aspx.

70   See the brochure, *Postcards from the Piazzas*.

Another pedestal pays silent homage to the origins of soccer in 1565 in Santa Croce Square in Florence. Still another celebrates the intrepid voyages of Marco Polo to Asia, one of the peninsula's original immigrants. An emerald colored map depicts his voyages, while the shape of the column recalls the architecture in Piazza San Marco.

And so on. Again, as with the murals, a wonderfully inspired idea is too often lost in the arbitrary nature of the individual themes spread over the sidewalks of Preston Street. Nothing really connects the pedestals beyond the uniqueness of the artist's perspective and the intentioned cultural walk of the willing participant. Perhaps a more localized subject-matter connecting the art pieces to Preston Street and the local community, rather than an idealistic attempt to bring the best of Italy (of which most immigrants, sadly, would have no clue) to the grey landscape of *Little Italy* would have given the postcards a more vital and grounded narrative.

Gateway Plaza

In May 2008, the rehabilitation of the Preston streetscape (beyond sewer and watermain replacement, eventual benches) was enhanced by the creation of a public plaza at the intersection with Gladstone Avenue. The plaza continued a consolidated a concerted effort by the BIA to identify the area's unique features and animate the street with viable cultural icons. Again, public art was at the center of a project for the visual renewal of Preston Street. But was it successful?

Towering stylized statues of 11 (the on-field number of a team) soccer players, immediately baptized *I bambini*, were erected at the intersection with four similar players located on the south east corner and seven more players located on the northeast corner. Designed by Stantec Engineering, the 11 field players are made of colored precast concrete, granite heads and tempered colored glass. The players apparently dribble soccer balls and we can only imagine that they are inviting passersby to do the same. According to Stantec: Working closely with the city and local community representatives, we addressed the practical requirements of the street by balancing the needs of traffic with transit, cyclists, pedestrians, businesses, and residents. The rejuvenation also provided places for the street to come alive through inviting streetscapes that include gardens, tree plantings, flowerbeds, wide sidewalks, piazzas, and patios. It also included elements of art and welcoming gateway features aimed at highlighting the area's culture.[71]

In other words, Preston Street was turned into just another semi-gentrified street in Ottawa (see Wellington Street, Elgin Street, Bank Street, to cite only a few) with similar accouterments employed to beautify the streetscape. But if towering soccer players just don't seem to fit the urban mix on these other streets, here they are actually a derogatory feature implying stereotypes of soccer fans and soccer mania amidst what is supposedly a street that *should* recall, highlight, promote, and possibly extemporize historico-cultural memories of the community. The overwhelming figures are thus visually underwhelming, the intended magic evaporates in all that zooming traffic.

Operative questions should have been: If you wish to see *Preston Street/Corso Italia*, is this exhibition helpful, illuminating, fun? Does it gather significant or representative examples from neighbothood's past? Does it overlook important aspects of the neighborhood's people, their art? Does it skew the sampling of the street in some detrimental way? Within these bounds, individual preferences can be usefully expressed.

---

71   See: *Preston Street Rehabilitation - The Heart of Ottawa's Little Italy: Bringing a Tired Street Back to Life.* https://www.stantec.com/en/projects/canada-projects/p/preston-street-rehabilitation

Portal Archways

On 6 June 2002, four polished autumn-brown Caledonia granite columns, two per each side of the street, were erected at the intersection of Carling Avenue and *Preston Street/Corso Italia*. The imposing columns rose 16 feet and, when connected with a 73 feet long curved tubular steel arch that crossed over the Preston roadway, formed a Portal Archway. A neon sign centered on the archway welcomes friends and visitors alike to *Little Italy*.

The architectonic landmark was a gift to the community by the Preston Street BIA. The project was spearheaded by Leo Bortolotti. The granite columns were produced in Quebec and assembled in Montreal by Les Granits Montval. The Durie Commercial Contracting company was responsible for installation. The tubular steel arch was rolled, fitted, welded and polished by Carleton Iron Works of Ottawa. Appropriately, Roger Pilon, an original *Village* boy, born and raised on Preston Street, was especially proud of the monumental project.

The intention of the Portal Archway and the Gateway Plaza is to create a delimited destination area similar, perhaps, to an Italian piazza. In the best of Italian architectural tradition, piazzas are the center of public life normally surrounded by the buildings that define its nature. They are threshold spaces, a third place filled with third places; always pedestrian-oriented and designed to be the heart of a town . . . or neighborhood.

And so, we return to our opening remarks that defined the schizofrenic nature of Preston Street: half transportation artery, half pedestrian mall. A thoroughfare seeking to defend an uneasy balance of wishful Italian pedestrian pleasure and Canadian economic utility, and not succeeding well in either. Future eyes and real estate signs point toward Preston Street. It is hoped that further revitalization and beautification projects contribute to a more nostalgic and authentic Italian feel before the street becomes a mere wind tunnel gateway to the eternally prorogued redevelopment fields of Lebreton Flats.

AFTERWORD
THE FUTURE AND SUSTAINABILITY

As Preston Street moves beyond its ethnic past and incorporates an amalgamated future, a tired proletarian street will be brought to life and become, the new beating heart in the center of a much larger city. According to plans: "A vibrant urban village will sprout up in *Little Italy* in the coming years, with a multimillion-dollar mixed use development project spearheaded by the Ottawa Community Housing Corporation (OCH). Gladstone Village will offer mixed-income housing, retail, commercial and green spaces, and a French language elementary school."[72] In the same article, Yasir Naqvi, Ottawa Centre MPP and Attorney General of Ontario, stated: "I'm confident that this is going to be a flagship project in demonstrating how to build complete communities, how to build vibrant, healthy and sustainable communities right in the core of the city." The new streetscape will shape the way residents experience the city, increase neighborhood safety, promote equitable access, and hopefully provide aesthetically pleasing public spaces for social gathering.

Just as lumber, fire and politics shaped the past of Preston Street, urbanization, multiculturalism, and gentrification will forge *Corso Italia's* destiny; intensification will transform the neighborhood in ways scarcely imaginable to its early pioneer residents and perhaps unsettling for its current ones. Bountifully crowded sidewalks, new major investments, inviting neighborhood coffee shops, boutique grocery stores to pick up dinner while strolling to a 45th floor Claridge Icon apartment overlooking Dow's Lake, will detail the future streetcape and provide the lifeblood of an appealingly modern and youthful community. But the transformation of the *ethnic Village* into a viable and contemporary

---

72   Paula McCooey, "Multimillion-dollar Mixed Use, Mixed Income Village Coming to Preston Street Area," *Ottawa Citizen*, 24 May 2017.

upscale and gentrified *generic Village* of sustainable development is fraught with uncertainty. Regeneration, renewal, revitalization, and beautification are buzz words for the trendy North American rehabilitation of its many worn urban storefronts and visually tired neighborhoods. The original businesses on Preston Street survived for two reasons: the ethnic (read family) nature of the enterprise and/or the relatively low rent when compared to property in the downtown core. Traffic was the area's lifeblood. In tomorrow's neighborhood, both the number and quality of the businesses would improve if the fast and heavy traffic were redirected elsewhere, thereby encouraging more leisurely walk-in trade.

More importantly, beyond the relatively innocuous pseudo-Italian signage and artworks that now animate the landscape, the street itself remains devoid of any truly identifiable ethnicity or culturally defining space. Though the same can be said of many other urban shopping streets in the City of Ottawa, the flavor of this particular street as an enduring Italian-Canadian enclave suffers if one considers its purported, and desperately desired, Italian roots. Preston Street and the surrounding area will continue its present pace of evolution and become a major artery of an expanding downtown core.

When examined from this vantage, Preston Street is replete with socio-cultural happenings, socio-historical importance, and alive with a trendy local vibe that continues to grow, consolidate, and animate its streetscape. These factors alone ensure a sustainable future. That future, however, is neither ethnic nor Italian-Canadian.

Perhaps the gravest sin the Italian-Canadian community has committed over the years was working against its own enduring sociohistorical sustainability. The historical and social niceties that rendered the Preston Street area a haven for ethnic pride are slowly slipping into the trendiness of gentrified upscale living, brogue-heeled hipsters, and latte-sipping bohemians.[73] As boutique condos and trendy

---

73 The phenomenon of gentrification was noted by Marxist sociologist Ruth Glass in 1964. She coined the term to describe the movement of London bohemians with cash to long-standing blue-collar communities (notably Islington and Notting Hill) thereby displacing hard-working laborers who could no longer afford to live there. Though defenders view this

pubs replace friendly barber shops, compact diners and tired storefronts, the original eateries and family-run businesses, once the sole reason to visit the street, have either succumbed to market pressures or become upscale vanilla businesses, attracting a sophisticated clientele that demands novelty in lieu of tradition. Though the arrival of encroaching bike lanes and towering river-view apartments signal the beginnings of an urban renaissance, the influx of speculative investors with the inevitable proliferation of skyward condominiums and cookie-cutter chain stores marks the destruction of neighborhood authenticity.[74] All the things that marked the area and make it attractive as a community haven, will be displaced if not destroyed.

And yet, interestingly, perhaps Preston Street is finally achieving the dream first envisioned by Sir Preston himself as he surveyed the land south of the flats as prime investment property for his settlers on river's edge. Indeed, the street now more than ever looks northward towards the river's edge of Lebreton Flats where multi-billion dollar investments are reclaiming indigenous land (remember the neighborhood was razed in the early 60s) and creating a new, up-scale urban playscape that will forever alter the landscape and flavor of the entire area.[75] Preston Street will indeed become a new liveable public space, compact and complex, offering flexible options and access to all the requisite social infrastructure: health, school facilities, entertainment, and workplaces.

But what will happen to the Italian-Canadian community? Will it grow with the process, or remain distanced from its own purported roots? Will the community ever escape its future?

---

repopulating of city cores and rebuilding of derelict sites as the creation of sustainably dense and architecturally resplendent neighborhoods, detractors argue that such newly designated heritage zones favor the rich and drive-out the artists, designers, young entrepreneurs, and original communities that helped save the areas in the first place.

74 The first chain store to visit the area will surely be a major supermarket, a sorely needed, according to the BIA, commodity that will anchor the neighborhood.

75 In 1962, the Diefenbaker government decided to clear what had become for many an industrial slum that was unbefitting of the nation's capital. The expropriation of the 2800 residents still living in the area began in April 1962. The last building was torn down at the end of 1966.

Separateness, and its propensity to establish clichés rather than foster harmony and union, have long plagued the Italian-Canadian community of Ottawa. We are referring to questions of identity and how that identity must be defined by a genuinely self-conscious social unit that places community above individuality and considers comunal memory vital source of individual pride. This sort of strong and viable local identity was never really fostered in the Italian-Canadian community.

If we are to sustain a genuine Italian-Canadian culture in the City of Ottawa, each individual must feel the need to fulfill the community's ethnic potential by fully expressing its unique Italian immigrant profile within the larger multicultural network. The Italian-Canadian community needs to help its longstanding (and often moribund) institutions continue the evermore difficult task of carving a genuine ethnic niche, or risk melting into its own unstirring indifference.

We must see to it that the process of engraining tradition not end with elementary-age youth but that it corresponds to a continuous and integrated experience for all members of the community, young and old.

That it not be limited to trendy wood-oven baked thin crust pizza and glistening autos but instead privilege the memories, myths, symbols and traditions that are the bedrock of the Italian experience in Canada.

Only then can a more beneficial evolution and sustainability of the Italian-Canadian community occur and realistic goals for a visionary future be posited and achieved. Only then will it persist and survive.

In a truly sustainable community, art, politics, and culture are partners that enable all individuals to shape and develop local society by by promoting participation which in turn underpins the essence of democratic culture. Creativity, trust, mutual respect and support, and critical thinking are just as important as the ecological and economic fundamentals that sustain any community.

These goals should include the vitalization of a new sense of Italian-ness in this city (*Italianicity*) that privileges tradition but does not preclude either youth or their youthful ideas. We must develop a sociopolitical map of Italian-Canadians in Ottawa that reflects present sociocultural realities rather than the tired and redundant political and economic social geography that once centered in-and-around Preston Street. This versatile map must include concepts that respect both the history of the group while acknowledging its evolving ethnic character.

The well-intentioned gasping of those local Preston Street/*Corso Italia* inhabitants to leave a lasting mark for future generations with landmarks that declare the area *Italian* are perhaps too late in coming and possibly misdirected. A community's future sustainability resides in its youth, in their *real* understanding of their own culture, both Italian and Italian-Canadian, in their willingness to *live* in the hallowed hallways of their heritage, not in the shadows of tubular arches and concrete statues while consuming the occasional panino eaten on an ever more anecdotal Preston Street, once *Corso Italia*.

BIBLIOGRAPHY

A Journey of Faith — A History of St. Anthony of Padua Church: 1913-2013. Montreal: Longbridge Books, 2015.

Alini, Erica. "When Italy met Canada." *Mcleans,* 4 October 2011.

Amariles, David. *Locality, Community, Ethnic Community. The Italians with Special Reference to the Italian Residents of Dalhousie.* Ottawa: D.A. Dirks, 1976.

Anonymous. "Reflections of the History of Italian Immigration to Ottawa." *Italian Week Brochure,* 1983.

_____. "All Italians and Germans Required to Register." Tornoto Globe and Mail, 15 June 15 1940.

Ben-Ghiat, Ruth and Stephanie Malia Hom, eds. *Introduction to Italian Mobilities.* New York: Routledge, 2016.

Brault, Lucien. *Ottawa Old and New.* Ottawa: Ottawa Historical Information Institute, 1946.

Brown, Dave. "Old Gang" Brown's Beat, *The Citizen,* 19 January 1980.

Conner, Conner. "Third-generation Italian-Canadians more interested in preserving their heritage than previous generation, SFU study finds," *The Vancouver Sun,* 03 March 2015.

Conzen, Kathleen Neils. "Immigrants, Immigrant Neighborhoods, and Ethnic Identity: Historical Issues." *The Journal of American History* 66. 3 (1979): 603-615.

Conzen, Kathleen Neils et al., "The Invention of Ethnicity: A Perspective from the USA," *Journal of American Ethnic History* 12 (1992): 3-41.

Dare, Patrick. "Residents Aim to Save Last of LeBreton." The Ottawa Citizen, 21 July 2006. https://www.pressreader.com/canada/ottawa-citizen/20060721/textview.

Di Santo, Odoardo. "'Tempo di migrare: Abruzzesi in Canada." *A Monument for Italian-Canadian Immigrants: Regional Migration from Italy to Canada*. The Department of Italian Studies, University of Toronto and the Italian-Canadian Immigrant Commemorative Association: November. 1988.

Durkeim, Emile. *The Elementary Forms of Religious Life (1912)*. Translated by Carol Cosman, edited by Mark S. Cladis. Oxford: Oxford Classic, 2008.

Edmonston, Barry. "Canada's Immigration Trends and Patterns." *Canadian Studies in Population* 43, no. 1-2 (2016): 78-116.

Elenco Telefonico Italiano/Italian Telephone Directory. Ottawa.

Elliot, Bruce. "*The City Beyond: A History of Nepean, Birthplace of Canada's Capital, 1792-1990*. Montreal: McGill UP, 1991.

Eyles, John and Perri, Eugenio. "Life History as Method: An Italian-Canadian Family in an Industrial City." *The Canadian Geographer* Vol. 37 No. 2 (1993): 104 -19.

Filoso, Angelo; Dal Farra Hostetter, Ariella; L'Orfano, Francesca. *Memories to Memorial: The Internment of Ottawa's Italian Canadians during the Second World War*. Italian Canadian Community Centre of the National Capital Region: 2001.

Fitzpatrick, J.P. "The Importance of Community in the Process of Immigrant Assimilation," in W. E. Mann, ed., *The Underside of Toronto*. Toronto: McClelland, 1970.

Fletcher, Katharine. *Capital Walks: Walking Tours of Ottawa*. Toronto: McClelland &Stewart, 1993.

fleury, cj. http://www.masconline.ca/en/artists/directory/cj-fleury.aspx.

Frutkin, Mark and Cole T.W.. "Italia Mia: Italy is alive and well and living in Centretown." *Ottawa Magazine*, July 1985: 14-17 +28-30.

Gambino, Richard. *Blood of my Blood: The Dilemma of the Italian-Americans*. New York: Doubleday, 1974.

Giornalisti Italiani nel Mondo. www.giornalistiitalianinelmondo.net.

Gonella, Luciano. "Addio 'Caro e vecchio' Giovanni's Snack Bar." *L'Ora di Ottawa*, 4 February 2008. p.2.

Harney, Robert F.. "Chiaroscuro: Italians in Toronto, 1815-1915." *Polyphony* Vol.6, 1984: 44-49.

Helmer, Aedan. "Murals Offer Glimpse into Colourful Past." *Ottawa Sun*, 28 June 2007, p. 4.

Holland, Carroll. "Departed Families Left 'Real Vacuum' – Father Ferraro," *The Ottawa Journal*, 14 February 1970.

Hurturbise, Pierre, McGowan, Mark G., and Savard, Pierre. *Planted by Flowing Water - The Roman Catholic Diocese of Ottawa, 1847-1997*. Ottawa: Saint Paul University, 1998.

Iacovetta, Franca, "From Contadina to Worker: Southern Italian Immigrant Working Women in Toronto, 1947-1962", (in *Immigration in Canada: Historical Perspectives*. Gerald Tulchinsky, ed. Toronto: Copp Clark Longmano, 1994: 380-402.

Iacovetta, Franca, *The Writing of English Canadian Immigrant History*, Canadian Historical Association, Ottawa, 1997.

Iacovetta, Franca., Perin, R., Principe, A., eds. *Enemies Within: Italian and Other Internees in Canada and Abroad*. Toronto: Toronto UP, 2000.

Jenkins, Phil. *An Acre of Time: The Enduring Value of Place*. Toronto: Macfarlane Walter & Ross, 1996.

Johnson, Jeff. "Battle of LeBreton Flats Warms Up," *The Citizen*, 19 December 1979.

Lofaro, Tony. "Big Changes Brewing in Little Italy." *Ottawa Citizen*, 30 June 2007.

Lynch, Anne. *The French and Italian Communities in Dalhousie*. Ottawa: A. Lynch, 1976.

Lynch, Kevin. *The Image of the City*. Cambridge: Harvard UP, 1960.

McCooey, Paula. "Multimillion-dollar Mixed Use, Mixed Income Village Coming to Preston Street Area. *Ottawa Citizen*, 24 May 2017.

McCormick, Rankin and Associates. *Preston/Somerset Zoning and Traffic Impact Analysis Study*. Ottawa: McCormick Rankin, 1995.

Memorials in Ottawa. *Bambini.* 17 April 2016. http://ottmem.blogspot.com/2016/04/bambini.html.

Mika, Nick and Helma. *Bytown: The Early Days of Ottawa.* Belleville: Mika Publishing Company, 1982.

Moss, Leonard. "Voluntary Association in South Italy and Detroit." *The Family and Community Life of Italian Americans.* Richard N. Juliani ed. Proceedings of the Thirteenth Annual Conference of The Italian American Historical Association 209: 11-22. file:///C:/Users/fricci/Downloads/d61435d4-51bf-47bf-ad26-affd8d85bc12.pdf.

Murphy, Terrence and Perin, Roberto, eds. *A Concise History of Christianity in Canada.* York: Oxford UP, 1996.

National Congress of Italian Canadians. *A National Shame: The Case for Redress.* February 1992.

National Congress of Italian Canadians. *Redress.* March 2000.

New Oxford Annotated Bible, Michael D. Coogan, ed. Oxford University Press, 2007.

Panofsky, Erwin. *Meaning in the Visual Arts.* Woodstock, NY: Overlook, 1974.

Picato, Joseph. "A History of Italian-Canadian Writing." *The Canadian Online Encyclopedia, 4 November 2008.*

Preston Street Rehabilitation - The Heart of Ottawa's Little Italy: Bringing a Tired Street Back to Life. https://www.stantec.com/en/projects/canada-projects/p/preston-street-rehabilitation.

Ramirez, Bruno, *On the Move, French-Canadian and Italian Migrants in the North Atlantic Economy, 1860-1914.* Toronto: McClelland and Stewart, 1991.

Rev. Father Fortunato, O.M.C. "The Founding of St. Anthony's Church in 1903," *L'Angelo delle Famiglie,* January-February 1930. http://ilpostinocanada.com/ottawaitalians/Community/theFoundingOfStAnthonysChurch.htm.

Rogers, Dave and Young, Kathryn. "Arabic Speakers Change the Face of Ottawa." *Canada.com.* 2 April 2008.

Sankey, John. *Outdoor Murals of Ottawa Canada: Corso Italia Heritage Mural.* www.johnsankey.ca/mural4.html.

Skerry, Peter. "Assimilation is a Brutal and Necessary Bargain." Law and Liberty Blog, 20 October 2014. https://www.lawliberty.org/.

Sollers, William. *Beyond Ethnicity: Consent and Descent in American Culture.* Oxford: Oxford UP, 1986.

Spada, A. V. *The Italians in Canada.* Montreal: Canada. Riviera Printers and Publishers Inc., 1969.

Stanford Encyclopedia of Philosophy. https://plato.stanford.edu/entries/associationist-thought.

Sturino, Franc. "Contours of Postwar Italian Immigration to Toronto." *Polyphony,* Summer 1984: 127-130.

Talarico, Kathleen E. *Standing Shoulder to Shoulder. The Experiences of Southern Italians Who Immigrated to Ottawa in the Postwar Period.* Research Essay submitted to Carleton University. 25 August 2008. Carleton Library Call Number M.A. 2008 T35.

Taylor, John H. *Ottawa: An Illustrated History.* Toronto: James Lorimer and Company, 1986.

Tomchuk, Travis and Giesbrecht, Jodi. *Redress Movements in Canada.* Ottawa: Canadian Historical Association, 2018.

Waldseemüller, Martin. *Cosmographiae Introductio (1507).* See Charles G. Herbermann, ed. (1907*). The Cosmographiæ introductio of Martin Waldseemüller in facsimile, followed by the Four voyages of Amerigo Vespucci, with their translation into English.* New York: The U.S. Catholic Historical Society.

Werner Sollors, *Beyond Ethnicity: Consent and Descent in American Culture.* New York: Oxford UP, 1986.

Whalen, Michael. "Stove Pipe Village." *Corso Italia News,* Vol. 2 No.1, November 2004, p. 7.

Waters, Mary C. *Ethnic Options: Choosing Identities in America.* Berkeley: California UP, 1990.

Zucchi, John E. *Italians in Toronto: Development of a National Identity, 1875-1935.* Montreal: McGill-Queens UP, 1988.

Government Reports and Studies

Biles, John. "Ottawa-Carleton: An EthniCity in the Making?" Third International Metropolis Conference. Israel, 30 November 1998.

Dalhousie North Redevelopment Plan. Ottawa: City of Ottawa, Department of Community Development, Planning Branch, 1980.

Frojmovic, Michel. *Preston Street Business Improvement Area Census Project 2018.* 15 September 2018.

Government of Canada. *Commons Debates,* Vol.1, 1940: 658.

Government of Canada, *The Civil Service List for the year 1912.* Department of the Civil Service. Ottawa: 1912. Printed by the Printer to the King's Most Excellent Majesty.

Kin in the Game. PwC Family Business Survey 2010/11 Price Waterhouse Cooper. https://www.pwc.com/gx/en/pwc-family-business-survey/assets/family-business-survey-2010-2011.pdf.

Mohamoud, Hindia. *Immigration, Ethnicity, and Languages in Ottawa: Fast Facts from the 2001 Census.* The Social Planning Council of Ottawa. www.spcottawa.on.ca.

Immigrants in Ottawa: Socio-cultural Composition and Socio-Economic Conditions. Social Planning Council of Ottawa. United Way, December 2004. ISBN# 1895732-36-0.

Italian Week in Ottawa 1976. Ottawa. L.F. Mastromonaco.

The Italians of Ottawa. Ottawa, Department of The Secretary of State.

Ottawa in Maps, 1825-1974, Library and Archives, Canada, 1974. No ISBN, p. 35.

Our Little Italy. Canada's Digital Collections. https://www.ottawaitalians.com/index.htm.

Planning Branch. *Preston Street Neighbourhood Study.* Ottawa, 1965. Preston Street Gateway. Ref N°: ACS2010-ICS-CSS-0013. 23 July 2010.

Recommendations for Full-Time Recreation Co-ordinators for Dalhousie.

Redress Committee Public Hearings, Toronto, 24 March 1991.

Resources in Dalhousie, Centretown, and Ottawa West. Working Paper. Social Planning Team of Ottawa City Council. December 1975.

Updating of the Neighbourhood Improvement Committee's September 1971 Progress Report. Community Organization and Development.

Urban Renewal in Ottawa and Hull, Central Mortgage and Housing Corporation: Architectural and Planning Division, February 1971, 3-4.

Census Information

Canadian censuses are a key starting point for discovering vital details on immigration years, occupations and so much more. www.ancestry.ca/cs/census, and/or Statistics Canada.

1881 Census of Ottawa. www.familysearch.org.

1901 and 1911 Census of Canada Records. www.automatedgenealogy.com.

1911 Census of Victoria Ward, Ottawa, Canada. www.automatedgenealogy.com.

Obituaries from the *Ottawa Citizen* 1950-1967. www.bytown.net/citizensearch.htm.

Registers of St. Anthony of Padua Roman Catholic Church, Ottawa, Ontario, Canada, 1908-1963. Online images available in the DROUIN Collection.

ACKNOWLEDGEMENTS

The persons interviewed for this study are too numerous to mention. Places, faces, questions, and answers blur over the years to create a nebula of wonderful memories and impressions that I hope to have translated into a fitting homage to the community.

I would be remiss, however, not to mention the elder members of the community who graciously gave their time to an upstart outsider inquiring about community gossip. A few are no longer with us: Lucio Appolloni, Nello Bortolotti, Elio Coppola, Joe Corda, Luigi Mion, Padre Sebastiano Pagano, Saro Panuccio, Italo Tiezzi. Others are community icons: Pasqualina (Pat) Adamo, Joe Cama, Salvatore (Sal) Pantalone, Rafaela Plastino, Luciano Pradal, Angelo Filoso.

During my seemingly interminable community foraging, I met many of the original Village People. These gracious and spirited old timers meet weekly to relive bonds of life-long friendship. I met regularly with two of these groups at their respective hangouts: Pasticceria Italiana on Sunday mornings, Local Heroes on Wednesdays. Though their stories are often ribald and their prankish personal jibes colored with their past exploits, their words drip with the legacy of experience and love for the close-knit gang that once was The Village.

I extend a warm hug and my heartfelt gratitude to Trina Costantini Powell whose deeply innate love of community and relentless passion for heritage was both inspirational and conducive to the successful completion of this study. Trina is not only a font of information, anecdotes, old photographs, and memorabilia regarding the Italian community and anything Canadian, but she graciously offered her professional editorial skills and uncensored opinions regarding my style, the form and content of these pages.

I would like to thank my dear friend Lucia Alloggia, artist at large whose work is truly inspiring. Thank you for encouraging community dialogue with your beautiful and thoughtful book cover, and for conveying in images what often cannot be expressed in words.

Finally, I thank the community at large for acknowledging this Italian-American in their midst, and for allowing me the space to remain Italian within a Canadian context.

ABOUT THE AUTHOR

DR. FRANCO RICCI (O.M.R.I.) is Professor of Italian Studies at the University of Ottawa. An eclectic researcher, his numerous publications cross multiple disciplines that broadly address narratives of human experience. He has garnered much acclaim for his recent book *The Sopranos: Born Under a Bad Sign* and was awarded Honorable Mention for the prestigious Marraro Prize for his book *Painting with Words, Writing with Pictures* by the Modern Language Association of America.

He is knight commander (*Commendatore*) in the Order of Merit of the Republic of Italy by Presidential decree.

When he is not writing or teaching, he spends his time reading, cooking, traveling and photographing the region of Abruzzo . . . his other world. A longtime resident of Ottawa, he is a proud Italian-American with deep Canadian roots.

VIA Folios
A refereed book series dedicated to the culture of Italians and Italian Americans.

MIKE FIORITO. *The Hated Ones.* Vol. 153. Literature.
PATRICIA DUNN. *Last Stop on the 6.* Vol. 152. Novel.
WILLIAM BOELHOWER. *Immigrant Autobiography.* Vol. 151. Literary Criticism.
MARC DIPAOLO. *Fake Italian.* Vol. 150. Literature.
GAIL REITANO. *Italian Love Cake.* Vol. 149. Novel.
VINCENT PANELLA. *Sicilian Dreams.* Vol. 148. Novel.
MARK CIABATTARI. *The Literal Truth: Rizzoli Dreams of Eating the Apple of Earthly Delights.* Vol. 147. Novel.
MARK CIABATTARI. *Dreams of An Imaginary New Yorker Named Rizzoli.* Vol. 146. Novel.
LAURETTE FOLK. *The End of Aphrodite.* Vol. 145. Novel.
ANNA CITRINO. *A Space Between.* Vol. 144. Poetry
MARIA FAMÀ. *The Good for the Good.* Vol. 143. Poetry.
ROSEMARY CAPPELLO. *Wonderful Disaster.* Vol. 142. Poetry.
B. AMORE. *Journeys on the Wheel.* Vol. 141. Poetry.
ALDO PALAZZESCHI. *The Manifestos of Aldo Palazzeschi.* Vol 140. Literature.
ROSS TALARICO. *The Reckoning.* Vol 139. Poetry.
MICHELLE REALE. *Season of Subtraction.* Vol 138. Poetry.
MARISA FRASCA. *Wild Fennel.* Vol 137. Poetry.
RITA ESPOSITO WATSON. *Italian Kisses.* Vol. 136. Memoir.
SARA FRUNER. *Bitter Bites from Sugar Hills.* Vol. 135. Poetry.
KATHY CURTO. *Not for Nothing.* Vol. 134. Memoir.
JENNIFER MARTELLI. *My Tarantella.* Vol. 133. Poetry.
MARIA TERRONE. *At Home in the New World.* Vol. 132. Essays.
GIL FAGIANI. *Missing Madonnas.* Vol. 131. Poetry.
LEWIS TURCO. *The Sonnetarium.* Vol. 130. Poetry.
JOE AMATO. *Samuel Taylor's Hollywood Adventure.* Vol. 129. Novel.
BEA TUSIANI. *Con Amore.* Vol. 128. Memoir.
MARIA GIURA. *What My Father Taught Me.* Vol. 127. Poetry.
STANISLAO PUGLIESE. *A Century of Sinatra.* Vol. 126. Popular Culture.
TONY ARDIZZONE. *The Arab's Ox.* Vol. 125. Novel.
PHYLLIS CAPELLO. *Packs Small Plays Big.* Vol. 124. Literature.
FRED GARDAPHÉ. *Read 'em and Reap.* Vol. 123. Criticism.
JOSEPH A. AMATO. *Diagnostics.* Vol 122. Literature.
DENNIS BARONE. *Second Thoughts.* Vol 121. Poetry.
OLIVIA K. CERRONE. *The Hunger Saint.* Vol 120. Novella.
GARIBLADI M. LAPOLLA. *Miss Rollins in Love.* Vol 119. Novel.
JOSEPH TUSIANI. *A Clarion Call.* Vol 118. Poetry.
JOSEPH A. AMATO. *My Three Sicilies.* Vol 117. Poetry & Prose.
MARGHERITA COSTA. *Voice of a Virtuosa and Coutesan.* Vol 116. Poetry.
NICOLE SANTALUCIA. *Because I Did Not Die.* Vol 115. Poetry.
MARK CIABATTARI. *Preludes to History.* Vol 114. Poetry.

HELEN BAROLINI. *Visits*. Vol 113. Novel.
ERNESTO LIVORNI. *The Fathers' America*. Vol 112. Poetry.
MARIO B. MIGNONE. *The Story of My People*. Vol 111. Non-fiction.
GEORGE GUIDA. *The Sleeping Gulf*. Vol 110. Poetry.
JOEY NICOLETTI. *Reverse Graffiti*. Vol 109. Poetry.
GIOSE RIMANELLI. *Il mestiere del furbo*. Vol 108. Criticism.
LEWIS TURCO. *The Hero Enkidu*. Vol 107. Poetry.
AL TACCONELLI. *Perhaps Fly*. Vol 106. Poetry.
RACHEL GUIDO DEVRIES. *A Woman Unknown in Her Bones*. Vol 105. Poetry.
BERNARD BRUNO. *A Tear and a Tear in My Heart*. Vol 104. Non-fiction.
FELIX STEFANILE. *Songs of the Sparrow*. Vol 103. Poetry.
FRANK POLIZZI. *A New Life with Bianca*. Vol 102. Poetry.
GIL FAGIANI. *Stone Walls*. Vol 101. Poetry.
LOUISE DESALVO. *Casting Off*. Vol 100. Fiction.
MARY JO BONA. *I Stop Waiting for You*. Vol 99. Poetry.
RACHEL GUIDO DEVRIES. *Stati zitt, Josie*. Vol 98. Children's Literature. $8
GRACE CAVALIERI. *The Mandate of Heaven*. Vol 97. Poetry.
MARISA FRASCA. *Via incanto*. Vol 96. Poetry.
DOUGLAS GLADSTONE. *Carving a Niche for Himself*. Vol 95. History.
MARIA TERRONE. *Eye to Eye*. Vol 94. Poetry.
CONSTANCE SANCETTA. *Here in Cerchio*. Vol 93. Local History.
MARIA MAZZIOTTI GILLAN. *Ancestors' Song*. Vol 92. Poetry.
MICHAEL PARENTI. *Waiting for Yesterday: Pages from a Street Kid's Life*. Vol 90. Memoir.
ANNIE LANZILLOTTO. *Schistsong*. Vol 89. Poetry.
EMANUEL DI PASQUALE. *Love Lines*. Vol 88. Poetry.
CAROSONE & LOGIUDICE. *Our Naked Lives*. Vol 87. Essays.
JAMES PERICONI. *Strangers in a Strange Land: A Survey of Italian-Language American Books*.Vol 86. Book History.
DANIELA GIOSEFFI. *Escaping La Vita Della Cucina*. Vol 85. Essays.
MARIA FAMÀ. *Mystics in the Family*. Vol 84. Poetry.
ROSSANA DEL ZIO. *From Bread and Tomatoes to Zuppa di Pesce "Ciambotto"*. Vol. 83. Memoir.
LORENZO DELBOCA. *Polentoni*. Vol 82. Italian Studies.
SAMUEL GHELLI. *A Reference Grammar*. Vol 81. Italian Language.
ROSS TALARICO. *Sled Run*. Vol 80. Fiction.
FRED MISURELLA. *Only Sons*. Vol 79. Fiction.
FRANK LENTRICCHIA. *The Portable Lentricchia*. Vol 78. Fiction.
RICHARD VETERE. *The Other Colors in a Snow Storm*. Vol 77. Poetry.
GARIBALDI LAPOLLA. *Fire in the Flesh*. Vol 76 Fiction & Criticism.
GEORGE GUIDA. *The Pope Stories*. Vol 75 Prose.
ROBERT VISCUSI. *Ellis Island*. Vol 74. Poetry.
ELENA GIANINI BELOTTI. *The Bitter Taste of Strangers Bread*. Vol 73. Fiction.
PINO APRILE. *Terroni*. Vol 72. Italian Studies.
EMANUEL DI PASQUALE. *Harvest*. Vol 71. Poetry.
ROBERT ZWEIG. *Return to Naples*. Vol 70. Memoir.

AIROS & CAPPELLI. *Guido*. Vol 69. Italian/American Studies.
FRED GARDAPHÉ. *Moustache Pete is Dead! Long Live Moustache Pete!*.
  Vol 67. Literature/Oral History.
PAOLO RUFFILLI. *Dark Room/Camera oscura*. Vol 66. Poetry.
HELEN BAROLINI. *Crossing the Alps*. Vol 65. Fiction.
COSMO FERRARA. *Profiles of Italian Americans*. Vol 64. Italian Americana.
GIL FAGIANI. *Chianti in Connecticut*. Vol 63. Poetry.
BASSETTI & D'ACQUINO. *Italic Lessons*. Vol 62. Italian/American Studies.
CAVALIERI & PASCARELLI, Eds. *The Poet's Cookbook*. Vol 61. Poetry/Recipes.
EMANUEL DI PASQUALE. *Siciliana*. Vol 60. Poetry.
NATALIA COSTA, Ed. *Bufalini*. Vol 59. Poetry.
RICHARD VETERE. *Baroque*. Vol 58. Fiction.
LEWIS TURCO. *La Famiglia/The Family*. Vol 57. Memoir.
NICK JAMES MILETI. *The Unscrupulous*. Vol 56. Humanities.
BASSETTI. ACCOLLA. D'AQUINO. *Italici: An Encounter with Piero Bassetti*.
  Vol 55. Italian Studies.
GIOSE RIMANELLI. *The Three-legged One*. Vol 54. Fiction.
CHARLES KLOPP. *Bele Antiche Stòrie*. Vol 53. Criticism.
JOSEPH RICAPITO. *Second Wave*. Vol 52. Poetry.
GARY MORMINO. *Italians in Florida*. Vol 51. History.
GIANFRANCO ANGELUCCI. *Federico F*. Vol 50. Fiction.
ANTHONY VALERIO. *The Little Sailor*. Vol 49. Memoir.
ROSS TALARICO. *The Reptilian Interludes*. Vol 48. Poetry.
RACHEL GUIDO DE VRIES. *Teeny Tiny Tino's Fishing Story*.
  Vol 47. Children's Literature.
EMANUEL DI PASQUALE. *Writing Anew*. Vol 46. Poetry.
MARIA FAMÀ. *Looking For Cover*. Vol 45. Poetry.
ANTHONY VALERIO. *Toni Cade Bambara's One Sicilian Night*. Vol 44. Poetry.
EMANUEL CARNEVALI. *Furnished Rooms*. Vol 43. Poetry.
BRENT ADKINS. et al., Ed. *Shifting Borders. Negotiating Places*.
  Vol 42. Conference.
GEORGE GUIDA. *Low Italian*. Vol 41. Poetry.
GARDAPHÈ, GIORDANO, TAMBURRI. *Introducing Italian Americana*.
  Vol 40. Italian/American Studies.
DANIELA GIOSEFFI. *Blood Autumn/Autunno di sangue*. Vol 39. Poetry.
FRED MISURELLA. *Lies to Live By*. Vol 38. Stories.
STEVEN BELLUSCIO. *Constructing a Bibliography*. Vol 37. Italian Americana.
ANTHONY JULIAN TAMBURRI, Ed. *Italian Cultural Studies 2002*.
  Vol 36. Essays.
BEA TUSIANI. *con amore*. Vol 35. Memoir.
FLAVIA BRIZIO-SKOV, Ed. *Reconstructing Societies in the Aftermath of War*.
  Vol 34. History.
TAMBURRI. et al., Eds. *Italian Cultural Studies 2001*. Vol 33. Essays.
ELIZABETH G. MESSINA, Ed. *In Our Own Voices*.
  Vol 32. Italian/American Studies.
STANISLAO G. PUGLIESE. *Desperate Inscriptions*. Vol 31. History.

HOSTERT & TAMBURRI, Eds. *Screening Ethnicity.*
  Vol 30. Italian/American Culture.
G. PARATI & B. LAWTON, Eds. *Italian Cultural Studies.* Vol 29. Essays.
HELEN BAROLINI. *More Italian Hours.* Vol 28. Fiction.
FRANCO NASI, Ed. *Intorno alla Via Emilia.* Vol 27. Culture.
ARTHUR L. CLEMENTS. *The Book of Madness & Love.* Vol 26. Poetry.
JOHN CASEY, et al. *Imagining Humanity.* Vol 25. Interdisciplinary Studies.
ROBERT LIMA. *Sardinia/Sardegna.* Vol 24. Poetry.
DANIELA GIOSEFFI. *Going On.* Vol 23. Poetry.
ROSS TALARICO. *The Journey Home.* Vol 22. Poetry.
EMANUEL DI PASQUALE. *The Silver Lake Love Poems.* Vol 21. Poetry.
JOSEPH TUSIANI. *Ethnicity.* Vol 20. Poetry.
JENNIFER LAGIER. *Second Class Citizen.* Vol 19. Poetry.
FELIX STEFANILE. *The Country of Absence.* Vol 18. Poetry.
PHILIP CANNISTRARO. *Blackshirts.* Vol 17. History.
LUIGI RUSTICHELLI, Ed. *Seminario sul racconto.* Vol 16. Narrative.
LEWIS TURCO. *Shaking the Family Tree.* Vol 15. Memoirs.
LUIGI RUSTICHELLI, Ed. *Seminario sulla drammaturgia.*
  Vol 14. Theater/Essays.
FRED GARDAPHÈ. *Moustache Pete is Dead! Long Live Moustache Pete!.*
  Vol 13. Oral Literature.
JONE GAILLARD CORSI. *Il libretto d'autore. 1860 - 1930.* Vol 12. Criticism.
HELEN BAROLINI. *Chiaroscuro: Essays of Identity.* Vol 11. Essays.
PICARAZZI & FEINSTEIN, Eds. *An African Harlequin in Milan.*
  Vol 10. Theater/Essays.
JOSEPH RICAPITO. *Florentine Streets & Other Poems.* Vol 9. Poetry.
FRED MISURELLA. *Short Time.* Vol 8. Novella.
NED CONDINI. *Quartettsatz.* Vol 7. Poetry.
ANTHONY JULIAN TAMBURRI, Ed. *Fuori: Essays by Italian/American
  Lesbiansand Gays.* Vol 6. Essays.
ANTONIO GRAMSCI. P. Verdicchio. Trans. & Intro. *The Southern Question.*
  Vol 5. Social Criticism.
DANIELA GIOSEFFI. *Word Wounds & Water Flowers.* Vol 4. Poetry. $8
WILEY FEINSTEIN. *Humility's Deceit: Calvino Reading Ariosto Reading Calvino.*
  Vol 3. Criticism.
PAOLO A. GIORDANO, Ed. *Joseph Tusiani: Poet. Translator. Humanist.*
  Vol 2. Criticism.
ROBERT VISCUSI. *Oration Upon the Most Recent Death of Christopher Columbus.*
  Vol 1. Poetry.

www.ingramcontent.com/pod-product-compliance
Lightning Source LLC
Chambersburg PA
CBHW030103170426
43198CB00009B/472